Best Rail Trails
ILLINOIS

Help Us Keep This Guide Up to Date

Every effort has been made by the author and editors to make this guide as accurate and useful as possible. However, many things can change after a guide is published—trails are rerouted, regulations change, facilities come under new management, and so forth.

We would love to hear from you concerning your experiences with this guide and how you feel it could be improved and kept up to date. While we may not be able to respond to all comments and suggestions, we'll take them to heart, and we'll also make certain to share them with the author. Please send your comments and suggestions to the following email address: editorial@GlobePequot.com

Thanks for your input, and happy trails!

Best Rail Trails
ILLINOIS

ACCESSIBLE AND CAR-FREE ROUTES FOR WALKING, RUNNING, AND BIKING

SECOND EDITION

TED VILLAIRE

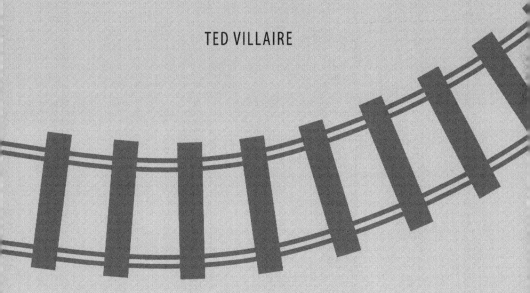

FALCON GUIDES

GUILFORD, CONNECTICUT

FALCONGUIDES®

An imprint of Globe Pequot, the trade division of The Rowman & Littlefield Publishing Group, Inc.
4501 Forbes Blvd., Ste. 200
Lanham, MD 20706
www.rowman.com
Falcon and FalconGuides are registered trademarks and Make Adventure Your Story is a trademark of The Rowman & Littlefield Publishing Group, Inc.

Distributed by NATIONAL BOOK NETWORK

Photos by Ted Villaire unless noted otherwise.

Maps by The Rowman & Littlefield Publishing Group, Inc.

British Library Cataloguing in Publication Information available

Library of Congress Cataloging-in-Publication Data
ISBN 978-1-4930-6947-7 (paper: alk. paper)
ISBN 978-1-4930-6948-4 (electronic)

♾™ The paper used in this publication meets the minimum requirements of American National Standard for Information Sciences—Permanence of Paper for Printed Library Materials, ANSI/NISO Z39.48-1992.

Printed in the United States of America

The author and The Rowman & Littlefield Publishing Group, Inc. assume no liability for accidents happening to, or injuries sustained by, readers who engage in the activities described in this book.

CONTENTS

CENTRAL ILLINOIS

SOUTHERN ILLINOIS

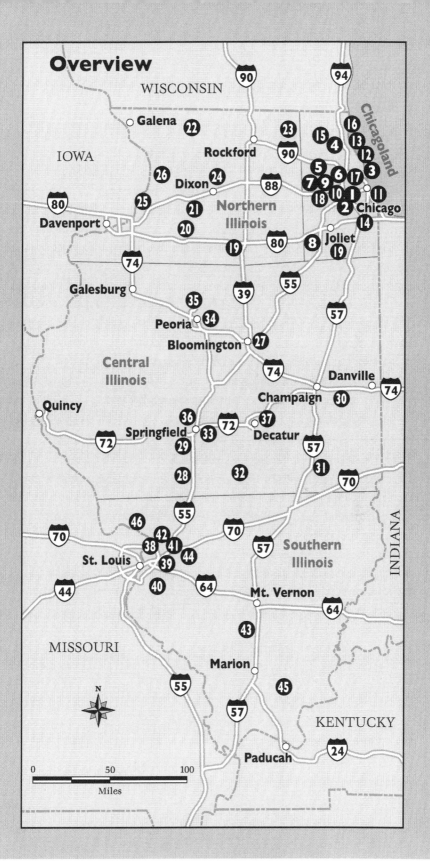

ACKNOWLEDGMENTS

Illinoisans are fortunate to have many people in state and local governments who see the value in creating recreation trails within easy reach. My gratitude goes to the agencies that maintain these trails, often on a shoestring budget. We're fortunate also to have a host of advocacy organizations that work to create, protect, and maintain rail trails in the state. It's an honor to have Dave Simmons, executive director of the Illinois statewide bike advocacy organization Ride Illinois, contributing the foreword to this book. I'm indebted to my colleagues at the Active Transportation Alliance for sharing their knowledge over the years about how to assess the quality of trails and how to advocate for them. In particular, thanks to my colleague Maggie Czerwinski for providing thoughtful feedback on sections of this book. Thanks to all the friends, acquaintances, and strangers who shared with me a wealth of information about local rail trails.

Despite all the helpful guidance from others and my own extensive research, errors can occur. Those errors are no one's fault but my own. But keep in mind that trails change and amenities change. If you spot an error or information in the book that is out of date, or if you have specific questions not answered in the book, please email ted@tedvillaire.com.

Pursuing a long project such as this guide would have been so much more difficult without the unflagging encouragement from a spectacular group of family members and friends. I'm particularly grateful to friends who accompanied me while exploring these trails, especially Tim Merello, whose plant identification skills helped me appreciate and share with readers more of the natural beauty along the way. Thanks goes to my sister Ann, one of my favorite companions for exploring trails. Thank you to my wife Christine for her patience, her enthusiasm, and her love.

FOREWORD TO THE SECOND EDITION

As an advocate for many years and the current executive director of Illinois's statewide, nonprofit bike advocacy organization, Ride Illinois, I've had the unique opportunity to witness the impact trails have on individuals, communities, and entire regions of the state. Developing new trails and improving existing trails has proven, time and again, to be a wise investment. Repurposing an abandoned rail line as a rail trail is truly a path of least resistance!

Effective advocacy takes time, creativity, patience, persistence, and support from others. Ride Illinois has led successful efforts related to legislation, education, and policy. Our work has been most fruitful when partnering with like-minded individuals and organizations. We're thankful for Rails-to-Trails Conservancy for spearheading efforts to breathe new life into decommissioned rail lines for nearly forty years. The results are impressive with over 1,000 miles of rail-trails in Illinois! As this guidebook goes to print, Rails-to-Trails Conservancy, Ride Illinois, and other organizations are working to close four gaps in The Great American Rail Trail in Illinois. When that effort is complete, The Great American Rail Trail will offer a contiguous route across Illinois. And for a shameless plug, we encourage you to support local, state, and national advocacy organizations so they can continue their important, meaningful work.

A typical trail offers many opportunities for recreation and transportation on foot or by bike, serves as links between nearby communities, and provides an escape from the complexity of life in the twenty-first-century for children and adults. If ten people were asked, "What does a trail mean to you?" chances are we'd receive ten different answers. Before flipping the page, ask yourself that question and take a moment to ponder your answer. Are you smiling yet?

It's been said before but bears repeating—there's simply no better way to fully appreciate your surroundings than doing so on a bicycle. When traveling by bike, one can't help but become immersed in the surroundings and gain a keen sense of place. The sights, smells, and sounds are inescapable—in a good way most of the time. In recent years, I have allowed my senses to guide me when I'm wandering on my bike. My sense of smell has become increasingly sharp, as it is the strongest of our senses.

From a coffee shop with that inviting aroma to the fresh, earthy smell of a lowland area to the sweet smell of honeysuckle in early summer—your sense of smell is strongly tied to your memory. So, the next time you're on a trail, breathe deep and connect the smells to the area you're passing through.

No matter if you're walker, cyclist, or a runner, this unique guidebook by Ted Villaire provides a wealth of information for everyone to use when planning their next adventure. With useful details, practical tips, and recommendations related to over forty rail trails in the Land of Lincoln, there's no lack of adventure awaiting you!

Dave Simmons
Executive Director
Ride Illinois

INTRODUCTION

It all started in the mind of a Chicago-area woman. In 1963 the late naturalist May Theilgaard Watts kicked off the national rail trails movement when she wrote a letter to the Chicago Tribune proposing that the abandoned rail line near her suburban Chicago home be converted to a long trail. Watts wrote, "The right-of-way of the Aurora electric road lies waiting. If we have the courage and foresight . . . then we can create from this strip a proud resource." Her idea caught on, and eventually that rail line became the Illinois Prairie Path, the centerpiece of Chicagoland rail trails. Inspired by this example in Chicago's western suburbs, rail trail projects were soon under way all over the country. While the Prairie Path wasn't the first rail trail in the nation, Illinoisans can take pride in their state's role in starting the rail trails movement and helping to inspire the creation of more than 25,000 miles of trails throughout the United States.

Thanks to Watts and many others who have volunteered their time and effort over the years, Illinois claims more than 1,000 miles of existing rail trails and is in eighth place among the states for rail trail mileage. As you'll see in this book, these trails allow you to explore some of the state's most beautiful settings. We have 80 miles of rail trails along the shore of the Mississippi River that run through charming river towns and nationally protected wetlands. In southern Illinois the Tunnel Hill Trail extends for nearly 50 miles through the bottomland woods of the Cache River Wetlands and the rugged terrain at Shawnee National Forest. Ambitious trail users can cross nearly the entire northern part of the state by hopping from the Old Plank Road Trail to the I&M Canal Trail to the Hennepin Canal Trail.

Illinois rail trails are not confined to the state's rural terrain and scenic natural areas. While the most rail trail mileage exists around the metropolitan areas of St. Louis and Chicago, there are excellent trails in the central Illinois cities of Bloomington, Decatur, Springfield, and East Peoria. These urban and suburban trails introduce you to local neighborhoods, city parks, and downtown districts. You'll learn plenty about local history, too. In many cases, you'll have the opportunity to combine your trip with visits to museums, restaurants, and shops.

The What and Why of Rail Trails

Rail trails are the perfect answer to the question of what to do with innumerable miles of abandoned railway throughout the nation. Rail trails provide answers to other pressing questions, too, such as: How do you encourage more people to exercise and spend time outdoors? How do you foster alternative modes of transportation? How do you preserve the rich history that developed alongside thousands of miles of national railroads? How do you connect communities and make them more walkable and bikeable?

Rail trails offer exercise and relaxation, scenery and tranquility, and more and more serve as a place for social engagement. South of Chicago, the pleasant little town of Frankfort holds a farmers' market each weekend during the summer along the Old Plank Road Trail. Trail users stop in at the market for their lunch and then sit down to enjoy live music on the adjoining village green. Spontaneous conversations are unavoidable. Healthful locally produced food is de rigueur. Some trail users have taken full advantage of this alliance and make weekly trips along the trail specifically for visiting the farmers' market.

Whether you're cycling, walking, running, in-line skating, cross-country skiing, riding a horse, or using a wheelchair, rail trails offer a peaceful setting to pursue these activities. Sure, users must negotiate cross streets with traffic, but generally multiuse paths provide welcome relief from tailpipe emissions, noise, and the hazards of traffic. This is why parents find rail trails an especially attractive option for getting outdoors with kids.

In urban and suburban areas, multiuse trails have started taking the next evolutionary step: They have become routes for transportation as well as recreation. The Lakefront Trail in Chicago, for example, hosts throngs of bike commuters throughout the day. With the awareness of climate change growing and the cost of operating an automobile climbing, the appeal of rail trails as a transportation option continues to grow stronger. The transportation role played by rail trails will only increase in years to come.

Illinois Railroads

It's fitting that the state considered the nation's railroad hub should contain an impressive collection of rail trails. Following Texas, Illinois hosts the most miles of railway in the country. Efficient movement of coal, grain, lumber, and passengers enabled Illinois to become the agricultural, manufacturing, and cultural center of the Midwest. In 1939 thirty-three interstate railroads ran into multiple Chicago train stations. The stations themselves often were magnificent structures that celebrated the ascendancy of the railroad.

The Illinois railroad boom began in 1850 when the Illinois Central Railroad received 2.5 million acres as a federal land grant to build what would be the longest railroad in the world at that time. Between 1851 and 1856, as many as 10,000 workers at a time were engaged in building the railroad. Initially the 700-mile Illinois Central Railroad ran down the length of the state, but eventually it expanded, laying down thousands of miles of track in other states.

The Illinois Central Railroad had a profound effect on the direction and pace of development of central Illinois. In the 1850s, when the middle of the state possessed a meager population, the railroad laid out towns every 10 miles along the train route. Within these towns, main streets often led to the train depots. Typically the north–south streets were numbered and east–west streets were named after trees. And of course the railroad company named the town—typically for company bigwigs. By 1884 the Illinois Central Railroad had named thirty-two Illinois towns.

In coming years, dozens of railroad lines sprang up in every corner of the state. Some were just a few miles long; some branched out over North America. Railroads were the primary means of long-distance transport for almost a century. Then in the mid-twentieth century, when the automobile became affordable for the average family and trucks started transporting more goods, the railroads lost ground and many lines were abandoned.

Why Rail Trails Are Important Right Now

It's no secret that many people discovered a new love of trails in recent years. During the onset of the COVID-19 pandemic, the number of people using trails surged as we sought convenient places to experience nature, decompress, and get some exercise. As a result, more government agencies and advocacy groups realized the essential role that trails can play in people's lives. It also showed the necessity of having trails close to where people live.

As digital screens proliferate and social media continues to pull our attention every which way, we need places to slow down and let our minds and bodies settle into the calming influence of the natural world. In addition to being low-stress restorative places, trails are also places where we can see our neighbors and get to know them. After walking, running, and biking thousands of miles of trails in Illinois and throughout the Midwest, I've decided that people are at their best while on trails. Friendliness prevails. Relationships are strengthened. A spirit of helpfulness is inescapable. Need to renew your affection for your fellow humans? It may sound a little silly, but trails can actually do that. I'm often taken aback at how something so seemingly mundane as a trail can have such a magical effect.

How Are the Trails in Your Community?

If you've used state-managed trails and parks in Illinois during the past couple of decades, you've probably noticed that many of these facilities have been struggling keep up with basic maintenance needs. The I&M Canal Trail, for example, regularly has detours or blockages because of maintenance issues. Indeed, the Illinois state park system has had a long list of park maintenance and improvement projects that have been ignored and delayed. Moreover, the state hasn't built a major multi-use trail in many years. This is not the case in plenty of other states.

Most of the trails in this book were built and are maintained by county and municipal agencies. Some local communities put a priority on trails, but many don't. When trails are given a short shrift, trail maintenance and trail amenities fall by the wayside. New trail projects get passed up or deferred indefinitely. Even in communities where good trails exist, there's still work to be done. Here are some often-overlooked questions to ask about trails in your community:

- Can the trails be safely accessed by people on foot, on a bike, and those using a wheelchair? Requiring a car to reach trails could keep many people from using them.

- Do the trails connect with key destinations in the community? Can trails in your community be connected with one another?

- Are the street crossings safe? High visibility crosswalks and flashing beacons improve the safety of trail users.

Another key question is equitable access. A long history of racist policies and segregation have prevented people of color from enjoying the outdoors and using trails. Making everyone feel welcome on trails means that parks, management agencies, and tourism bureaus need to do a better job of connecting with people of color. Another important step is supporting organizations like Outdoor Afro—a national group with a chapter in the Chicago area—that encourages African Americans to get outside by organizing group outdoor activities like hiking and biking excursions. And finally, a crucial way to open up the outdoors to more people of color is by building trails close to where people live. Ensuring that trail options exist close to where people live can help reverse the dearth of green space in marginalized communities.

Get Involved

Many of the trails listed in this book would not exist—or would only exist in a scaled-back version—if not for local volunteer trail groups. These groups work to establish and expand local trails, keep them maintained, and spread the word about their existence. It's often local volunteers who pressure the management agencies to make trails a priority. All of us who use the trails regularly owe a debt of gratitude to those who spend their free time expanding and improving local trails. (For each trail listing, I have added contact information for local volunteer groups.)

In addition to local organizations, there are regional, state-wide, and national organizations that deserve our support. For more than a decade, I have worked for the Active Transportation Alliance, which, among other goals, seeks to expand and improve the trail system around Chicagoland. The state-wide organization Ride Illinois has done an enormous amount of work to help fund trail development and gather local support. Nationally, the Rails to Trails Conservancy has been a key player in drumming up support for rail trails around the country.

So what can you do to improve the quality and accessibility of trails in your community? Get involved. Elected officials are responsive to the needs of residents, but they must know about your concerns—that you want not only well-maintained and accessible trails, but you also want to see your trail system expanded and improved. Let your political representatives know you care. While you'll often hear that no money is available for such things, there are always opportunities for reallocating public tax dollars.

As you use this book to explore Illinois rail trails, consider this advice: Don't take these trails for granted. If you want to ensure the continued existence and upkeep of your local rail trails, consider helping out. The success of a rail trail depends upon citizen participation. Here are just a few ways you can lend a hand to guarantee the future of these trails:

- Get involved with a local trail advocacy organization.

- Write a letter or send an e-mail to your city, county, or state elected official in favor of improving and expanding multi-use trails.

- Contact your local publications, offering praise for a local trail. Describe why you, your family, and your friends value this treasure.

- Attend a local hearing to express support for a local trail project.

- Start a petition on behalf of a trail project. When you can clearly show public support, public officials are far more likely to provide funding and resources.

- Attend a trail cleanup event. Many of the trails described hold annual cleanup activities and volunteers are needed.

- Most importantly, get out and use the trails: Take your kids and your friends. Lead a group of scouts or organize an outing for seniors.

USING THIS GUIDE

Trail Selection

My hope was to include the best rail trails in the state and offer generous variety in terms of length, location, and scenery. By and large I think I succeeded with this project. Unfortunately, for the sake of space some trails didn't make the cut. Usually a trail was left out because it was less than 4 to 5 miles, but in some cases there was an abundance of trails in the area and some picking and choosing had to occur. In the back of the book, you'll find a listing of Honorable Mention trails, which didn't make the main list but are well worth exploring.

It's true: Not all the trails described in this guide follow the routes of former rail lines. While the vast majority of the trails presented here are genuine rail trails, some of the trails also follow the routes of canals, levees, shorelines, rivers, and highways. In all these cases the trail adheres to the spirit of a rail trail by serving as a linear multiuse pathway.

After reading my trail descriptions and looking at my maps and you're still undecided about which trail to explore, here are a few more considerations:

- Take a look at aerial photos available at caltopo.com and google.com. You'll get a better sense of tree cover, nearby businesses, busy street crossings, and natural areas.

- If you have kids along, choose a trail with fewer street crossings and perhaps choose a shorter trip with some kid-friendly amenities along the way.

- Consider wind direction and sun exposure, both of which can make a big difference, depending on the day's weather.

When planning your trip, here are a few of suggestions that may add some variety to your trail experiences.

- Let your stomach guide you. Many of these trails pass in the vicinity of restaurants. Another option is to pack a meal and have a picnic at a park or scenic spot along the trail.

- Make it an overnighter. Illinois is fortunate to have some long trails with camping options—as well as B&Bs and hotels—along the way (my book *Camping Illinois* offers details about the camping alongside Illinois rail trails).

- Consider a one-way trip. While many people prefer the simplicity of out-and-back trail excursions, there are several ways to make it a one-way trip. You can spot a vehicle at one end or, if using urban and suburban trails, use public transportation for the return trip. Even better is using public transit for the trip between home and the trailheads.

When selecting a trail from this book, keep in mind that this is journalistically prepared information that has no agenda other than sharing details that will help you make an informed choice about where to go and have an enjoyable experience once you're there. My years of performing on-the-ground research and writing an engaging, accurate account of what I've learned offer a sharp contrast to most of information about trails that you'll find on the web. Reviews of trails online are often problematic. You never know if someone has actually used the trail, if they have an agenda, or if they simply are not a good source of information. Guidebooks like this one offer warts and all coverage as well as history, context, and expert recommendations compiled for your convenience.

Trail Surface

Illinois rail trails generally possess two types of trail surface: asphalt or crushed gravel. While this is not always the case, most urban trails have a smooth, asphalt surface; the rural trails tend to be surfaced with finely crushed gravel. Suburban trails will offer one or the other or a mix of both. The surprisingly flat and smooth surface of crushed gravel is great for bicyclists, walkers, runners, horseback riders, and wheelchair users. It's inadequate, however, for in-line skaters and skateboarders. On those rare occasions when the trail surface gets rough, such issues will be noted in the trail specifications so that you can plan accordingly. Even though road bikes with skinny tires work fine on a crushed gravel surface, you'll likely have a better experience using beefier tires that absorb bumps and grip the surface better.

Mileage and Maps

While exploring each of the trails described in this guide, I used a Global Positioning System (GPS) device to continuously track the route via satellite. After completing each trail, I loaded the GPS routes to a mapping software program and then marked mileage with the software. Most of the maps for this guide are based on the maps I created with the mapping software. I have found this procedure to be fairly accurate in determining the route and the mileage for trails. Unfortunately, it doesn't mean our numbers will match up precisely. If you're a cyclist using a bike odometer, keep in mind that these have to be calibrated carefully; just changing to a larger tire can make a noticeable difference.

While GPS devices are generally more accurate, they too can lead you astray. If you do any backtracking or pursue a side trip and forget to subtract this distance from the total mileage covered, that will throw off the mileage reading.

Trails in Winter

Since each destination covered in this guide is open year-round, you shouldn't let winter months keep you from enjoying rail trails. In addition to hiking, many rail trails are good places to do cross-country skiing and snowshoeing during the winter. Because the days are short in winter, I like to get out early. It's when you'll most likely see animals and it allows you to avoid the experience of racing back to the trailhead as dusk sets in. There's much to enjoy on winter trails if you're patient and willing to look for it. Getting out on a trail after a recent snowfall, for example, allows you to experience the profound stillness of the landscape and see imprints left by paws, hooves, and claws. (I have a lengthy list of tips for using trails during winter at tedvillaire.com/winter-hiking).

Each Trail Provides the Following Information

Activities: A list of icons tells you what kinds of activities appropriate for this trail.

Location: The general location where the trail description starts and the area through which the trail travels.

Length: Length of the described trail.

Wheelchair access: Indicates the ease of wheelchair access and challenges that wheelchair users may face on the trail.

Difficulty: Describes how challenging the trail is based on factors like length, trail surface, on-street navigation, and exposure to wind and sun.

Restrooms: If a restroom is available along the trail, it's indicated here and on the map. Water fountains are also mentioned here.

Maps: While each trail described in the book includes a map, it never hurts to look at other maps.

Hazards: Learn about anything you should be prepared for: extraordinarily busy trails, precarious street crossings, tricky navigation, or a lack of amenities.

Access and parking: This section guides you to the starting point and end point parking areas, as well as a few parking options in between. These start and end point parking areas are not necessarily the beginning and end points of the trail. The starting point corresponds with the "Start" point on the map and includes Universal Transverse Mercator (UTM) coordinates to use with a GPS device. The UTM coordinates are to be used with North American Datum of 1927 (NAD 27) datum rather than WGS83 or WGS84. Along with the UTM coordinates, the zone is also given. All coordinates were generated using mapping software rather than "in the field" readings.

Transportation: Learn if you can lighten your carbon footprint by accessing the trail with public transportation. This section will offer contact information for local public transit agencies.

Rentals: If bike rentals or bike-sharing options are available near the trail, it will be indicated here.

Contacts: The name and contact information for the trail management agencies is provided here.

Trail description: Get the information you need for the best possible experience on the trail: local attractions, recommendations for rest spots, and suggested side trips. Many of the descriptions include sidebar text that delve a little deeper into points of interest, local history, and the like.

Major milepoints: Many of the trails include short on-street sections, which will be described here. In almost every case, the on-street sections follow quiet roads and bike-route signs clearly point the way.

Local information: Tourism bureaus, chambers of commerce, and local trail-related groups will be listed here.

Local events/Attractions: Learn about museums, amusement parks, community parks, and other attractions either on the trail or close to it.

Restaurants: These listings highlight either specific restaurants or nearby areas where you're likely to find food. Restaurants swiftly come and go, so be sure to investigate options beforehand.

Accommodations: If you're staying overnight, here's where you can learn about nearby hotels, B&Bs, and campgrounds. These options change over time so be sure to inquire well in advance.

Rules of the Trail

One of the beauties of rail trails is that they are built to accommodate a variety of users. This great triumph of rail trails highlights a small drawback. With all these different trail users, opportunities abound for everyone to get confused about issues of right-of-way and trail etiquette. Knowing the following rules will help ensure an enjoyable experience for all trail users:

- Cyclists and skaters yield to walkers. Control your speed, especially near people walking.

- Cyclists, skaters, and walkers yield to equestrians.

- Keep to the right except when passing. This is especially important on trails that have a steady stream of users.

- Move off the trail when stopped. This is for your own safety as well as that of others.

- Call out when passing. It's better not to surprise your fellow trail users. Also, if they know you're approaching, they won't unexpectedly move in front of you or move into you as you're passing.

- Keep a close eye on young children when cyclists, skaters, and equestrians are near.

- Keep dogs on a short leash, and clean up after them.

- If using a listening device, keep one ear open so that you can hear others approaching.

- Take extra care when approaching blind corners, entering the trail, and changing direction.

- Approach road crossings with care.

- Respect the rights of property owners along the trail.

- If on an e-bike or e-scooter, make sure your ride is allowed. Some trails restrict class 3 e-bikes and electric scooters.

- Share your plans with others when going solo on a trail, particularly on trails that are more remote with fewer users. In these places, be prepared for limited cell phone reception.

- Bring snacks and water, and if you're on a bike, a repair/patch kit.

Legend

Local Roads	────────
State Roads	───(7)───
US Highway	───(55)───
Interstate	───(80)───
Main Route	─ ─ ─ ─ ─ ─
Other Trail	-- -- -- -- --
State Line	░░░░░░░░
Rivers/Creek	────────
Ocean/Lake/Pond	▭
Park	▭
Camping	🔺
Information	Ⅰ
Parking	P
Point of Interest	■
Rentals	R
Restrooms	🚻
Start/End	START END
Town	○

Key to Activities Icons

	Bird-watching		Mountain Biking
	Camping		Paddlesports
	Cross-country Skiing		Road Bicycling
	Fishing		Running
	Historic Sites		Swimming
	Horseback Riding		Walking/Day Hiking
	In-line Skating		Wildlife Viewing

Chicagoland

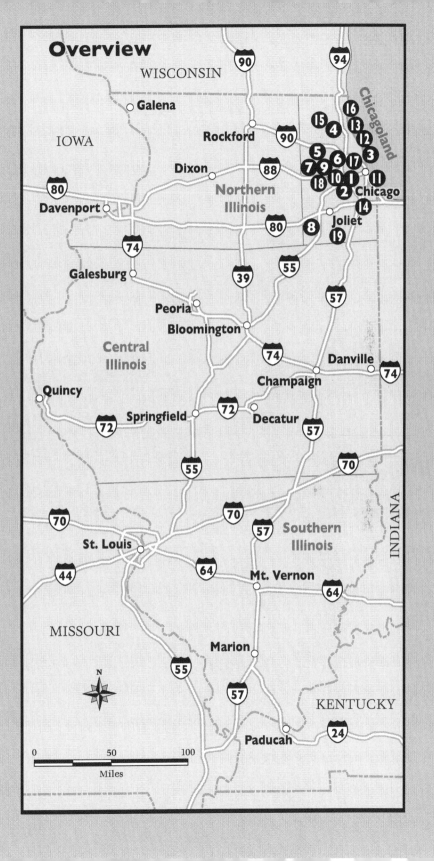

Overview

WISCONSIN

IOWA

Galena

Rockford

Dixon

Northern Illinois

Davenport

Galesburg

Peoria

Bloomington

Central Illinois

Quincy

Springfield

Decatur

Champaign

Danville

Chicagoland

Chicago

Joliet

Southern Illinois

St. Louis

MISSOURI

Mt. Vernon

INDIANA

Marion

KENTUCKY

Paducah

N

0   50   100
Miles

Chicago-area residents are fortunate to live within not only the most extensive system of rail trails in the state, but also the entire the Midwest. Spend some time on these rail trails and you'll see places that you never knew existed. You'll be introduced to countless towns and suburbs and dozens of parks containing woods, prairie, rivers, and lakes. Chicagoland rail trails provide a perfect escape from the cheek-to-jowl living that occurs within a metro area of nearly ten million people. Some Chicagoans I know regularly pack up their cycling panniers and let local rail trails lead the way to places like Milwaukee, Starved Rock State Park, and Lake Geneva, Wisconsin.

The centerpiece of Chicago's rail trail system is the Illinois Prairie Path, one of the first rail trails in the nation. Located in the western suburbs, the Prairie Path consists of a main stem and several branches and spurs that run through countless towns, parks, and residential neighborhoods. Each branch connects with the Fox River Trail, another prized local rail trail. The Fox River Trail traces the wooded banks of the Fox River for 30 miles between Aurora and Algonquin and runs through urban riverfront areas with parkland, gardens, walkways, and pleasant shopping areas. Taken together, the Prairie Path and the Fox River Trail are favorite destinations for local rail trailers because they're very accessible and because they allow various-size trail loops.

The honor for the longest and most historically interesting Chicago-area rail trail goes to the I&M Canal Trail. The 60-mile-long segment of the canal trail that runs from Joliet to LaSalle has locks, aqueducts, and locktenders' houses that allow visitors to learn much about nineteenth-century canal transportation. In addition to the human history, the natural beauty along the canal can be breathtaking. Near Channahon, for example, the trail follows a thin sliver of land bordered by the Des Plaines River on one side and the canal on the other.

While recreation and exercise are the focus of most trail users, more and more people also use the trails for transportation and commuting. For much of the year, weekday mornings bring a steady stream of bike commuters to the Lakefront Path, the Prairie Path, and others. The same scene occurs along local rail trails that run next to any school, whether it's a college or an elementary school. With a growing network of trails and more opportunities for combining modes of transportation on a single trip, rail trails will only become more of a draw for the transportation minded. Often, Metra train stations are located right on or within several blocks of the trail, allowing both bike commuters and recreational riders to combine their trail ride with a train trip.

1 CAL-SAG TRAIL

Get a taste of Chicago's southwest suburbs and enjoy plenty of striking natural scenery on this trail as it threads its way alongside a historic shipping channel. You'll find two excellent parks along the way: one of the biggest and best county parks in the region and a small but lovely urban park where you can watch waterbirds from a bench on the shore of a small lake.

Location: Begin in Chicago's southwest suburbs near the intersection of Archer Ave. and IL 83 and follow the Cal-Sag Channel to Cicero Ave.

Length: 11.5 miles one-way.

Surface: Asphalt.

Wheelchair access: The trail is wheelchair accessible, except for the on-street section on 117th St. and the 127th St. Bridge.

Difficulty: Easy.

Restrooms: There are public restrooms at the west end (Sag Quarries parking area), Teason's Woods parking area, Lake Katherine, the Schaaf Athletic Complex, and the parking area at the east end of the trail (Freedom Park).

Maps: calsagtrail.org/map; fpdcc.com.

Hazards: If biking, watch your speed on a handful of blind turns. Use care when crossing 127th St. and when sharing a short stretch of road with traffic on 117th St.

Access and parking: The ride description starts at Sag Quarries parking lot in the Palos Forest Preserve in Lemont. From I-55, head south on IL 83. After crossing several waterways, look for the parking area on the left. The trail starts at the parking area at the end of the park road.

IL 83 offers access to other parking areas: Teason's Woods, 86th Ave., Lake Katherine, and Freedom Park (turn left on Cicero Ave. to cross the channel and then right on 131st St.) Plans are afoot to extend this trail to the east.

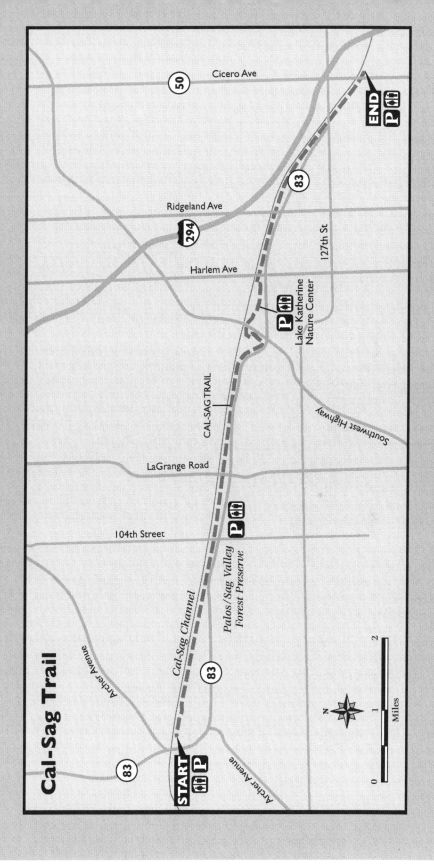

Cal-Sag Trail

Cicero Ave
50

Ridgeland Ave
294

Harlem Ave

83

127th St

Lake Katherine
Nature Center

END P

CAL-SAG TRAIL

Southwest Highway

LaGrange Road

104th Street

P

Palos/Sag Valley
Forest Preserve

Cal-Sag Channel

83

Archer Avenue

83

START P

Archer Avenue

N

0   1   2
Miles

Transportation: Metra's Southwest Service and its Heritage Corridor both offer access to the trail, as well as Pace buses 379, 769, and 383.

Rentals: 2 Bici Bike Shop, 8695 S. Archer Ave., Willow Springs, (708) 330-5234; 2bici.com.
      Cook County Forest Preserve might be offering a bike-sharing option in the area.

Contacts: Cook County Forest Preserve, (800) 870-3666, fpdcc.com. The trail cuts through the Palos/Sag Valley Forest Preserve, which offers 15-plus miles of multi-use trails, as well some of the best hiking and mountain biking trails in the region.

For an urban trail like this one, it's surprising how much striking natural scenery you'll encounter along the way. The entire trail follows the wooded banks of the Cal-Sag Channel, a 16-mile waterway that was built between the Little Calumet River to the east and the Sanitary and Ship Canal to the west.
      Along with its natural beauty and rich history, the Cal-Sag Trail is unique because it came together thanks to community members partnering with local decision makers. After many years of writing letters, holding events, and gathering support, the dream slowly took shape and the trail has become one of the favorites in the region.

Palos Forest Preserve

Starting at the west end of the Cal-Sag Trail and tracing the route of the channel, you'll get a pleasing introduction to the biggest—and many would say the best—park in Cook County, Palos/Sag Valley Forest Preserve. Wooded bluffs rise in the distance on either side, and wetlands come and go as the trail threads its way through prairie bordered by woodland. On the opposite shore of the straight-as-an-arrow canal, you can see the layers of limestone that had to be blasted through when the channel was built in 1911. Further along the trail, you'll see high mounds of stone excavated from the channel.
      The trail turnoff for Teason's Woods appears at about 4 miles, connecting you with some 15 miles of multi-use trails at Palos/Sag Valley Forest Preserve, a trail network that feels surprisingly remote for being situated

in one of the populous counties in the nation. Also, at this turnoff, you can hop on the 104th St. Bridge and cross the channel to visit Saganashkee Slough, a 377-acre lake popular with birdwatchers and anglers.

After ducking under 104th St. and then LaGrange Rd., the trail begins running even closer to the channel while burrowing through a tunnel of mature trees. The feeling that you're far off in the countryside somewhere is amplified when the trail crosses Mill Creek, where you'll see low rocky falls made from stone excavated from the channel. While admiring the falls, listen for the chattering sound of kingfishers, a small blue and white bird that scouts for meals in the canal. Or you may hear the prehistoric-sounding rattling call of sandhill cranes, a large waterbird that was scarce in Illinois not so long ago.

Lake Katherine and the East End of the Trail

Soon you'll arrive at the only place where the trail curves away from the channel and follow a mile or so of side path along a couple of busy roads through the town of Palos Heights. It may occur to you along this stretch that you haven't crossed a single road so far while following this trail—a true rarity on an urban trail like this one.

The side path ends, directing you on to 117th St. and sharing the road with traffic for a very brief stretch, before arriving at the shoreline of Lake Katherine Nature Center and Botanic Gardens. Nestled alongside the Calumet-Sag Channel, this compact park features an attractive lake, an arboretum, a waterfall garden, an herb and a conifer garden, a picnic area, and kayak rentals. After a peaceful break watching people, birds, and maybe a muskrat from the shore of the small lake and enjoying the park's very natural-looking—but artificial—waterfalls on its east end, you'll continue ahead on the trail passing under the Harlem Ave. Bridge.

Across the channel, more artificial waterfalls are visible, but these have a specific function. This is one of a handful of facilities along the channel and the Little Calumet River that clean the water by having it flow down big concrete steps, cooling it and increasing its oxygen content, while also providing a pleasant recreation spot for residents.

In 1955, the Army Corp of Engineers widened the Cal-Sag Channel, piling up excavated rock into a thirty-foot-high ridge along the many stretches of the trail. These mounds—laden with cottonwood, elm, hickory, and half-buried chunks of limestone—are visible to the right as you continue east from Lake Katherine. A series of walking trails trace the tops of these mounds, offering a bird's eye view of the channel.

The final few miles of the trail bring into focus the large industrial presence in Chicago's south and southwest suburbs, a place where waterways, train tracks, heavy industry, and wide arterial roads give the area a bustling atmosphere. As the trail squeezes between the channel and a long stretch of athletic fields, you'll see and hear I-294 on the other side of the channel. A concrete production plant and other heavy industries become visible as you cross the 127th St. and accompany the same street on a bridge path over the channel. The east end of the trail arrives after crossing under Cicero Ave.

The Cal-Sag Channel

The primary purpose of the Cal-Sag Channel is to connect Calumet Harbor, the largest harbor on the Great Lakes, with the Mississippi River. Also, like the North Shore Channel to the north, the Cal-Sag Channel was built to serve as a giant septic system, preventing polluted water from entering Lake Michigan, keeping Chicago's drinking water safe and clean. First completed 1922 and then widened and dredged in 1955, it continues to be a key shipping route for cargo such as coal, fuel oils, and gravel.

Local Information
- Friends of the Cal-Sag Trail; calsagtrail.org. Group instrumental in getting the trail built.
- Lake Katherine Nature Center and Botanic Gardens, (708) 361-1873, lakekatherine.org.

Local Events/Attractions
- The Forge adventure park; 1001 Main Street, Lemont; forgeparks.com. Family-oriented outdoor activities, located just south of the starting point.

The Cal-Sag Trail runs beside the historic shipping canal.

- Imperial Oak Brewing, 501 Willow Boulevard, Willow Springs; (708) 330-5096; imperialoak-brewing.com. Located several miles north of starting point; check the website for food truck schedule.

Restaurants

- A handful of restaurants and stores where you can buy snacks are located at the major intersections closest to Lake Katherine: College Drive and Southwest Highway to the west and College Drive and Harlem Avenue to the east. Use care: neither of these intersections have good infrastructure for people walking and biking.
- Al Basha Mediterranean Restaurant; 7216 W. College Drive, Palos Heights; (708) 671-1440. Very close to Lake Katherine.
- Frangella Italian Market, 11925 S. 80th Avenue, Palos Park; (708) 448-2598; frangellaitalian-market.com. Deli sandwiches and soups served for past thirty years just one block from the trail.

Accommodations

- DoubleTree Hotel, 5000 W. 127th Street, Alsip; (708) 371-7300; hilton.com. One of several mid-range hotels located very close to the east end of the trail; indoor pool and restaurant.

2 CENTENNIAL AND I&M CANAL TRAILS

This route is jammed with scenic vistas and fascinating local history. While tracing the route of the Des Plaines River, the Chicago Sanitary and Ship Canal, and the I&M Canal, you'll pass two museums, several parks, and a couple of historic sites. Much of the northern half of the route offers a surprisingly remote feel as it cuts through many acres of wetlands and bottomland woods.

Location: Beginning at Columbia Woods Forest Preserve on Willow Springs Rd. in southwest Cook County, the trail runs south beside the Des Plaines River and the Chicago Sanitary and Ship Canal to Joliet.

Length: 20.1 miles one-way.

Surface: Paved for the first 9.2 miles in Cook County; crushed gravel surface for the remaining 10.9 miles in Will County.

Wheelchair access: The trail is wheelchair accessible, but the 3-mile section upon entering Will County has a gravel surface that is rough in places.

Difficulty: The length of this trail gives it an easy-to-medium level of difficulty.

Restrooms: There are public restrooms and water at Columbia Woods Forest Preserve, the Isle a la Cache Museum (0.3 mile off the trail), and the Gaylord Building Historic Site in Lockport.

Maps: fpdcc.com; reconnectwithnature.org.

Hazards: Watch for trucks while traveling along the on-street section of the route.

Access and parking: From I-55 head south on US 12/20 (La Grange Rd.). Turn right onto IL 171 (Archer Ave.). Turn right again onto Willow Springs Rd. Turn left into Columbia Woods Forest Preserve after crossing the Chicago Ship and Sanitary Canal and the Des Plaines River. In the forest preserve, stay left to reach the trailhead. UTM coordinates: 16T, 426593 E, 4620585 N.

To reach the parking area on Kingery Hwy. (IL 83), head south on Kingery Hwy. from I-55. After crossing the Des Plaines River, park in the small lot on the right.

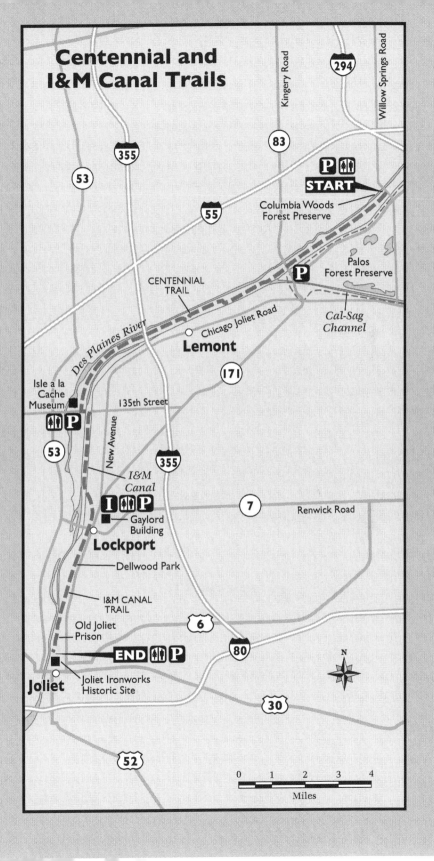

To park at the Schneiders Passage parking area on 135th St., head south on Weber Rd. from I-55. Turn left onto 135th St. Look for the parking area on the left after crossing the Des Plaines River.

To park in Lockport, head south on Weber Rd. from I-55. Turn left onto Renwick Rd. In Lockport turn left onto State St. and then left again onto Eighth St. Park in the lot on the right next to the Gaylord Building.

Transportation: The trail can be accessed by taking Metra trains to Willow Springs, Lemont, Lockport, and Joliet. In Lockport the Heritage Corridor Metra train stops mere yards from the trail.

Contact: I&M Canal National Heritage Area, 754 First Street, LaSalle; iandmcanal.org.

Cook County Forest Preserve District, 536 N. Harlem Avenue, River Forest; (800) 870-3666; fpdcc.com.

Will County Forest Preserve District, 17540 W. Laraway Road, Joliet; (815) 727-8700; fpdwc.org.

The first half of this route follows the Centennial Trail as it threads its way between the Des Plaines River and the Chicago Sanitary and Ship Canal, and the second half follows the historic I&M Canal. This second half of the route is one of three different segments of the I&M Canal Trail in the Chicago region.

Centennial Trail

Heading south from Columbia Woods, as the trail traces the top of a small bluff, the Des Plaines River appears on the right, fringed by moisture-loving trees such as box elder, maple, and cottonwood. Amid the dense bottom-land woods along the trail, you'll see piles of limestone excavated from the digging of the canal. Finished in 1900, the Sanitary and Ship Canal reversed the flow of the Chicago River in order to flush waste away from Chicago toward the Mississippi.

Soon the Des Plaines River meanders away from the trail and is replaced by a remarkably quiet stretch of open grassland. A bit farther south, the first bridge you pass under, IL 83 (Kingery Rd.), offers an opportunity for an extended side trip. A trail over the bridge leads to the northernmost section of the I&M Canal Trail on the opposite side of the Sanitary and Ship Canal. The path is 8.6 miles long and contains two connected loops that run beside the former shipping canal.

Continuing south on the Centennial Trail, you'll soon encounter a small lighthouse-looking structure that marks the confluence of the Sanitary and Ship Canal and the Calumet Sag Channel. Barges and tugboats chug along the Cal-Sag Channel on their way to and from Calumet Harbor, the largest industrial port on Lake Michigan. (About one mile to the east is the western end of a trail that follows this canal, the Cal-Sag Trail, also covered in this book.)

The next stretch of trail runs through wetland, bottomland woods, and patches of savanna before meeting up with a heavily industrial area crowded with barge offloading facilities. Near the town of Lemont, the Centennial Trail shares its route with Canal Bank Rd. (Despite all the industrial facilities and piers along this route, the road is fairly quiet.) One offloading area contains mountains of salt; another is piled high with landscaping mulch.

As you pass under I-355 and enter Will County, you'll follow a raised embankment through wet bottomland woods at the edge of the Des Plaines River for the next 3 miles. The Centennial Trail ends with a crossing of a 300-foot-long historic swing bridge that once spanned the Sanitary and Ship Canal, nearby on 135th St. The bridge, still with its pilothouse up top for controlling the bridge's movement, was transferred to this spot in 1990.

At the end of the Centennial Trail, you may enjoy a quick trip to the Isle a la Cache Museum, which focuses on local Native American culture and early European explorers and trappers in the area. The museum contains a birch bark canoe, an example of American Indian lodging used in the area, and items that were commonly traded between the Europeans and Indians. A handful of pleasant picnicking spots overlooking islands within the Des Plaines River backwater sit behind the museum. To reach the museum from the parking area at the end of the Centennial Trail, go several hundred yards to the right on 135th St.

I&M Canal Trail

As you make your way alongside the I&M Canal Trail from the 135th St. Bridge for a few miles south to Lockport, you'll pass an enormous coal-fired power plant and then cut through an open area that once was the site of a massive oil refinery.

Once you arrive in Lockport, be sure to check out some of the historic attractions that are remnants from the days when the town hosted the headquarters for the I&M Canal. One of these is the Gaylord Building, which served as a warehouse for materials used in building the canal. The building now contains a museum focusing on the history of the canal, a visitor center, and an upscale restaurant.

In the museum you'll learn that the canal was built to provide the final shipping link between the East Coast of the United States and the Gulf of Mexico. From Chicago the canal angled southwest, running halfway across the state, first beside the Des Plaines River and then beside the Illinois River to where the Illinois was deep enough for boat traffic. After it was finished in 1848, the 96-mile-long canal catapulted Chicago into its position as the largest and most efficient grain market in the world.

Another historic structure alongside the path in Lockport is the Norton Building, which was used for grain storage and as a grocery store. Today the Norton Building houses a state-run art gallery that focuses on past and present Illinois artists. South of Lockport you'll find the first of many locks canal boats would encounter after leaving Chicago.

Getting closer to Joliet, a spur trail heads left into Dellwood Park, followed by a section of trail that zigzags back and forth across the canal as it passes a jumble of bridges, railroad tracks, and another lock.

Just after passing the Old Joliet Prison on the other side of the railroad tracks, you'll pass through the Joliet Ironworks Historic Site, which provides a snapshot of how a large-scale iron-making operation worked more than one hundred years ago. In the nineteenth century, Joliet was known as the City of Steel and Stone. The stone was quarried from the nearby banks of the Des Plaines River, while the steel was produced here at the ironworks. Through interpretive signs posted among the crumbling ruins, you can trace the practice of iron making from raw materials to the casting bed. Constructed in the 1870s, the Joliet Ironworks employed some 2,000 workers when production reached its peak at the turn of the twentieth century. Much of the steel made in Joliet was used in the production of barbed wire and train rail.

This historic swing bridge was moved to this location at the south end of the Centennial Trail in 1990.

Old Joliet Prison

Near the south end of this route, you'll see the castle like guard tower of the Old Joliet Prison, built with locally quarried limestone in 1858 and codesigned by the same architect who designed Chicago's famous Water Tower. During its heyday, the infamous prison was the largest and most state-of-the-art facility in the nation, housing notable criminals like Nathan Leopold and Richard Loeb, and Baby Face Nelson. Numerous films, including The Blues Brothers, have used the prison as a movie set.

Major Milepoints:

6.2   Keep straight to begin a 1.1-mile-long on-street section of the route that follows Canal Bank Rd.

7.3   Pick up the trail again on the right.

Local Information

- Chicago Southland Convention and Visitors Bureau, 19900 Governors Drive, Suite 200, Olympia Fields; (708) 895-8200 or (888) 895-8233; visitchicagosouthland.com
- Joliet Visitors Bureau, 30 N. Bluff Street, Joliet; (815) 723-9045; visitjoliet.org

Local Events/Attractions

- Joliet Area Historical Museum, 204 N. Ottawa Street, Joliet; (815) 723-5201; jolietmuseum.org. The museum offers a thorough introduction to the history of the Joliet area.
- Old Joliet Prison; 1125 Collins Street, Joliet; jolietprison.org. The biggest tourist attraction in Joliet offers a variety of tours.
- Lockport Gallery, 201 W. 10th Street, Lockport; (815) 838-7400; illinoisstatemuseum.org. The gallery, located in a historic building alongside the trail, features Illinois artists.
- Gaylord Building Historic Site, 200 W. Eighth Street, Lockport; (815) 838-9400; gaylordbuilding. org. Contains permanent and temporary exhibits that relate to the canal and local history.

Restaurants

- Merichka's, 604 Theodore Street, Crest Hill; (815) 723-9371; merichkas.com. Serving up American food since 1933; try the poor boy sandwich.
- Public Landing Restaurant, 200 W. Eighth Street, Lockport; (815) 838-6500; publiclandingrestaurant.com. Fish, seafood, and steak; sandwiches served at lunch. Located next door to the Gaylord Building.

3 CHICAGO LAKEFRONT TRAIL

The list of things to see and do along Chicago's Lakefront Trail will make your head spin: two dozen beaches, three golf courses, two skate parks, Soldier Field Stadium, Buckingham Fountain, a handful of world-class museums, and a free public zoo. And don't forget the stellar views of the downtown skyline against the big lake.

Start: After starting at the South Shore Cultural Center, at the corner of 71st St. and South Shore Dr., the trail follows the Chicago lakefront north to Ardmore Ave.

Length: 17.7 miles one-way.

Surface: Asphalt.

Wheelchair access: The entire trail is wheelchair accessible, but be aware that the north half of this trail gets extremely crowded at peak times during the summer.

Difficulty: Expect a medium level of difficulty due to length, crowds, and exposure to sun. Wind can be an enormous challenge, depending on its direction and speed.

Restrooms: There are public restrooms at the South Shore Cultural Center, 63rd St. Beach, 57th St. Beach, Promontory Point, 47th St., 31st St. Beach, along the Chicago Harbor near the Chicago Yacht Club, the North Ave. Beach House, Belmont Harbor, and Foster Ave. Beach House. Water fountains appear frequently along the trail.

Maps: bit.ly/lftmap.

Hazards: As one of the busiest trails in the nation, expect a leisurely pace and stay aware of what's happening on the path ahead of you. If stopped, step off the trail. People on bikes must yield to people on foot.

Access and parking: Exit I-94 at 71st St. and head east. Getting close to the lake, enter the South Shore Cultural Center on the left. Park in the lot on the west side of the building. Return to the main entrance and turn right, following the trail (it looks like a wide sidewalk at this point) north on the east side of South Shore Dr. UTM coordinates: 16T, 453025 E, 4624009 N.

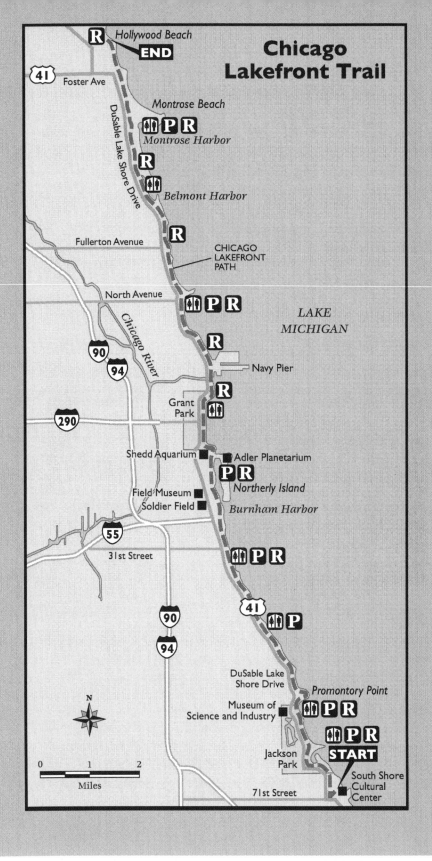

To park at Promontory Point, exit DuSable Lake Shore Dr. at 57th St. Turn right immediately onto Everett Ave. Turn right onto 56th St. and then left onto South Shore Dr. Park to the right on 55th St. Take the tunnel under DuSable Lake Shore Dr. to reach the Lakefront Trail.

To park at 31st St. Beach, take Lake Shore Dr. to the 31st St. exit. Turn east onto 31st St. and follow the driveway to the parking lot on the right. Alternatively, if you're approaching via I-90/I-94, exit onto 31st St. and head east toward the lake.

To park at the Adler Planetarium, go east on McFetridge Dr. from DuSable Lake Shore Dr. Park in the free lot at 12th St. Beach.

To park at the North Ave. Beach House, exit DuSable Lake Shore Dr. at North Ave. and go east.

To park at Montrose Harbor, exit DuSable Lake Shore Dr. at Montrose Ave. and head east.

To park at the north end of the trail at Foster Ave. Beach, exit DuSable Lake Shore Dr. at Foster Ave. and head east.

Transportation: The South Shore station on the Metra Electric Line is practically across the street from the South Shore Cultural Center, where the route begins. The Bryn Mawr station on the Red Line "L" train is just a few blocks west of the northern terminus of the Lakefront Trail. There are dozens of other options for using public transportation to access the path. Visit rtachicago.com for an online public transportation trip planner.

Rentals: Divvy, Chicago's bikesharing program, offers app-based hourly bike (and ebike) rentals along the trail. (855) 553-4889; Divvybikes.com.

Bike Chicago, 1600 N. DuSable Lake Shore Drive, Chicago; (773) 327-2706; bikechicago.com; located in the North Ave. Beach House.

Lakeshore Bike, 3650 North Recreation Drive, Chicago; (847) 742-6776; lakeshorebike.com; located next to the path at the Waveland Tennis Courts; seasonal.

Contact: Chicago Park District, 541 N. Fairbanks Court, Chicago; (312) 742-7529; chicagoparkdistrict.com.

C hicago would be unthinkable without the great expanse of Lake Michigan at its doorstep. The Lake Michigan shoreline not only offers city dwellers refuge from the relentless concrete grid, but also if you live in Chicago, it's probably the most accessible place to run, walk, cycle, or skate uninterrupted for miles. Indeed, for a great number of Chicagoans, a trip to the lake is synonymous with following this path as it snakes by harbors, museums, high rises, and acres of moored boats. This trail also offers a nice way to combine a shoreline stroll or bike ride with a visit to one of the world-class museums along the way (and avoid the high cost of parking downtown or near the museums).

The South Side

Before starting your journey northward, poke your head inside the grand South Shore Cultural Center, a landmark on Chicago's south side that was saved from demolition by residents. Built in 1907 as a swanky country club, membership reached its peak in the 1950s. The country club continued to exclude Black people into the 1970s, even when the surrounding neighborhoods were becoming heavily settled by African Americans. The country club is no more, but the golf course and the beach remain, as well as a small nature sanctuary in back of the building.

Heading north from the center alongside DuSable Lake Shore Dr. takes you by the 63rd St. Beach House, an attractive structure featuring open-air balconies and grand porticos. As you get farther into Jackson Park, you'll see remnants of one of the most important events in Chicago history: an enormous fair called the World's Columbian Exposition of 1893. A glance down Hayes Dr. reveals a shining gold statue called The Republic, a replica of a much larger statue built for the exposition. The Museum of Science and Industry, visible along the trail at 57th St., is one of the only buildings remaining from the event.

After passing the museum and the 57th St. Beach house, take the path to the right as it loops around Promontory Point, perhaps the best slice of open parkland in the city. The park occupies a small piece of land jutting into the lake and offers plenty of benches and big rocks from which to enjoy the city skyline, about 9 miles north.

As the journey north continues, a few small hills come and go, as do beaches and the occasional bridge allowing access over DuSable Lake Shore Dr. Open parkland prevails, but the main spectacle is the big blue lake. Lake watchers will testify to this body of water's frequently changing appearance. On some days, factors such as atmosphere, sunlight, and water temperature conspire to give the water a dazzling blue glow.

Downtown

With all the lovely scenery along the trail, what more could anyone want? How about a rather ugly building that serves as the world's largest convention hall? Thankfully the small bird sanctuary that occupies a fenced-in prairie south of the building helps humanize the giant black metal box of McCormick Place. Ditto the nearby flower garden and several small sculptures that are part of a memorial to Chicago firefighters and paramedics who died in the line of duty.

McCormick Place is situated at the mouth of Burnham Harbor, opposite Northerly Island. Built in 1925, Northerly Island was conceived by Daniel Burnham, an architect and urban planner known for helping plan the Columbian Exposition and for his Plan of Chicago, a comprehensive design for the city. Northerly Island was to be the first of a five-island chain of parks heading south, but the Great Depression came and the other four islands were never built. Some years later the city turned the island into a little peninsula by building a roadway to it. Northerly Island, well worth a side trip, now hosts a planetarium, a performance venue, a lovely beach, and a park with a multi-use trail.

As you pass Burnham Harbor, Soldier Field appears on the left. Built in 1922, the stadium received a controversial face-lift in 2003 when a glass-and-steel top section was added to the existing neoclassic structure. Just north of Soldier Field is the Field Museum, one of the world's best natural history museums. This enormous marble structure, also designed by Burnham, houses a vast collection of exhibits on anthropology, zoology, botany, and geology. The main floor lobby contains the skeleton of the largest and most complete T. rex ever found.

Continuing ahead through the museum campus, the trail gains a bit of elevation and then drops down to a tunnel under Solidarity Dr., which leads out to Adler Planetarium and Northerly Island. As the trail circles the rear of the John G. Shedd Aquarium, paneled glass walls offer a glimpse of the oceanarium—the world's largest indoor saltwater pool and home to a family of beluga whales and a handful of performing dolphins.

As you pass another big harbor on the right featuring acres of moored boats, the revered Buckingham Fountain appears in the midsection of Grant Park on the left (during water displays, the center jet shoots water 150 feet straight up). Passing the Chicago Yacht Club, continue alongside the shoreline as it bends right and runs alongside more tied-up boats and a large passenger ship. This is where you'll mount a new pedestrian and biking bridge that took decades to get built. The bridge leads you over the Chicago River, the Ogden Slip, and couple of busy streets, depositing you at the Ohio St. Beach.

After crossing the bridge, the opportunity to experience Illinois's biggest tourist attraction beckons (or repels, as the case may be). Navy Pier, two blocks to the right, offers oodles of tourist-oriented shops and an array of overpriced restaurants and bars on a pier jutting more than one-half mile into the lake. It also contains the Chicago Children's Museum, the Chicago Shakespeare Theatre, a monster Ferris wheel, and tour boats in a range of sizes offer water tours from the pier's south side. If you happen to pass Navy Pier during a less busy time, it can be an enjoyable spot for an open-air stroll out into the lake. North of Navy Pier and east of the trail is Milton Lee Olive Park, a pleasant little patch of green space with benches, water fountains, and great views.

The North Side

For the next 2.7 miles the greenery goes on hiatus as the trail is squeezed—sometimes uncomfortably—between DuSable Lake Shore Dr. and the lake. After the shoreline curves left, you'll encounter Oak St. Beach, often a hotbed of activity during the summer, whether that's jugglers, BMX trick riders, or in-line skaters whizzing through a slalom course. Watch the action while dining at a small seasonal restaurant.

The crowds and the people-watching opportunities continue to grow at North Ave. Beach and Fullerton Ave. During summer, North Ave. Beach sprouts an impossible number of beach volleyball courts. The North Ave. Beach House, topped off with a rooftop café, was built to look like a big ocean liner parked in the sand. Continuing north, the trail skirts the Fullerton Pavilion, a Prairie-style structure built in the early twentieth century as a "fresh air sanitarium" to promote health among the infirm. Now the building is home to a restaurant and a summer theater that's been staging plays for fifty years.

Within Belmont Harbor you'll likely see boat owners tending to their yachts and sailboats. A small fenced-off bird sanctuary appears on the right, followed by the English Gothic–style park field house with a clock tower overlooking a public golf course. The real avian action happens during spring and fall migrations at Montrose Nature Sanctuary, a lightly wooded area on a small hill at the eastern tip of the jetty that forms Montrose Harbor.

Navigating the Crowds on the Lakefront Trail

During the summer, 100,000 people may use Chicago's Lakefront Trail in a single day, making it one of the busiest trails in the nation. If you're not accustomed to using a trail that can get this crowded, it can be stressful navigating the most congested areas, which tend to be near downtown and on the northern half of the trail. In addition to the trail etiquette and safety tips provided in this book's introduction, here are a few additional pieces of advice to make your Lakefront Trail experience safe and comfortable:

- The entire trail has separate pathways for people walking and biking, and the arrangement of the pathways changes frequently. Keep an eye on pavement markings to make sure you're in the right place.

- People on foot always have the right of way.

- Riding two abreast might not be safe or courteous when the trail is busy.

- The Lakefront Trail is a challenging environment for young kids; keep them very close.

- Ditch the earbuds or at least use only one earbud at a time.

- Want to ride fast? Consider a different location.

The Chicago Lakefront Trail has become easier to use since the city has installed separate lanes—and in some cases separate paths—for people walking and people biking.

As you approach Montrose Harbor, watch for the signs directing people on bikes to keep to the right around the sports fields and the famous sledding hill, whereas people on foot will continue straight ahead. Montrose Beach appeals to many because it's a great big swath of sand and water and because, unlike many other Chicago beaches, it's located a comfortable distance away from DuSable Lake Shore Dr.'s six lanes of heavy traffic. From Montrose Harbor it's a short jaunt through grassy parkland to the end of the trail at Hollywood Beach.

Local Information
- Chicago Convention and Tourism Bureau, 2301 S. DuSable Lake Shore Drive, Chicago 60616; (312) 567-8500; choosechicago.com.

Local Events/Attractions
- The Field Museum, 1400 S. DuSable Lake Shore Drive, Chicago; (312) 922-9410; fieldmuseum. org.

- John G. Shedd Aquarium, 1200 S. DuSable Lake Shore Drive, Chicago; (312) 939-2438; shed-daquarium.org.
- Museum of Science and Industry, 5700 S. DuSable Lake Shore Drive, Chicago; (773) 684-1414; msichicago.org. The museum contains an OMNIMAX theater and a working coal mine.
- Navy Pier, 600 E. Grand Avenue, Chicago; (800) 595-PIER (7437); navypier.com. It's the main tourist attraction in the state of Illinois; ride the Ferris wheel and arrive at the restaurants with low expectations.

Restaurants

- In recent years, more seasonal restaurants have sprung up along the Lakefront Trail. Ranging from snack counters to a more upscale experience, your best bets are at 63rd St. Beach, 31st Beach, Navy Pier, Ohio St. Beach, Oak St. Beach, North Ave. Beach, Theater on the Lake at Fullerton, the Clock Tower near Irving Park Rd., and Montrose Harbor. Since restaurants in these locations come and go with regularity, be sure to do some investigating beforehand.

Accommodations

- The trail grazes the edge of downtown Chicago, which, of course, features an enormous selection of hotels. More affordable options are further away from downtown and into the nearby suburbs.
- J. Ira and Nicki Harris Family Hostel, 24 E. Congress Parkway, Chicago; (312) 360-0300; hichicago.org. A huge, clean, and affordable hostel located downtown; dorm-style rooms and a limited number of private rooms.

4 DES PLAINES RIVER TRAIL

If you like riparian landscapes, you'll love the Des Plaines River Trail as it winds alongside tree-laden riverbanks, through dense bottomland woods, alongside ponds, and over footbridges. Quiet oak savannas and many acres of tallgrass prairie thick with goldenrod, asters, and big bluestem prairie grass decorate the trail borders. Spanning nearly the entire length of Lake County, the trail gives visitors an extended encounter with this attractive river and the surrounding—mostly wet—landscape.

Location: From Half Day Forest Preserve in southeast Lake County, head north alongside the Des Plaines River to Van Patten Woods Forest Preserve, nearly at the Illinois–Wisconsin border.

Length: 24.8 miles one-way.

Surface: Crushed gravel.

Wheelchair access: Both the trail and the parking areas are wheelchair accessible.

Difficulty: The length and the gentle roll of the landscape create a medium level of difficulty.

Restrooms: There are public restrooms and water at Half Day, Old School, and Independence Grove Forest Preserves; you can also find restrooms at Growe Park, north of Wadsworth Rd.; and the north trailhead at Russell Rd.

Maps: lcfpd.org; lakecountyil.gov.

Hazards: There are many trail junctions along the way, but the plentiful trail signs make navigation easy. Thanks to careful planning, the trail runs under most of the busy roads. Occasionally, the rising river swallows up these underpasses. The county posts signs during flooding, in which case you cross the road at street level instead. Check the status of underpasses at lcfpd.org.

Access and parking: Several miles north of where I-294 and I-94 converge, exit I-94 at Half Day Rd. and head west. At IL 21 (Milwaukee Ave.) turn right. The entrance is on the right. UTM coordinates: 16T, 422931 E, 4673708 N.

To reach the IL 60 parking area, exit I-94 at IL 60 and head west. Park on the left just across the river.

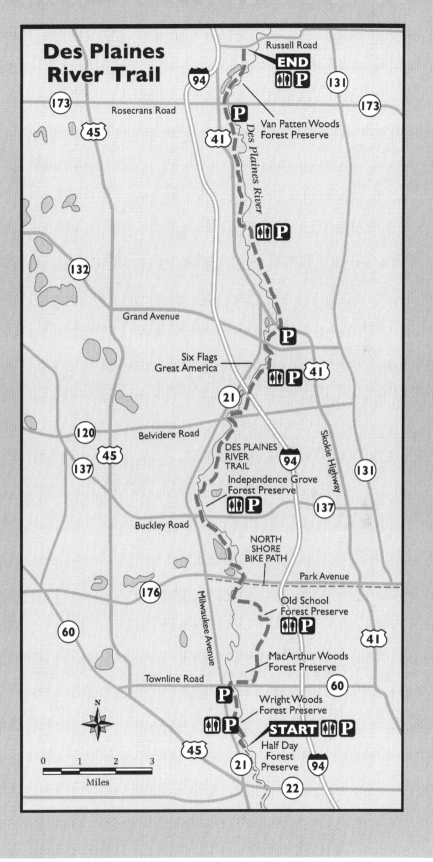

Des Plaines River Trail

Russell Road

END

Van Patten Woods
Forest Preserve

Des Plaines River

Rosecrans Road

Grand Avenue

Six Flags
Great America

Belvidere Road

DES PLAINES
RIVER
TRAIL

Independence Grove
Forest Preserve

Buckley Road

Skokie Highway

NORTH
SHORE
BIKE PATH

Park Avenue

Old School
Forest Preserve

MacArthur Woods
Forest Preserve

Townline Road

Wright Woods
Forest Preserve

START

Half Day
Forest
Preserve

Milwaukee Avenue

N

0 1 2 3
Miles

To park at Old School Forest Preserve, exit I-94 at IL 176 and head west. Turn left onto St. Mary's Rd. The entrance to the preserve is on the left.

To access the trail from Independence Grove Forest Preserve, exit I-94 at IL 137 and drive west. The preserve is on the right.

To reach the Kilbourn Rd. parking area, exit I-94 at IL 132 and drive east. Turn left onto Kilbourn Rd.; the parking area is on the left.

To reach the Wadsworth Rd. parking area from the south, exit I-94 at IL 132 and drive east. Turn left onto IL 21 (Milwaukee Ave.). Turn left again onto US 41 and then right onto Wadsworth Rd. Parking is on the right.

To park at the Russell Rd. parking area, exit I-94 at Russell Rd. and head east. The parking area is on the right.

Transportation: The Milwaukee District/North Metra Line stops in Libertyville less than 1 mile from the Des Plaines River Trail. The route from the train station to the trail runs along quiet streets and has paths and sidewalks along the way. Just north of where the train crosses IL 21, turn right onto Appley Ave. and then left onto Oak Spring Rd. The trail crosses the road after you pass Minear Lake on the left.

Rentals: George Garner Cyclery, 740 N. Milwaukee Avenue, Libertyville; (847) 362-6030; georgegarnercyclery.com.

Contact: Lake County Forest Preserves, 2000 N. Milwaukee Avenue, Libertyville; (847) 367-6640; lcfpd.org.

||||||||||||||||||||||||||||||||||||||||||||||||||||||||||||||||||||||||||||||||||||||||

Given all the development in the area surrounding the Des Plaines River, it may come as a surprise to see how much nature lines the river. Indeed, the many forest preserves that accompany the Des Plaines River in Lake and Cook Counties serve as the longest greenway in the Chicago region. In Lake County no fewer than ten forest preserves lie along a continuous path within the Des Plaines River Valley as it runs from Vernon Hills to the Wisconsin border. (To the south in Cook County, the Des Plaines River Trail runs for about another 20 miles or so—although not continuously.)

In addition to the many benefits these greenways provide for humans, ecologists will attest to the advantages of long, extended natural areas for local plants and animals too. Plants and animals tend to be healthier when they are not cut off from one another and are part of a larger gene pool. Animals also are more likely to thrive if they have room to move around and don't have to cross busy roads regularly.

Half Day and MacArthur Woods

As you start heading north along the trail from Half Day Forest Preserve, you'll cross a footbridge that sits in an especially attractive setting: Half Day Forest Preserve is on one side and Wright Woods Forest Preserve on the other. Before the trail takes you beneath IL 60, you'll cross two more footbridges and pass through bottomland woods alongside the river and stretches of prairie.

The next stretch of trail threads its way through two more attractive forest preserves. The first, MacArthur Woods, offers a mix of savanna and woodland. Among the hickories, maples, and oaks, look for birds such as brown creepers, red-shouldered hawks, and pileated woodpeckers. The next forest preserve, Old School, takes you through a great expanse of prairie decorated, depending on the time of year, with goldenrod, heath and sky-blue asters, and big bluestem prairie grass.

Returning to the river, the path curls to the right and passes a housing development and thick bottomland woods and then brushes against a pond before heading under IL 176 and the North Shore Bike Path. (The North Shore Bike Path shadows IL 176 for 7.5 miles between Mundelein to the west and Lake Bluff to the east. In Lake Bluff you can connect with the Robert McClory Trail.)

Independence Grove

After you cross Oak Spring Rd., a small lake appears over the embankment on the left. Like many of the lakes and ponds along the river, this lake— called Minear Lake—was created by a former gravel mining operation. Up ahead, a sign points up the bluff to Adler Park, which contains picnicking areas and a Frisbee golf course. At Independence Grove Forest Preserve, the trail mounts a hill that allows an expansive view of the pleasant and highly manicured 1,110-acre preserve and the 6 miles of trails that wrap around the 115-acre lake (also a former gravel pit).

North of Independence Grove, the trail winds through prairie, savanna, and woodland and then weaves through a power line right-of-way before passing under IL 120. For the next 3.5 miles, between encounters with five busy roads, the trail runs intermittently alongside the river and through bottomland woods. Just before the Washington St. underpass, the roller coasters at Six Flags Great America Amusement Park appear above the trees to the west.

Wetlands and Ponds

For those intrigued with floodplain forests and wet prairies, the next 4 miles after US 41 offer a special treat. First the trail mounts a raised bed and cuts through an area with dozens of little ponds surrounded by dense stands of elm, hickory, and maple trees. Beyond this very wet woodland, the trail skirts the edge of a pleasant expanse of water fringed by willows

Dense woodland dominates the MacArthur Woods section of the Des Plaines River Trail.

and cottonwood. The body of water seems to be a lake but is actually one of the pools of the river. After the pool, the trail swings left into open grassy wetlands, where you'll see groves of enormous oaks, a string of ponds to the left, and large spreads of cattails and wet prairie. The trail winds through more stunning wetlands, open prairie, and groves of oak after crossing Wadsworth Rd.

Before reaching the end of the trail, you'll encounter Sterling Lake—another former gravel pit that is now an attractive lake fringed by grassland and savanna. North of Sterling Lake the path runs through more prairie and savanna before hitting the Russell Rd. parking area at end of the trail.

Local Information

- Lake County Convention and Visitors Bureau, 5465 W. Grand Avenue, Suite 100, Gurnee; (847) 662-2700; lakecounty.org.

Local Events/Attractions

- Six Flags Great America, 1 Great America Parkway, Gurnee; (847) 249-1776; sixflags.com/greatamerica. Located mere blocks from the trail, a trail connects the park to the Des Plaines River Trail.
- The Des Plaines River Trail continues south for about 25 miles from Half Day Forest Preserve, where this route starts. After 5.5 miles, you'll pass from Lake County into Cook County and the trail has interruptions and a dirt surface that is prone to flooding and mud. Cook County is planning on upgrading the trail in coming years. Visit fpdcc.com.

Restaurants

- The Café at Independence Grove Forest Preserve, 16400 W. Buckley Road, Libertyville; (847) 968-3499; lcfpd.org/IG. While the café is limited to hamburgers, hot dogs, pizza, and the like, this is a peaceful spot with wonderful views. There's also a beer garden and boat rentals.
- Loads of restaurant options are available in Vernon Hills just west of where the trail crosses IL 60 (E. Townline Rd.). It's a sprawling suburban shopping area that's not very welcoming to people walking and biking, but it's very close to the trail and easy to access. While many of them are chain restaurants, there's a good selection of local options, too. Exit the trail at the IL 60 canoe launch and take the path left on IL 60.
- A small collection of restaurants is available in Gurnee just west of the trail on Washington St. Two strip malls with food options are easy to access with a trail heading west from the Des Plaines River Trail on Washington.

Accommodations

- Illinois Beach State Park, Zion; (847) 662-4811; www2.illinois.gov/dnr. The park has many campsites a stone's throw from Lake Michigan. Follow Wadsworth Rd. east to the lake.
- Lincolnshire Marriot Resort, 10 Marriott Drive, Lincolnshire; (847) 634-0100; marriot.com. Multiple restaurants, a golf course, and a theater with live performances; the trail runs through the resort just a couple miles south of the starting point at Half Day Forest Preserve.

5 FOX RIVER TRAIL

Located only 30 miles west of downtown Chicago, the Fox River Trail has plenty of great things going for it. As this pathway hugs the Fox River between Aurora and Algonquin, it passes numerous community parks and forest preserves. The towns the trail passes through—Elgin, St. Charles, Geneva, Batavia, Aurora—contain plenty of dining options as well as attractive urban riverfront areas with flower and sculpture gardens, pedestrian bridges, and scenic walkways.

Location: From Algonquin in southeast McHenry County, head south following the route of the Fox River to downtown Aurora.

Length: 32.8 miles one-way.

Surface: Asphalt.

Wheelchair access: The trail is wheelchair accessible, except for the two on-street sections around St. Charles.

Difficulty: The trail is flat and shaded for most of the route. Difficulty level increases in a few spots where you must climb river bluffs.

Restrooms: There are public restrooms at the Algonquin Rd. trail access (water), Fox River Shores Forest Preserve (water), East Dundee Depot (water), Trout Park, Tekakwitha Woods Forest Preserve, Island Park in Geneva (water), and Les McCullough Park.

Maps: northernfoxrivervalley.com; kdot.countyofkane.org.

Hazards: Watch carefully for bike route signs while following brief on-street sections in St. Charles. Watch for traffic in the handful of places where the trail crosses busy streets. Sections of this trail are closed periodically for construction. Signs usually direct trail users along detours. Check with the Kane County Forest Preserve District for the latest construction news (see contact information below).

Access and parking: From I-90 west of the Fox River, head north on IL 31 toward Algonquin. In Algonquin turn left onto Algonquin Rd. Turn right onto Meyer Dr. and then left into the Algonquin Rd. Trail Access parking area. UTM coordinates: 16T, 392651 E, 4669502 N.

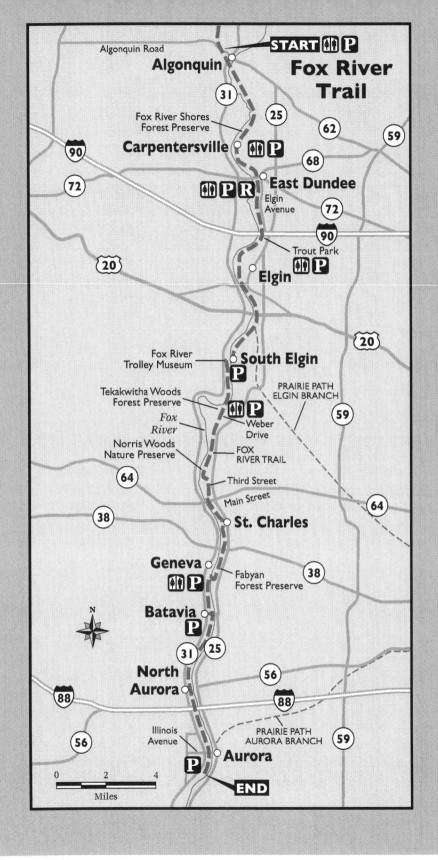

NOTE: During winter, when this trailhead parking area is closed, use a parking lot at Towne Park in Algonquin. Also, as the trail runs through a string of small towns, there is nearly always free on-street parking next to the trail.

To park at Fox River Shores Forest Preserve, head north on IL 25 from East Dundee. Turn left onto Lake Marian Rd. and then right on Williams Rd.

To park in South Elgin, head south on IL 31 from Elgin. Turn left onto State St. and then right onto Water St. Park and catch the trail as it runs through the riverside park.

To park at the Fabyan Forest Preserve, head south on IL 25 from Geneva. The parking area is just after the windmill on the right.

To park near the south end of the trail at River St. Park in Aurora, head south on IL 31 from I-88. At Park Ave. turn left, and then turn right onto River St. The park and the trail are on the left.

Transportation: Metra trains bring you close to the trail in Elgin, Geneva, and Aurora. In Elgin the Milwaukee District West Metra line stops across the river from the trail. In Geneva, the Union Pacific West Metra line stops about 0.5 mile from the trail. From the station, go north on Third St. and then turn right on South St. The BNSF Railway Metra line stops in Aurora across IL 25 from the trail.

Rentals: Main Street Bicycles, 39 E. Main Street, Carpentersville; (847) 783-0362; mainstbicycles.com; located on the trail.

Mill Race Cyclery, 11 E. State Street, Geneva; (630) 232-2833; millrace. com; located on the trail.

Contact: Kane County Forest Preserve District, 719 S. Batavia Avenue, Geneva; (630) 232-5980; kaneforest.com.

||||||||||||||||||||||||||||||||||||||||||||||||||||||||||||||||||||||||||||||||

While following the Fox River Path, you'll encounter towns of varying size; many scenic natural areas; and a host of parks, museums, and options for dining and shopping. The many towns along the way contain an assortment of restaurants, ice cream parlors, coffee shops, and watering holes. These are places where you can see historic architecture; stroll along pleasant river walks; and drop in museums, cafés, and shops. If you're keen on a longer trip, the trail allows you to hook up with a handful of other Chicagoland recreation trails. Heading north, for example, connects you with the Prairie Trail, which runs all the way to the Wisconsin border.

Elgin

The first mile of the trail after starting in Algonquin, you'll make a dramatic crossing of the Fox River on a soaring pedestrian bridge. For the next couple of miles, you'll get one of the best tours of wooded backyards that Illinois has to offer. Before reaching Fox River Shores Forest Preserve (where you'll find a perfect picnicking spots on the shore of the river), the trail meets up with a wide spot in the river where kingfishers and great blue herons loiter on the deadfall in the river.

It may be difficult to get through East Dundee without stopping at one of the coffee houses, brew pubs, restaurants, or ice cream shops—many of which are just steps from the trail. You'll also pass a former train depot with picnic tables at which you can sit to admire the handsome historic architecture on the surrounding streets.

On the way into Elgin, the trail runs through a long wooded stretch parallel to Elgin Ave. Along the way is a remarkable brick house built to resemble a small tower. You'll also encounter Trout Park, which contains a rich display of spring wildflowers, and a pedestrian bridge that crosses the Fox River.

In Elgin, the development of water-powered mills and hydroelectric generators in the late nineteenth century allowed a variety of local businesses to thrive, including the Elgin National Watch Company, once the world's largest watch manufacturer. In place of these riverside industries, you'll now find walkways planted with trees and flowers, benches, and arched pedestrian bridges. There are also a couple of small islands in the river connected to trail with foot bridges. If you have kids along, they'll be thrilled with the imaginative sculptures and playground equipment at Festival Park, located just upstream from Elgin's riverboat casino.

After passing the Elgin Spur of the Prairie Path, the trail runs through the arched opening of a stone train bridge. From there you'll take a roller-coaster ride up and down a series of river bluffs. After crossing the river in South Elgin, the trail runs through a couple of riverside parks and an outdoor railroad museum. Chicago's rich railroad legacy is on full display at the Fox River Trolley Museum. Some of the train cars at this museum ran along the "L" tracks in Chicago and others were owned by the Chicago, Aurora and Elgin Railroad, an interurban passenger train service that operated on the Fox River Trail. During the summer, you can board a historic trolley at the museum for a several-mile trip along the river.

St. Charles and Fabyan Forest Preserve

The splendor of the Fox River takes center stage about 5 miles south of Elgin, where a 250-yard-long footbridge connects two wooded parks just before the river takes a hairpin curve. Downstream from the bridge is an island covered by a fairy-tale forest. After crossing the bridge, you'll follow the trail up a steep 120-foot bluff that, from a distance, resembles a vertical wall.

Once past that grueling climb, you can catch your breath on a mile-long segment of modestly trafficked road with no sidewalks on

A Dutch windmill from 1915 overlooks the Fox River Trail in the Fabyan Forest Preserve.

Weber Dr. Closing in on St. Charles, you'll return to the trail and then snake through the thick bottomland woods at Norris Woods Nature Preserve. As you navigate the residential streets of St. Charles for another mile of on-street travel, trail signs direct you through the town's historic district, past a bookstore, a coffee shop, gift shops, and restaurants.

A couple miles past St. Charles the trail rambles through a series of riverside parks in Geneva. After passing through Island Park, you'll encounter a couple of local landmarks at the Fabyan Forest Preserve: the Dutch windmill, built in 1915, and a Japanese garden—a carefully landscaped environment with ponds, walkways, and a small arched bridge. The park also contains the Frank Lloyd Wright–designed Villa Museum, which showcases the history of the park and the family who once owned it. The trail runs on both sides of the river for the next 5 miles south of Fabyan Forest Preserve. If following the trail on the east side, cross back over to the west side in Batavia or in North Aurora.

Batavia and Aurora

In Batavia you'll pass an old train depot that now serves as a local history museum. A series of twenty-foot-tall windmills along Batavia's river-walk honor the town's former specialty—manufacturing water-pumping windmills. While tracing the top edge of a small bluff for the final 7 miles between Batavia and Aurora, big views of the river open up to the trail, revealing a progression of wooded islands.

A series of gentle curves in the river guides you into Aurora, which welcomes you with open grassy riverside parks. The trail ends across the river from an island in the Fox River that once served as the city's administrative center. A stroll around this large island takes you to a casino, a historical theater, and a couple of museums.

In Aurora, you have the option to connect with several other trails, including the Virgil Gilman Trail and the Aurora Branch of the Illinois Prairie Path, both covered in this book. There's also a 5-mile-long south section of the Fox River Trail that you can catch a half mile to the south.

The Fabyan Estate

In Geneva, the trail passes through a forest preserve that was the former estate of George Fabyan, an eccentric millionaire whose property once sprawled along the riverbank. In addition to the five-story Dutch windmill he erected in 1915, Fabyan's estate included a private zoo and a laboratory that performed research on acoustics, code cracking, and—surprisingly—human levitation. Fabyan's Japanese garden remains, as does his farmhouse, which was remodeled by Frank Lloyd Wright. Now the house serves a museum focusing on Fabyan's estate and the artifacts he collected over the years.

Major Milepoints

19.8 Turn right on Third Ave. to begin a 1.2-mile-long on-street section of the route in St. Charles.

20.2 Turn right on North Ave.

20.6 Turn left on Second Ave.

20.8 Turn right on State Ave.

20.9 Turn left on First Ave. and cross IL 64.

21.0 Return to the Fox River Trail.

Local Information

- Aurora Area Convention and Visitors Bureau, 43 W. Galena Boulevard, Aurora; (630) 256-3190; enjoyaurora.com.
- Explore Elgin, 60 S. Grove Avenue, Elgin; (847) 695-7540; northernfoxrivervalley.com.

Local Events/Attractions

- The Depot Museum, 155 Houston Street, Batavia; (630) 406-5274; bataviahistoricalsociety.org. The museum, which sits alongside the trail, chronicles the local history of Batavia.
- Fox River Trolley Museum, 361 S. LaFox Street, South Elgin; (847) 697-4676; foxtrolley.org. Old trolleys on display. The museum operates a trolley along a 4-mile section of track that parallels the Fox River Trail.

Restaurants

- Plenty of restaurants can be found close to the trail in Elgin, East Dundee, St. Charles, Geneva, Batavia, and Aurora.
- Batavia Creamery, 4 N. Island Avenue, Batavia; (630) 482-3729; bataviacreamery.com. Great selection of premium ice creams. Located on the trail.

Accommodations

- The Mansion Bed and Breakfast, 305 Oregon Avenue, West Dundee; (847) 426-7777; themansionbedandbreakfast.com. Turn-of-the-twentieth-century iron-ore baron's estate; affordable rates.
- Oscar Swan Country Inn Bed and Breakfast, 1800 W. State Street, Geneva; (630) 232-0173; oscarswan.com. English country manor with eight guest rooms.

6 GREAT WESTERN TRAIL—DUPAGE COUNTY

As the Great Western Trail makes a straight shot west from Villa Park, it cuts through residential areas and brushes against community parks and forest preserves. Expect to see woods, prairie, and wetlands, particularly on the second half of the route where houses and trail users grow sparse. Consider short side trips to Churchill Woods Forest Preserve at the halfway point and Kline Creek Farm near the end of the trail.

Location: From Villa Park Museum in Villa Park, located about 20 miles west of downtown Chicago, the trail runs west to West Chicago.

Length: 11.7 miles one-way, with options for short side trips.

Surface: Crushed gravel.

Wheelchair access: The trail is wheelchair accessible.

Difficulty: The trail is mostly easy; some sections leave you fully exposed to the elements.

Restrooms: There are public restrooms and water at the Villa Park Museum, Lombard Commons Park, Churchill Woods Forest Preserve (restrooms about 0.5 mile off the GWT), and Kline Creek Farm (about 0.25 mile off the GWT).

Maps: dupagecounty.gov/bikeways.

Hazards: Use caution while crossing a few busy roads along the way.

Access and parking: To reach the Villa Park Museum, head west on St. Charles Rd. from I-290. In Villa Park turn left onto Villa Ave. Park in the lot at the museum on the right. The museum is located on the main stem of the Illinois Prairie Path. Catch the Great Western Trail by heading west on the Prairie Path and then following signs north one block via Myrtle Ave. UTM coordinates: 16T, 420174 E, 4637375 N.

The best place to start the trail from the west end is the Timber Ridge Forest Preserve parking area on Prince Crossing Rd. From I-355 head west on IL 64 and turn left onto Prince Crossing Rd. The parking area is on the left; the trail is twenty yards south of the parking area.

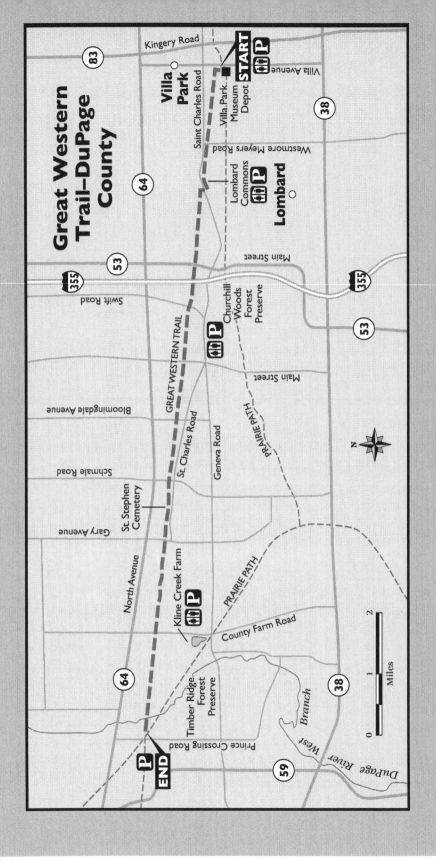

Transportation: The Villa Park station on the Union Pacific West Line is just 0.5 mile away from the trailhead. From the station, head south on Ardmore Ave. Look for the trail crossing after passing south of St. Charles Rd.

Contacts: DuPage County Division of Transportation, Jack T. Knuepfer Administration Building, 421 N. County Farm Road, Wheaton; (630) 682-7318; dupagecounty.gov/dot.

IIIIIIIIIIIIIIIIIIIIIIIIIIIIIIIIIIIIIIIIIIIIIIIIIIIIIIIIIIIIIIIIIIIIIIIIIIIIIIIIIIIIIIIIIIIIIII

Many people use this section of the Great Western Trail (GWT) as an alternative to the Illinois Prairie Path, which runs parallel to the GWT for its full distance. While the two trails hit some similar terrain, they also possess important differences. The GWT tends to go through fewer residential areas and as a result is less used than the Prairie Path. In this case, it also means fewer trailside amenities such as restrooms, drinking fountains, and benches. The GWT intersects the Prairie Path's Main Stem at the beginning of this route and intersects the Prairie Path's Elgin Branch at the end of the route.

There are two sections of the Great Western Trail. This eastern section of the trail, which runs across the northern section of DuPage County, does not directly connect with the western section of the Great Western Trail (also covered in this book), which starts in Kane County near St. Charles and runs west to Sycamore.

Churchill Woods

As you start the trail westward, the first few miles pass a couple of parks that are mixed in with residential backyards. In Lombard a trail leading into Westmore Woods Park branches right. This paved path hugs the shore of a small pond while taking a short trip to a grassy community park. Also in Lombard is a sprawling park called Lombard Commons, which contains more open grassy areas, a public pool, and multiple sports fields. Heading west from Lombard, more residential backyards appear as the path traces the top of a ten- to fifteen-foot railroad embankment.

After crossing I-355 at 4.2 miles, take the crushed gravel trail that branches left alongside Swift Rd. for a side trip to Churchill Woods Forest Preserve. On the left, a hiking trail winds through the second largest prairie in DuPage County. Prairie flowers such as asters, bottle gentian, and prairie sundrops decorate this grassland during spring and fall. Continue ahead on the main trail for a winding wooded route through Churchill Woods. At St. Charles Rd. go left and head through the underpass. On the other side of St. Charles Rd., continue ahead on the trail to a scenic picnic area alongside a series of islands within the East Branch of the DuPage River.

Two Local Landmarks

Back on the GWT, the path begins to do that magical thing that rail trails tend to do. The landscape surrounding the trail dips and rises, but thanks to surface grading for the railroad right-of-way, the trail remains extremely level.

Not far ahead, just after the path cuts straight through the middle of a gravel and concrete operation, you'll see the tiny St. Stephen Cemetery on the right. If the chain-link fence didn't prevent access, you would see that the gravestones date back to the 1850s, many with German names on them. When the Great Western Railroad was built, it cut off road access to the small cemetery, causing it to languish. An adjoining church was razed. The small patch of prairie to the west of the cemetery was intended to accommodate future gravesites, but it was never used. After being neglected for decades, the cemetery has been restored and protected in recent years.

At County Farm Rd. you'll have the opportunity to visit another local landmark—the Kline Creek Farm. Kline Creek Farm is a county-operated living-history farm that demonstrates local farm life in the 1890s. Along with livestock, there are several barns, an icehouse, a windmill water pump, and a farmhouse containing decor and furnishings of a DuPage County Victorian-era farm.

The final section of the GWT trail takes you on a very gentle downhill through rolling savanna and prairie in the Timber Ridge Forest Preserve. Wetlands with patches of open water and sedge grasses show up near the crossing of the West Branch of the DuPage River. The trail ends about

1 mile past the point where it intersects with the Elgin Branch of the Prairie Path.

Local Information

- DuPage Convention and Visitors Bureau, 915 Harger Road, Suite 240, Oak Brook; (800) 232-0502; discoverdupage.com.
- Friends of the Great Western Trail, friendsofthegreatwesterntrails.com; organizes events and trail improvements efforts.

Local Events/Attractions

- Kline Creek Farm, 1 mile south of North Avenue (IL 64); (630) 876-5900; dupageforest.org. Living-history farm with education programs and a visitor center.
- Villa Park Museum, 220 S. Villa Avenue, Villa Park; (630) 941-0223; vphistoricalsociety.com. The museum contains exhibits relating to the town and the railroad line; serves as the starting point for this route.

Restaurants

- Augustinos Rock and Roll Deli, 246 S. Schmale Road, Carol Stream; (630) 665-5585 augustinos.com. Burgers, pasta, pizza, and submarine sandwiches in a 1950s-style diner with outdoor seating. Located right on the path.

Accommodations

- Lynfred Bed and Breakfast, 15 S. Roselle Road, Roselle; (630) 529-9463; lynfredwinery.com. Luxurious and pricey; also a winery.

7 GREAT WESTERN TRAIL—KANE AND DEKALB COUNTIES

Setting out toward Sycamore from St. Charles, the first half of the path presents you with attractive woodland intermingled with housing developments. A rural landscape with big views takes over on the second half of the path as it slices through wide-open agricultural land alongside IL 64.

Location: From LeRoy Oaks Forest Preserve, northwest of St. Charles, the trail runs west to the outskirts of Sycamore, located just north of Dekalb.

Length: 17.1 miles one-way.

Surface: Crushed gravel with a short stretch of asphalt.

Wheelchair access: The trail is wheelchair accessible. Some of the bridges are arched and could be challenging to wheelchair users.

Difficulty: The length of the trail and its lack of amenities may offer a challenge to some trail users.

Restrooms: There are public restrooms at the LeRoy Oaks' Great Western Trail parking area (water), Campton Township Community Center (portable toilets), and Sycamore Community Park (just south of the Airport Rd. trailhead; water).

Maps: kdot.countyofkane.org.

Hazards: The trail crosses only a few busy streets; use caution while crossing these.

Access and parking: From I-355 go west toward St. Charles on IL 64. After passing through St. Charles, turn right onto Randall Rd. and then left onto Dean St. The Great Western Trail parking area is on the left. UTM coordinates: 16T, 388277 E, 4641642 N.

Most of the road crossings west of IL 47 have room for at least one car to park. Additional parking is available at the following areas:

To park in Wasco, head west from St. Charles on IL 64. In Wasco turn right onto Wasco Rd. Park on the right.

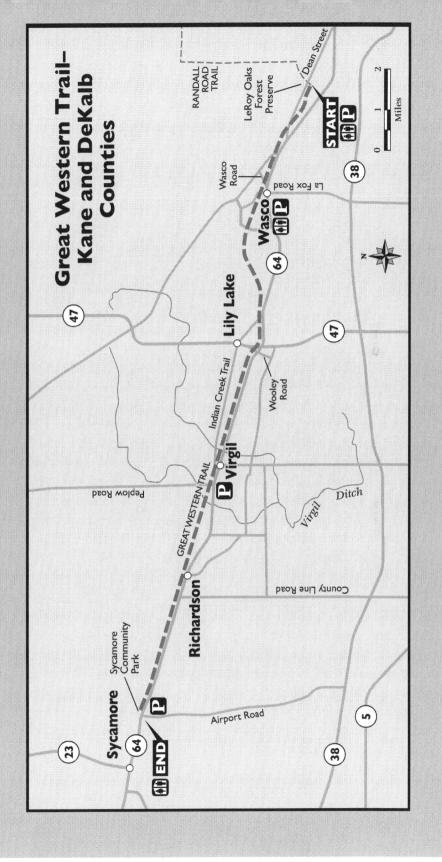

Great Western Trail–Kane and DeKalb Counties

RANDALL ROAD TRAIL

Dean Street

LeRoy Oaks Forest Preserve

START

Wasco Road

La Fox Road

Wasco

64

38

47

Lily Lake

Indian Creek Trail

Wooley Road

47

Virgil

Peplow Road

GREAT WESTERN TRAIL

Virgil Ditch

Richardson

County Line Road

Sycamore Community Park

Sycamore

Airport Road

END

64

23

38

5

N

Miles

0 1 2

To park at the west end of the trail in Sycamore, take I-88 to DeKalb and exit north onto Peace Rd. Follow Peace Rd. all the way to IL 64 and turn right. After passing through Sycamore, turn left onto Old State Rd. The parking area is immediately on the right.

Transportation: The Union Pacific West Metra line stops in Geneva about 5 miles southeast of the trailhead.

Contacts: Dekalb County Forest Preserve, 110 E. Sycamore Street, Sycamore; (815) 895-7191; dekalbcounty.org.

Kane County Forest Preserve, Building G, 719 Batavia Avenue, Geneva; (630) 232-5980; kaneforest.com.

First established in 1885 as a regional railroad between St. Paul, Minnesota, and the Iowa-Minnesota state line, the Chicago Great Western Railroad eventually linked Chicago, Minneapolis, Omaha, and Kansas City. The route—nicknamed the Corn Belt Route because it toured the most productive agricultural land within the Midwest—was mostly abandoned in 1968 when the railroad was merged with the Chicago and North Western Railway. Fortunately, long sections of the railroad in Illinois, Iowa, and Minnesota have been transformed into rail trails, including two sections in northern Illinois. In addition to the section described here, an 11.5-mile section of the railroad between Villa Park and West Chicago has been developed as a rail trail (also covered in this book).

LeRoy Oaks and Wasco

Starting in LeRoy Oaks Forest Preserve, the trail launches you into a large prairie fringed by woods and wetlands. After a sharp turn to the right, you'll arrive on the railroad right-of-way and then pass above Peck Rd. on an arched metal bridge. Initially, new housing developments peek through the woods now and then. But soon you'll have little doubt that local homebuilders have done a brisk business in the past decade. Shortly after crossing another arched bridge over Hidden Oaks Rd., the trail pulls alongside IL 64. As the trail follows IL 64, the woodland along the trail grows thin, reducing the shade but increasing the views. Briefly the trail plunges through one of those human-made ravines designed to make the railroad run level.

After passing through Wasco, the trail, which becomes asphalt for a stretch, temporarily breaks away from IL 64. Woodlands intermittently appear alongside the trail, as do marsh grasses and small ponds. Ferson Creek winds between the trail and the foot of the small bluffs rising on the right. Before the trail crosses IL 47 on an old train bridge, another small creek connects Ferson Creek with the wetlands on the left.

Big Views and Agricultural Land

After crossing IL 47, the remaining 9.5 miles of the trail closely parallels IL 64. This is where housing developments subside and agricultural land begins to dominate the scenery. Vegetation tends to be sparse as the path runs about thirty feet north of the highway; occasional stands of trees interrupt the shrubs and prairie grasses. The lack of dense greenery allows long views from atop the twelve-foot-high railroad embankment.

Before and after you bisect the hamlet of Virgil, the trail crosses arms of Virgil Ditch. In the little gathering of houses called Richardson, Friday and Saturday nights bring the roar of car engines at the Sycamore Speedway, located a few hundred feet north of the trail. The end of the trail in Sycamore offers a shaded picnic table to take a breather before returning to the trail's starting point.

Those with energy to burn may consider a couple of tempting side trips. At the end of the trail, go 0.25 mile south on Airport Rd. to the entrance of Sycamore Community Park on the right. At the end of the 1-mile-long trail through the park, cyclists have the opportunity to follow an on-street bike route through Sycamore and into DeKalb.

Another side trip can be explored at the beginning of the Great Western Trail in St. Charles. Follow the trail north through LeRoy Oaks Forest Preserve and then continue north along Randall Rd. for a 7-mile connection to the Fox River Path outside Elgin.

Local Information

- Sycamore Chamber of Commerce, 519 W. State Street, Sycamore; sycamorechamber.com.

The western trailhead for the Great Western Trail in DeKalb County.

Local Events/Attractions

- Downtown St. Charles. A charming small town just a couple miles from the trailhead. Plenty of shopping and dining options as well as pleasant walkways along the Fox River. This is also where you can connect with the Fox River Trail.
- Sycamore Speedway, 50W086 Highway 64, Maple Park; (815) 895-5454; sycamorespeedway. com. Stock car and drag racing on Friday and Saturday nights since 1960.

Restaurants

- There's a collection of restaurants near where LaFox Rd. crosses IL 64. They're easy to get to from the trail. You'll also find plenty of eating options in St. Charles and Sycamore.

Accommodations

- Hotel Baker, 100 W. Main Street, St. Charles; (630) 584-2100; hotelbaker.com; a historic hotel located in the charming downtown of St. Charles.
- Oscar Swan Country Inn Bed and Breakfast, 1800 W. State Street, Geneva; (630) 232-0173; oscarswan.com. English country manor with eight guest rooms.

8   I&M CANAL TRAIL

In 1848 the Illinois and Michigan Canal provided the final shipping link between the East Coast of the United States and the Gulf of Mexico. From Chicago the canal angled southwest, running beside the Des Plaines and Illinois Rivers halfway across the state. Thanks to the 96-mile-long canal, Chicago quickly became the largest and most efficient grain market in the world. The canal towpath, originally used by mules for pulling boats through the canal, has been transformed into a 61.9-mile crushed gravel path running from the outskirts of Joliet to the town of La Salle. From end to end, the route wanders through a variety of landscapes: dense woods, marshes, prairies, riverbanks, agricultural land, and small towns.

Location: From the southwest outskirts of Joliet, the trail runs west to the town of LaSalle.

Length: 61.9 miles one-way.

Surface: Crushed gravel.

Wheelchair access: Most of the trail is wheelchair accessible. There are several stretches where the trail shares the route with local roads.

Difficulty: The length of this trail may present a challenge even for well-prepared athletes. While amenities exist along the way, some sections are very remote.

Restrooms: There are public restrooms at Lower Rock Run Forest Preserve (water), Channahon State Park (water), McKinley Woods Forest Preserve (water), the Aux Sable Aqueduct, Gebhard Woods State Park (water), Marseilles, the riverside park in Ottawa, Utica (take pedestrian bridge on right after crossing IL 178; water), and the La Salle parking area (water).

Maps: idot.illinois.gov.

Hazards: The trail crosses a handful of busy roads. Use caution while crossing these. Small sections of the trail are occasionally closed due to erosion and bridges in need of repair. Call the trail's main office or contact the Illinois DNR (www2.illinois.gov/dnr) to learn about any detours or closed sections of the trail.

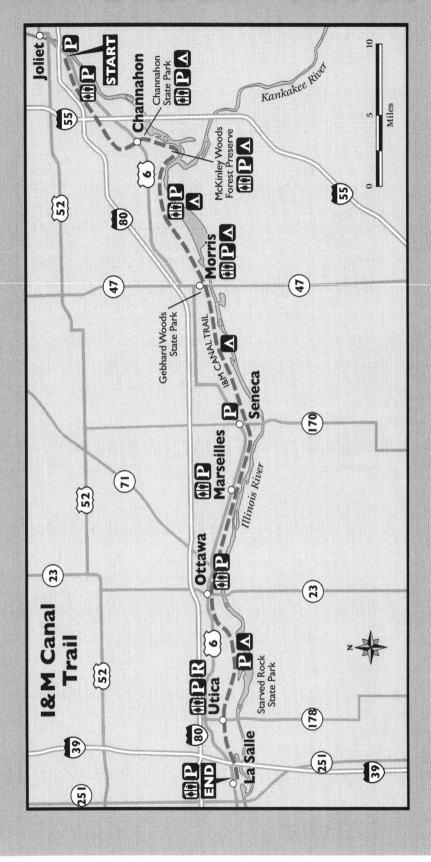

Access and parking: From I-55 head east on I-88. Go south on Raynor Rd. (exit 131). Continue ahead as Raynor Rd. swings to the right and turns into Meadow Ave. Turn left onto Brandon Rd. Turn right on Mound Rd. and the parking area is on the left. UTM coordinates: 16T, 407662 E, 4595096 N.

To park at Rock Run Forest Preserve, head south on Hollywood Rd. from I-80. The forest preserve is on the right.

To park at Channahon State Park, exit west on US 6 from I-55. In Channahon turn left onto Canal St. The entrance to the park is on the right.

To reach the Aux Sable Aqueduct parking area, take I-55 south to exit 248 and head southwest on US 6. Turn left onto Tabler Rd. and then right onto Cemetery Rd.

To park at Gebhard Woods State Park, head south from I-80 into Morris on IL 47. Turn right onto Jefferson St., which soon becomes Freemont St. Turn left onto Ottawa St.; the entrance to the park is on the left.

To park in Seneca, head south on US 6 from I-80. Turn left onto IL 170. Look for the trailhead on the right.

To park in Marseilles, head south from I-80 on 24th Rd. Look for on-street parking as you cross over the trail while following Main St.

To access the trail in Ottawa, head south on Columbus St. from I-80. Turn left onto Superior St. Before reaching the Fox River, park in the lot on the left.

To park in Utica, head south on IL 178 from I-80. Park in the lot on the right in Utica.

To park at the west end of the trail in La Salle, exit south onto St. Vincents Ave. from I-80. Keep straight ahead as St. Vincents Ave. becomes Joliet St. Look for the entrance to the parking area on the right.

Transportation: The Heritage Corridor and the Rock Island District Metra train lines both end in Joliet. The trailhead is several miles from the train station.

Rentals: Bike sharing stations are available in LaSalle, Utica, Morris, and Channahon; available April 1–November 30; iandmcanal.org/bike.

Contact: Lock 16 Café & I&M Canal Visitor Center; 754 First Street, LaSalle; canalcor.org.

The I&M Canal Trail is one of the unsung treasures of the state. Rich in history and natural beauty, it takes you through interesting but less known corners of northern Illinois. While it's a great trail for those seeking solitude and pristine landscapes, it's also a draw for people who like to explore the small, historic towns that grew up alongside the canal—before the railroad took centerstage. Unlike the Hennepin Canal Trail—Illinois's other long canal trail—I&M Canal Trail hits towns along the way, seven in total. Interspersed among the charming towns is no shortage of lovely parks alongside the trail.

Joliet to Seneca

Heading west from the Brandon Rd. parking area on the outskirts of Joliet, wetlands rule much of the landscape. There are algae-covered ponds littered with deadfall, huge expanses of cattails, and swaying stands of fifteen-foot-tall sedge grasses. Water-loving birds such as red-winged blackbirds, green night herons, and kingfishers seem unfazed by the sounds of heavy industry nearby on US 6.

Before reaching Channahon, short spur trails head left into Rock Run Forest Preserve and Channahon Community Park. Both parks are less than 0.25 mile off the I&M Canal Trail, and each have picnic areas, restrooms, and water. At Rock Run a short hiking trail leads to the shore of Rock Run Creek. After passing under I-55, the path runs through attractive bottom-land terrain alongside the canal's open water.

The diminutive Channahon State Park contains a tenting campground, a picnic area, a former canal lock, and one of only two locktender's houses remaining along the canal. Locktenders had to be available day or night to keep the boat traffic moving. They opened the gate for the canal boat to enter the twelve- by 100-foot lock, closed the gate, and then filled or drained the lock to raise or lower the boat. Fifteen locks were needed along the canal for 141 feet of elevation change between Chicago and the Illinois River.

After the path crosses the DuPage River and passes two more locks, you'll embark on one of the best stretches on the eastern side of the I&M Canal Trail. For most of the next 5.5 miles, the trail occupies a fifteen-foot-wide strip of land between two bodies of water: The twenty- to thirty-foot-wide canal is on the right; the broad and mighty Des Plaines River is on the left. The surrounding landscape is wooded and hilly with bluffs and patches of farmland. With good weather, expect to see plenty of pleasure boats on the Des Plaines. Barges may come lumbering by, too, some as long as two city blocks. At McKinley Woods a pedestrian bridge over the canal leads to a picnic area, a small campground, and the hiking trails that lead through the park's rugged terrain.

The bluffs continue beyond McKinley Woods all the way to the Dresden Lock and Dam. Near the dam is the only mule barn left standing along the canal. (Mule barns once were situated every 10 to 15 miles so that the mules and horses could eat and rest before their next haul.) Another locktender's house appears along the path at Aux Sable Creek. This is also where you'll find a small camping area and an aqueduct where the canal is directed over the forty-foot-wide creek.

A young man dressed in period attire shows how mules once pulled the boats through the I&M Canal.

Before passing downtown Morris you'll likely see some anglers and boaters in a riverside park. Morris's vibrant main strip runs straight north from a pedestrian bridge that spans the canal. Across the street from the bridge sits the Grundy County Historical Society.

After the aqueduct over Nettle Creek at Gebhard Woods State Park, the canal dries up and bottomland woods and sedge grasses take over. You'll see a small stream that trickles under the trail toward the Illinois River. Beyond the stream you'll duck under the curving wooden supports of a new bridge for Old Stage Rd. Dense stands of bottomland woods occasionally open up to reveal big sprawling wetlands sprinkled with downed trees and muskrat lodges.

Seneca contains the only grain elevator that still stands along the I&M Canal. Built in 1861 and placed on the National Register of Historic Places in 1997, the eighty-foot structure is a reminder of the cargo that weighed down most canal boats as they were hauled up and down the canal.

Seneca to La Salle

Leaving Seneca, the path follows a dirt road for a mile or so through farm fields. Once you've regained the trail, you'll catch glimpses of the Illinois River beyond the field on the left. In a residential area within the town of Marseilles, the trail passes a former lock beside the trail.

A dramatic crossing of the Fox River marks your arrival in Ottawa. Alongside the pedestrian bridge that takes you over the river is an enormous aqueduct that shuttled canal boats fifty feet above the Fox River. The riverside park on the west bank of the Fox River serves as a perfect picnicking spot. If you're in the mood for exploring, a few blocks south of the trail in Ottawa (on IL 71) is Washington Square, which hosted the first of the series of U.S. Senate debates between Abraham Lincoln and Stephen Douglas.

The remaining 15 miles of trail from Ottawa to LaSalle offer many scenic stretches of river bluffs, wetlands, and open water. Exposed sandstone appears now and then on the eighty-foot-high bluffs to the right. In some places the exposed rock is the result of dynamite used to clear the route for a railroad line that runs at the foot of the bluff.

For those with the time and inclination to explore the area, Buffalo Rock State Park is well worth a brief detour. At the Buffalo Rock parking area, you can cross Dee Bennett Rd. to visit this park perched on a bluff above the Illinois River. Buffalo Rock State Park is a reclaimed strip mine that contains five enormous earthen mounds depicting creatures commonly found near the river.

Entering Utica, the trail shares the route with a quiet country road.

At the parking area near the end of the trail in La Salle, you'll come upon a full-size replica of a canal boat that traveled the canal more than 150 years ago. The wooden boat is long and narrow, with an open-air deck on the second level. During an hour-long boat ride, tour guides dressed from the era provide narration. You can buy boat tickets at I&M Canal Visitor Center and café located just across the canal in downtown La Salle. At the end of the trail, about 1 mile beyond the parking area in La Salle, you can see the canal's confluence with the Illinois River off to the left.

Local Information

- Heritage Corridor Convention and Visitors Bureau, 2701 Black Road, Suite 201, Joliet; (844) 944-2282; heritagecorridorcvb.com.
- Joliet Bicycle club; jolietbicycleclub.com. Organizes regular rides, some on the I&M Canal Trail.
- Lock 16 Café and Visitor Center, 754 First Street, La Salle; (815) 223-1851; iandmcanal.org. The visitor center, located several blocks from the trail, contains exhibits, a café, and a gift shop. Buy tickets for mule-pulled boat ride in the canal.
- Ottawa Visitors Center, 1028 La Salle Street, Ottawa, (815) 434-2737; experienceottawa.com.

Local Events/Attractions

- Hegeler Carus Mansion, 1307 Seventh Street, La Salle; (815) 224-6543; www.hegelercarus.org. Huge mansion from 1874 occupies an entire city block; tours provided.
- Illinois Waterway Visitors Center, 950 N. 27th Road, Ottawa; (815) 667-4054. Observation decks allow you to watch the boats using the locks.
- Starved Rock State Park, at IL 178 and IL 71, Utica; (815) 667-4726; www2.illinois.gov/dnr Visit the canyons and bluffs at one of the state's best (and most popular) state parks.

Restaurants

- La Salle, Ottawa, and Morris all offer an assortment of dining and drinking options close to the trail. The smaller towns have fewer options.

Accommodations

- I&M Canal camping. From the east, tent camping is offered at Channahon State Park, McKinley Woods Forest Preserve, the Aux Sable Aqueduct, and three hike-in sites along the trail between the Aux Sable Aqueduct and Seneca. There's also camping at Gebhard Woods State Park and three hike-in sites on the trail west of the Buffalo Rock parking area. (My book *Camping Illinois* offers full descriptions of each camping location.)

- Starved Rock Lodge and Conference Center, One Lodge Lane, Oglesby; (800) 868-7625; starvedrocklodge.com. Guest rooms, cabins, and campground at the state park, located at IL 178 and IL 71.

9 ILLINOIS PRAIRIE PATH—AURORA AND ELGIN BRANCHES

These two connected branches of the Illinois Prairie Path take you through a suburban landscape that is largely residential, sometimes industrial, and often feels more remote than it actually is. As the route cuts through a number of forest preserves, the dense trailside greenery falls away, and majestic views of wetlands and prairie open up in front of you. At roughly the route's halfway mark, budget some time for checking out the shops and restaurants in Wheaton.

Location: From Veterans Memorial Island Park, just north of downtown Aurora, the trail runs northeast to Wheaton and then northwest to Elgin.

Length: 27.2 miles one-way.

Surface: Asphalt for the first mile or so; crushed gravel surface the rest of the way.

Wheelchair access: The trail is wheelchair accessible.

Difficulty: The trail offers a medium to high level of difficulty due to the length.

Restrooms: There are public restrooms and water at Veterans Memorial Island Park, in front of the Warrenville city offices, the junction with the Prairie Path Main Stem in Wheaton, and the Army Trail Rd. parking area.

Maps: ipp.org.

Hazards: The trail crosses a few busy streets; use caution while crossing these. Be mindful of other trail users, particularly on the busier sections of this trail.

Access and parking: From I-88 north of Aurora, head south on IL 31 (Lincoln St.). Turn left at Illinois Ave. Park at Veterans Memorial Island Park on the right. From the island, catch the trail by heading to the east shore of the Fox River and following the path left. UTM coordinates: 16T, 391214 E, 4624868 N.

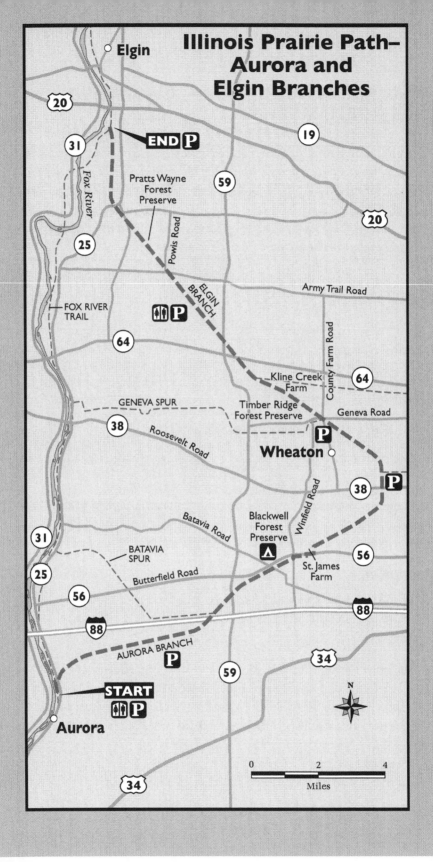

To park at the Country Lakes Forest Preserve parking area, head south from I-88 on IL 59. Turn right onto Diehl Rd. and then left onto Shore Rd. Park on the left.

To park at the Winfield Rd. parking area, head north from I-88 on Winfield Rd. Parking is on the left.

Wheaton contains many side streets where you can park at no cost near the trail. To park at Stevens Park on Lincoln Ave., go north on Main St. from Roosevelt Rd. Turn left on Lincoln Ave. and look for parking as you get near the trail.

To park at the corner of County Farm and Geneva Roads, head west from I-355 on IL 64. Turn left onto County Farm Rd. Park at the northwest corner of the intersection with Geneva Rd.

To park at the Army Trail Rd. parking area, head south on IL 59 from I-90. Turn right onto Army Trail Rd.

To park at the Raymond St. parking area, located at the north end of the route, head south on IL 59 from I-90. Turn right onto US 20 (Lake St.) and then left onto Raymond St. Park on the right.

Transportation: The Aurora stop on the BNSF Metra line is across the street from south end of the trail in Aurora. The Wheaton stop on the Union Pacific West Metra line is a couple blocks east of the trail. In Elgin, the National St. station on the Milwaukee District West line is less than a mile north of the north end of the trail.

Rentals: Fox Valley Bike Share system has bikes available in Aurora and Elgin; enjoyaurora.com.

Contact: DuPage County Division of Transportation, Jack T. Knuepfer Administration Building, 421 N. County Farm Road, Wheaton; (630) 682-7318

Illinois Prairie Path, P.O. Box 1086, Wheaton; (630) 752-0120; ipp.org.

B efore starting toward Elgin on the Prairie Path, you might consider taking a quick visit south to Aurora's riverside park, which contains a large outdoor performance venue, pleasant parkland, and a graceful curving bridge that connects to an island in the river and the opposite shore.

This will allow you to enjoy the Fox River for a spell before the trail quickly takes you away from the river.

Aurora Branch

The first section of the trail—called the Aurora Branch—offers a fairly even mix of suburban neighborhoods, industrial parks, and scenic parkland. The Fox River accompanies this route for just a brief moment before the path heads away from Aurora and then climbs the wooded river bluff. As you proceed, the greenery alongside the trail toggles between dense stands of trees and thick shrubbery. New residential developments proliferate, and this is where the trail shares a right-of-way with multiple power lines that crackle and hum overhead. After you cross Farnsworth Ave., a big grassy wetland opens on the left.

In Warrenville the trail shoots across the West Branch of the DuPage River and then brushes against two county-operated parks. First is Blackwell Forest Preserve, where there's a great collection of multi-use trails, as well as camping, boat rentals, and one of the most popular sledding hills around, and the second is St. James Farm, a former private estate that focuses on equestrian activities.

The route toward downtown Wheaton offers densely wooded terrain, well-kept backyards, and crossings of mostly low-traffic roads. You may also notice that this stretch of trail is well used by local residents. Proof of this path's popularity is demonstrated by homeowners posting HOUSE FOR SALE signs along the path.

Elgin Branch

Compared to the first half of this route, the second half of the route—called the Elgin Branch—is more scenic and peaceful as the trail carries you through a greater number of sleepy neighborhoods and more forest preserves. After passing the main stem of the Prairie Path in Wheaton and following a long pedestrian bridge over multiple railroad tracks, you'll soon come upon a park called Lincoln Marsh. A short time later pass through the lush and dense landscape at Kline Creek Farm preserve (at the corner of Geneva and County Farm Roads, a spur trail on the right leads to Kline Creek Farm, a living history museum operated by the county park system). Again, the path crosses the West Branch of the DuPage River. Near where the Great Western Trail intersects the Prairie Path on the right, you'll encounter a big swath of wetlands, ponds, and stands of cattails.

Soon you'll arrive at Pratts Wayne Forest Preserve, a generous-size natural area that contains prairies, sprawling wetlands, and a collection of fishing ponds. As you enter the forest preserve, thick woods and a dense, leafy canopy turn the trail into a shadowy tunnel. Wooden railings mark the spots where creeks pass underneath the trail. Occasionally, you'll catch fine views of cattail-fringed ponds, where you can look for waterbirds perched on fallen logs.

The final several miles of the path take you past former and current gravel mining operations and chunks of farmland. The trail ends at the Fox River Trail. Taking the Fox River Path right brings you to Elgin and eventually to the Wisconsin border along the Prairie Trail. Turning left takes you back to Aurora.

As the Elgin Spur of the Prairie Path runs through a collection of forest preserves, a remote ambiance prevails.

Local Information

- Aurora Area Convention and Visitors Bureau, 43 W. Galena Boulevard, Aurora; (630) 897-5581; enjoyaurora.com.
- DuPage Convention and Visitors Bureau, 915 Harger Road, Suite 240, Oakbrook; (800) 232-0502; discoverdupage.com.
- Elgin Area Convention and Visitors Bureau, 77 Riverside Drive, Elgin; (847) 695-7540; northern-foxrivervalley.com.
- Fox Valley Bicycle and Ski Club; fvbsc.org. Local club organizes bike rides and other activities in the area.

Local Events/Attractions

- Aurora Regional Fire Museum, 53 N. Broadway, Aurora; (630) 892-1572; auroraregionalfire-museum.org. Vintage firefighting equipment; located across the street from the trailhead in downtown Aurora.
- Blackwell Forest Preserve, Butterfield Rd., just west of Winfield Rd.; (630) 933-7200; dupage-forest.com. Boat rentals, campground, and lots of trails.
- Kline Creek Farm; 1 mile south of North Ave. (IL 64); (630) 876-5900; dupageforest.com. Living-history farm with animals, education programs, and a visitor center.
- St. James Farm, Butterfield Rd. east of Blackwell Forest Preserve, Wheaton; (630) 933-7200; dupageforest.com. Equestrian facilities; trails for hiking and riding; open seasonally on weekends.

Restaurants

- La Quinta de Los Reyes, 36 E. New York Street, Aurora; (630) 859-4000; laquintaaurora.com. Live music; courtyard area; located at the end of the trail in Aurora.
- Two Brothers Roundhouse, 205 N. Broadway, Aurora, (630) 264-2739; twobrothersbrewing.com. A local favorite brewpub located next to trailhead.
- Simply Thai Bistro, 563 W. Liberty Drive, Wheaton; (630) 765-7715; simplythaibistrowheaton.com. Basic Thai offerings; located on the Prairie Path Main Stem in Wheaton.

Accommodations

- Big Rock Forest Preserve, 46W499 Granart Road, Big Rock; (630) 444-1200; bit.ly/bigrockcg. Offers tent camping sites tucked away in a wooded area.
- Holiday Inn Express, 111 N. Broadway Avenue, Aurora; (630) 896-2800. Located in downtown Aurora, 1 block from the Hollywood Casino.

10 ILLINOIS PRAIRIE PATH—MAIN STEM

Stretching from Wheaton to Maywood, the main stem of the Prairie Path takes you through wooded parks and greenways and offers a taste of a handful of communities that grew up alongside this route. Along the way, you'll encounter pleasant towns like Glen Ellyn, Lombard, Villa Park, and Maywood.

Location: From Elmer J. Hoffman Park on the east side of Wheaton, the trail runs east to the Des Plaines River in Maywood.

Length: 13.4 miles one-way.

Surface: Crushed gravel for the 9.4-mile-long DuPage County section of the trail; asphalt for much of the 4-mile-long Cook County section.

Wheelchair access: The trail is wheelchair accessible, but there is a brief on-street section in Hillside.

Difficulty: The trail is easy.

Restrooms: There are public restrooms and water at Elmer J. Hoffman Park, the Villa Park Museum, Wild Meadows Trace Park in Elmhurst, and Berkeley Town Park.

Maps: ipp.org.

Hazards: Sections of this trail can get busy; be mindful of other trail users. Watch for broken glass on the paved sections. The trail crosses a few streets with very heavy traffic. Waiting to cross sometimes requires patience.

Access and parking: From I-355 head west on Roosevelt Rd. (IL 38). Turn right onto Lorraine St. Turn left onto Hill Ave. and then right onto Prospect Ave. Park at Elmer J. Hoffman Park and catch the trail just north of the parking area. UTM coordinates: 16T, 409942 E, 4635804 N.

In DuPage County, parking is available in all the communities along the trail. On weekends most leased parking spaces near the Metra stations are free, as are most metered parking spaces. Farther east in Cook County the path runs through residential areas where free parking is often available.

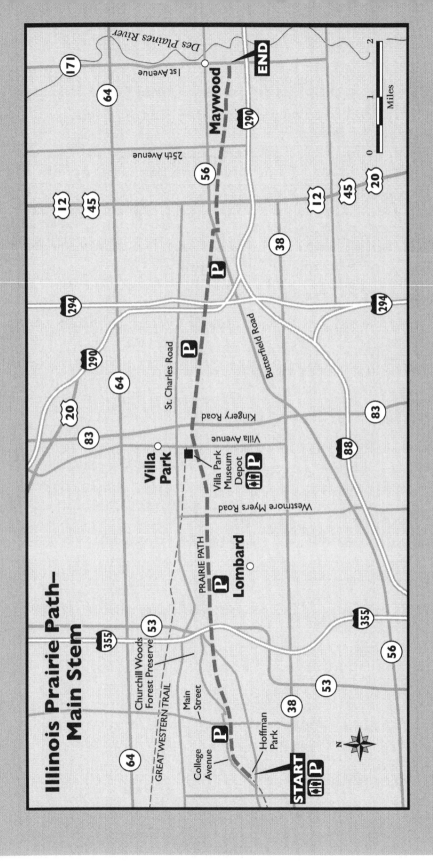

Illinois Prairie Path–Main Stem

To park at the trailside parking area in Lombard, head north on West-more Ave. from IL 38 (Roosevelt Rd.). The parking lot is on the left.

To park at the trailside parking lot in Elmhurst, head north from IL 38 (Roosevelt Rd.) on York Rd. Turn left onto Madison St. and then right onto Spring Rd.

Transportation: Take the Metra's Union Pacific West line to either the Wheaton or College Ave. stop. The trail runs alongside the tracks. In Lombard and Villa Park, catch trains on the same Metra line several blocks north of the trail.

Contact: DuPage County Division of Transportation, Jack T. Knuepfer Administration Building, 421 N. County Farm Road, Wheaton; (630) 682-7318.

Illinois Prairie Path, (630) 752-0120; ipp.org.

The Illinois Prairie Path was the brainchild of May Theilgaard Watts, a local artist, writer, horticulturist, and early environmentalist. In 1963, Watts set the ball rolling in creating one of the first rails-to-trails conversions in the nation by stirring the interest of local volunteers, promotors, and decision-makers. "We are human beings," she wrote in a letter to the *Chicago Tribune* that kicked off the effort. "We are able to walk upright on two feet. We need a footpath. Right now there is a chance for Chicago and its suburbs to have a footpath, a long one." Watts ended the letter with a call to action, telling readers that "many hands are itching" and "many bulldozers are drooling" for this land.

Shortly after the letter was published, eighty people turned out for a walk along the path. Watts spoke widely to local groups and municipalities to drum up support for the path. The path's eventual success owes much of its initial spark to Watts and a small group of volunteers who happened to be women.

Wheaton and Glen Ellyn

Before heading east on the trail, consider taking the 1.5-mile trip west along the path into downtown Wheaton, where restaurants, bars, and shops line the streets. Along the way you'll pass Wheaton College, which contains a museum focusing on the school's most famous alumnus, the evangelist Billy Graham. The trail also passes a large Romanesque-style courthouse built in 1896 that is now on the National Register of Historic Places. The building, topped off by a large clock tower, now contains condos. The west side of Wheaton is where the Prairie Path splits into two main branches; one goes to Aurora, the other to Elgin (these two branches are also included in this book).

Back at the starting point and now heading east on the path you'll soon encounter another pleasant downtown area in Glen Ellyn. Smaller than Wheaton, Glen Ellyn also has a collection of shops and restaurants within sight of the trail. On the way out of Glen Ellyn, the trail passes through a little ravine before shooting under I-355. In Lombard a leafy residential atmosphere dominates as the trail crosses numerous side streets.

The trail is accompanied by an attractive greenway as it proceeds through Villa Park, the next town along the route. At Ardmore St. you'll pass an old Prairie-style train depot built with river rock in 1910. Just ahead, another former depot contains a museum with a few small exhibits. The depot was built in 1929 of cut stone and stucco with wood trim. Inside you'll learn the Illinois Prairie Path runs along the route of the former Chicago, Aurora, and Elgin Railway, an electric railroad line that carried commuters and freight between Chicago and its western suburbs. The rail line stopped service in the late 1950s and was abandoned altogether in 1961. Signs near the museum point to the eastern terminus of the Great Western Trail (also included this book), which starts just one block north.

Elmhurst and Cook County

In Elmhurst the many patches of trailside greenery will likely catch your eye. Well-tended flower gardens decorate the residential backyards along the path, and cottonwood, sumac, and oaks occasionally conspire to create a tunnel of trees that encloses the trail. Near Spring Rd., community

Small Bridge, Big Headache

West of I-355, the Illinois Prairie Path crosses the East Branch of the DuPage River on a small bridge that had to be rebuilt five times during the trail's early years. Between 1969 and 1977, the bridge saw it all: vandalism, multiple floods, arson, and in one instance, the remaining structural support of an old steel railroad bridge was pulled down and fell the wrong way, seriously damaging the new bridge. Finally, local volunteers raised enough money to build a new, heavily reinforced steel bridge designed to last.

volunteers maintain a swath of restored prairie thick with such plants as milkweed, baby's breath, compass plants, shooting star, and goldenrod.

Passing under I-290 and I-294 signals your departure from DuPage County and your entry into Cook County. In Berkeley the path again runs through a wide greenway sprinkled with picnic tables, playgrounds, and ball diamonds. After a brief on-street section of the trail in the community of Hillside, small industrial businesses multiply. For the remainder of the path through Bellwood and the much larger town of Maywood, residential neighborhoods with modest, well-kept homes intermingle with industrial districts. Through much of this area, the path shares the route with a power line right-of-way.

Major Milepoints

10.2   Cross IL 56 and keep straight ahead on Forest Ave.

10.3   Turn left onto Warren Ave.

10.5   Cross Mannheim Rd. and resume traveling on the Prairie Path.

Local Information

- Choose Chicago, 301 E. Cermak Road, Chicago; (312) 567-8500; choosechicago.com.
- DuPage Convention and Visitors Bureau, 915 Harger Road, Suite 120, Oakbrook; (630) 575-8070; discoverdupage.com.

The Prairie Path's main stem often runs through a pleasant grassy parkland.

Local Events/Attractions

- Elmhurst Art Museum, 150 Cottage Hill Avenue, Elmhurst; (630) 834-0202; elmhurstartmuseum.org. Nice collection of contemporary art.
- York Theatre, 150 N. York Road, Elmhurst; (630) 834-0675. An impressive Spanish-style film theater first opened in 1924; the pipe organ is played before some shows.

Restaurants

- Dairy Queen, 205 S. Main Street, Lombard; (630) 627-6364. Ice cream only; look for the vintage neon sign a few blocks north of the trail.
- Roberto's Ristorante and Pizzeria, 483 Spring Road, Elmhurst; (630) 279-8474; robertosristorante.com. Slightly upscale, classic Italian food and thin-crust pizzas; located next to the trail.

11 MAJOR TAYLOR TRAIL

The first section of the Major Taylor Trail curves through Dan Ryan Woods Forest Preserve into the historic neighborhood of Beverly. After touring the neighborhoods of Beverly, Morgan Park, and West Pullman, a soaring pedestrian bridge takes you over the Little Calumet River to the Whistler Forest Preserve.

Location: From Dan Ryan Woods Forest Preserve, near the intersection of Western Ave. and 83rd St. on Chicago's South Side, the trail runs south to Whistler Woods Forest Preserve, located just south of the Little Calumet River in Riverdale.

Length: 8.6 miles one-way.

Surface: Asphalt.

Wheelchair access: The trail is wheelchair accessible; however, on-street sections may not all have ramped sidewalks.

Difficulty: This trail is easy.

Restrooms: There are public restrooms and water at Dan Ryan Woods and Whistler Forest Preserves.

Maps: chicagocompletestreets.org.

Hazards: Broken glass appears regularly on the trail. A handful of busy street crossings must be approached with caution.

Access and parking: Take I-94 south from downtown Chicago. Exit at 79th St. and head west to Damen Ave. Turn left onto Damen Ave. and then right onto 83rd St. Park in the Dan Ryan Woods Forest Preserve's groves 15 and 16, located on the right. Head north on the trail from the parking area and then follow it as it takes a sharp turn right, heading south. UTM coordinates: 16T, 443582 E, 4621316 N.

To park at the south end of the trail, take I-57 south to 127th St. Turn left onto 127th St. and then right onto Halsted Ave. After crossing the river, turn left onto Forestview Ave. Enter Whistler Forest Preserve on the left. The trail starts at the end of the park road.

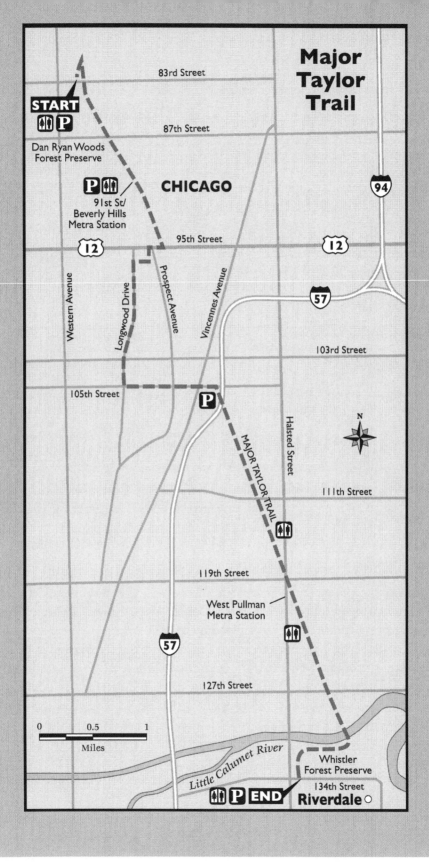

Transportation: Take the Rock Island Metra train line to the 91st St. station in Beverly. The Major Taylor Trail runs along the east side of the railroad tracks.

Rentals: Divvy is Chicago's bike sharing option; divvybikes.com.

Contact: Forest Preserve District of Cook County, 536 N. Harlem Avenue, River Forest; (800) 870-3666; fpdcc.com.

Chicago Park District, 541 N. Fairbanks Court, Chicago; (312) 742-7529; chicagoparkdistrict.com.

The Major Taylor Trail honors an African American athlete who dominated track cycling at a time when it was the most popular spectator sport in the country. Taylor was lauded for his strength and speed on a bike, especially for his tactical ability and his dazzling last-minute sprints. He made triumphant tours of Europe and Australia, defeating everyone he competed against. The title of his autobiography, The Fastest Bicycle Rider in the World, was no exaggeration. Despite harassment and frequent attempts to ban him from cycling because of his race, Taylor's prowess on the cycling track made him the wealthiest African American athlete in America.

Taylor lived in Chicago the final two years of his life after, sadly, losing his wealth on bad business deals. He died in 1932 while living at a YMCA in Chicago's Bronzeville neighborhood and is buried west of the trail in the Mount Greenwood Cemetery.

Dan Ryan Woods and Beverly

The first section of the Major Taylor Trail follows an old railroad embankment that gradually curves along the eastern edge of the Dan Ryan Woods Forest Preserve. Dense stands of trees rise high above the trail and lean overhead, creating a tunnel of branches and leaves. When the trail leaves the twenty-foot-high embankment and returns to street level, the forest preserve continues to sprawl on the right, occasionally dotted with wetlands and marsh grasses.

Known for its historic homes, tree-lined streets, and racially integrated population, Beverly is one of the most attention-grabbing neighborhoods in Chicago. The large lawns, hilly topography, and close-knit community atmosphere add to the area's appeal. Along Longwood Dr., which you follow during the on-street section of the route, you'll encounter a progression of mansions built in various styles, many with wooded, carefully landscaped yards and gardens. The first block on Longwood Ave. takes you past a couple of houses built in the Prairie style, one of which was designed by Frank Lloyd Wright (9914 S. Longwood Dr.). Probably the best-known community landmark is a replica of an Irish castle built in 1886 by real estate developer Robert C. Givins at 103rd St. and Longwood Ave. As the story goes, Givins built the limestone castle in an effort to woo a bride from Ireland. Owned by the Beverly Unitarian Church since 1942, the structure has an assortment of ghost stories attached to it.

Pullman the Little Calumet River

Once reunited with the trail, you'll start a several-mile-long journey through Morgan Park and West Pullman, a couple of Chicago's southernmost neighborhoods. After the trail crosses I-57, it angles alongside a power line right-of-way and through neighborhoods with modest working-class homes.

At 111th St., a 2-mile side-trip to the east will take you to the Pullman National Monument, a park commemorating a grandiose experiment in town planning and its beautiful old houses and public buildings. In 1881, George M. Pullman, inventor and manufacturer of the Pullman railroad sleeping car, built a town for the employees of his massive manufacturing plant. Simple but elegant row houses extend south to 115th Ave. At Cottage Grove Ave. stands Hotel Florence opposite the clock tower and the former factory, now operated by the National Park Service.

The final leg of the trail crosses a pedestrian bridge 60 feet above the Little Calumet River. The river, wider than the length of a football field, marks the boundary between Chicago and the suburban town of Riverdale. Looking west from the bridge, a string of riverside houses occupy the leafy north bank; the dense woods of Whistler Forest Preserve border the south bank.

The Major Taylor Trail brings trail users through a couple of leafy forest preserves on Chicago's far South Side.

Just before entering the forest preserve, the trail skirts the edge of a huge steel mill. Keep an eye peeled for the resident deer population scurrying into the shrubbery as you follow the trail into the dense woods of Whistler Forest Preserve.

Major Milepoints

2.0 From here, you'll need to travel 2.2 miles along city streets to reach the second part of the trail. Turn right at 95th St. Proceed with care; 95th is busy. (Option: For a shorter but less scenic on-street route, turn left onto Charles and left again onto 105th St. to return to the trail.)

2.2 Turn left onto Vanderpoel Ave.

2.3 Turn right onto 96th St.

2.5 Turn left onto Longwood Ave.

3.6 Turn left onto 105th St.

4.4 Turn right onto the trail.

Local Information

• Chicago Convention and Tourism Bureau, 2301 S. Lake Shore Drive, Chicago; (312) 567-8500; choosechicago.com.

- Friends of the Major Taylor Trail; local trail group that organizes rides, cleanups, and other activities. Check for its Facebook page.

Local Events/Attractions

- Beverly Arts Center, 2407 W. 111th Street, Chicago; (773) 445-3838; beverlyartcenter.org. Gallery exhibitions and a gift shop. The center hosts films and live music.

Restaurants

- The Good Life Soul Food Café, 11142 S. Halsted Street; (773) 264-5433; bit.ly/glsfood; casual soul food a few blocks from the trail.
- Southtown Health Foods, 2100 W. 95th Street; (773) 233-1856; southtownhealthfoods.com. Offers groceries and a smoothie bar.

Accommodations

- J. Ira and Nicki Harris Family Hostel, 24 E. Congress Parkway, Chicago; (312) 360-0300; hichicago.org. A huge, clean, and affordable hostel located downtown; dorm-style rooms and a limited number of private rooms.

12 NORTH BRANCH TRAIL

Like the river that it runs beside, the North Branch Trail never cuts a straight course for long: The trail continuously curves around little ravines, winds through picnic areas, and snakes along the tops of small river bluffs. For an urban trail, expect to see a surprising amount of woodland, prairie, and open grassy parkland as you make your way to the trail's glorious northern end point: the Chicago Botanic Garden.

Location: From LaBagh Woods Forest Preserve, at the corner of Cicero and Foster Avenues in Chicago, the trail heads north along the North Branch of the Chicago River to the Chicago Botanic Garden.

Length: 18.6 miles one-way.

Surface: Asphalt.

Wheelchair access: While the entire trail is wheelchair accessible, there are some busy road crossings and some steep overpass bridges.

Difficulty: The length and the small river bluffs give this trail a medium level of difficulty.

Restrooms: There are public restrooms at LaBagh Woods, Bunker Hill (water), Miami Woods, Linne Woods (water), Harms Woods, and Blue Star Memorial Forest Preserves and at the Chicago Botanic Garden (water).

Maps: fpdcc.com.

Hazards: There are multiple road crossings along the North Branch Trail. Be alert—some of these crossings are very busy with traffic. Fortunately traffic lights and overpasses simplify the busiest crossings. This trail can become congested on summer weekends.

Access and parking: Follow I-94 to Foster Ave. (exit 42) and turn right on Foster and then quickly turn right on Cicero Ave. The entrance to LaBagh Woods is on the right and you'll see the trail just after crossing I-94. UTM: 16T, 0438236 E, 4647667 N.

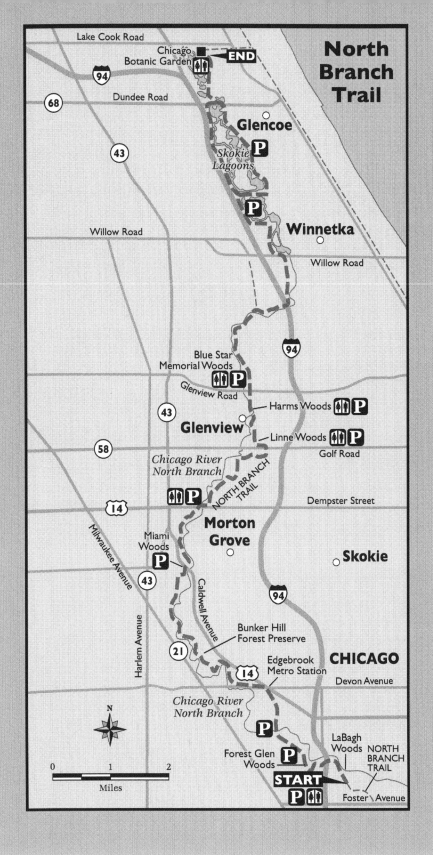

To park at Bunker Hill Forest Preserve, follow I-94 north to Caldwell Ave. (exit 41A) and head northwest. Enter Bunker Hill Forest Preserve on the left and park in any of the lots on the left near the entrance.

To reach Linne Woods Forest Preserve, take I-94 to Dempster St. (exit 37A). Head west on Dempster St. and enter the forest preserve on the right.

To catch the trail at Blue Star Memorial Woods, take I-94 north to Lake St. (exit 34B). Head west on Lake Ave. to the forest preserve entrance on the left.

To park at the Tower Rd./Skokie Lagoons parking area, take I-94 to Willow Rd. (exit 33A). Head west on Willow Rd. and turn right onto Central Ave. Bear left as Central Ave. becomes Frontage Rd. Turn right onto Tower Rd. and enter the parking area on the right.

To park at the Chicago Botanic Garden, head north on I-94. At exit 29, remain on the Edens Expressway (US 41) then take the next exit for Lake Cook Rd. Head east and travel for 0.5 mile to the botanic garden. Follow signs to the parking areas (fee).

Transportation: The Forest Glen and Edgebrook stations on the Milwaukee District North Line Metra train are both very close to the trail.

Rentals: Divvy is Chicago's bike sharing option; divvybikes.com.

Contact: Forest Preserve District of Cook County, 536 N. Harlem Ave., River Forest; (800) 870-3666; fpdcc.com.

If you look at a map of Chicago's northern suburbs and follow the routes of several streams that merge to form the North Branch of the Chicago River, it looks like strands of a rope gradually coming together. While much of the North Branch and its tributaries have fallen victim to campaigns to straighten the many bends, the sections of river along the North Branch Trail wriggle and twist through a corridor of county-owned forest preserves.

After the Chicago Lakefront Path, the North Branch Trail gets the second-place prize for the most beloved long trail in Chicagoland. The trail's popularity has much to do with its scenic beauty as well as its proximity to where many people live. A big attraction at the north end of the trail is a string of tree-fringed lakes called the Skokie Lagoons.

LaBagh Woods and Bunker Hill

Like many of the forest preserves along the North Branch Trail, LaBagh Woods, where the route starts, contains big strips of open, grassy picnic areas bordered by dense groves of oak and maple. The first few miles set the tone for much of the path to come: The North Branch of the Chicago River is not always visible, but it regularly peeks out from behind clusters of trees, through thick stands of brushes, and at the bottom of small ravines. Sometimes the path follows the top of a small bluff; sometimes it runs closer to the river. During spring and fall, in the absence of leafy cover, more miles of the twisting river will be visible along the path.

At Bunker Hill Forest Preserve, the trail cuts between the flood plain forest and the sprawling picnic areas. This park is usually busy with picnicking families and people of all ages enjoying the trail. Crossing Touhy Ave., the path winds along the top of a small bluff above the river's earthen banks where trees hang lazily over the river. As you enter the restored prairie at Miami Woods Forest Preserve, watch for hawks as they hunt for prey from above. After the prairie the path rambles through a gently rolling, wooded landscape and over a couple of trickling streams that drain into the river.

The Skokie River and Lagoons

With seven street crossings during the 6 miles between Dempster St. and the Skokie Lagoons, this stretch of trail gets interrupted regularly. Fortunately, there's plenty of visual charm along the way, such as the section north of Dempster St., where the trail runs through dense woodland strewn with deadfall and sprinkled with ponds and little ravines. North of Beckwith Rd. the landscape becomes less welcoming along a 1-mile stretch of trail that is bounded on each side with high chain-link fence. This is also where you'll start to see gravel bridle paths paralleling the main trail. At the pedestrian bridge that crosses to the west side of the river, look downriver to see the spot where the North Branch's Middle Fork joins up with its East Fork, often called the Skokie River.

Crossing Willow Rd. brings you into the wooded refuge of the Skokie Lagoons. To the right is Willow Rd. Dam—a favorite spot for local anglers. The county has worked hard over the years to keep the fish biting in these waters. After the lagoons were dug in the 1940s, the lagoons started slowly returning to their original state of marshland. Eventually both the stocked and native fish were unable to survive winters in water that was only five or six feet deep. To solve this problem, in 1988 the U.S. Environmental Protection Agency (EPA) deepened many of the lagoons to twelve feet, dredging one million cubic yards of sediment. Now the lagoons are some of Cook County's most productive fishing spots for bass, pike, and walleye.

As the trail curves left, the traffic noise of I-94 increases and you get farther into the wetlands and bottomland woods that border the lagoons. After crossing the bridge along Tower Rd. and embarking upon a rolling section of the path alongside Forest Way, you'll encounter big views of the lagoon's open water peppered with islands and fringed with dense woodland. Grassy picnic areas situated along the shore provide spots for viewing waterbirds that hang out in the shallows or float on the open water.

Chicago Botanic Garden and Beyond

If you love to see carefully selected flowers, trees, and bushes growing in perfectly landscaped environments, the final portion of the route as it passes through the Chicago Botanic Garden will be sure to quicken your pulse. Among the garden's 305 acres of artfully landscaped grounds are twenty-three distinct gardens, including Japanese- and English-style gardens, rose and bulb gardens, fruit and vegetable gardens, and gardens specially designed for children and for people with limited mobility. Along with the gardens, attractive bridges, statues, fountains, and plenty of scenic spots are situated among the nine islands and the surrounding shoreline.

Before entering the garden, you might take a break on one of the benches set within pleasant grassy lawns overlooking a few of the many

The Long History of the Skokie Lagoons

The Skokie Lagoons have undergone many changes since the area was a marshland that local Potawatomi Indians called Chewab Skokie, meaning "big wet prairie." Like so many other wetlands in the area, the marsh was drained by early white settlers. Their efforts to create farmland fell flat, however. During wet years the land still flooded. During dry years the peat contained in the marsh would actually catch fire. When Cook County acquired the marshlands in 1933, the Civilian Conservation Corps (CCC) started digging a series of connected lakes for flood control and recreation. Using mostly wheelbarrows, picks, and shovels, workers excavated four million cubic yards of earth in what became the largest CCC project in the nation. When work finished in 1942, 7 miles of waterway connected seven lagoons that were fed and drained by the Skokie River.

captivating islands containing flowering trees, bridges, and a waterfall. While at the garden, consider a visit to the restaurant within the main building. You also might consider a visit to Green Bay Trail (see page 74) by taking the trail that runs east for 1 mile from the botanic garden along Lake-Cook Rd. And in coming years, look for a new trail—the Weber Spur Trail—connecting to the North Branch Trail in LaBagh Woods, starting place for this route.

Local Information

- Chicago Convention and Tourism Bureau, 2301 S. Lake Shore Drive, Chicago; (312) 567-8500; choosechicago.com
- Chicago's North Shore Convention and Visitors Bureau, 8001 Lincoln Avenue, Suite 715, Skokie; (866) 369-0011; cnscvb.com
- The North Branch Restoration Project; northbranchrestoration.org; volunteer-run organization that hosts landscape restoration workdays throughout the year.
- The North Branch Trail Alliance; northbranchtrailalliance.com; a local organization that hosts events and rides.

Local Events/Attractions

- Chicago Botanic Garden, 1000 Lake Cook Road, Glencoe; (847) 835-5440; chicagobotanic.org. Visitor center, café, restrooms, gift shop. Pick up maps at the visitor center. Be prepared for a steep admission price.
- Ravinia Music Festival, 418 Sheridan Road, Highland Park; (847) 266-5000; ravinia.org. In operation for more than one hundred years, the festival hosts live concerts all summer long, primarily in its open-air theater. Lawn seats are a great deal.

Restaurants

- Garden Café, 1000 Lake Cook Road, Glencoe; (847) 835-3040; chicagobotanic.org. At the Chicago Botanic Garden; bakery items, soups, sandwiches, salads, and snacks.
- Superdawg Drive-in, 6363 N. Milwaukee Avenue, Chicago; (773) 763-0660; superdawg.com. Located close to the trail. A Chicago institution since 1948 serving all the menu items you'd expect, most of which are prefaced with the word "super."
- A few chain hotels are located along I-94 close to the trail. Several are located near the junction of Old Orchard Rd. and I-94.

13 NORTH SHORE CHANNEL AND GREEN BAY TRAILS

This route starts on Chicago's northwest side and follows the North Shore Channel's wooded banks through the communities of Lincolnwood, Skokie, and Evanston. In Skokie the route winds for 2 miles through an outdoor sculpture park before meeting up with the Green Bay Trail. The Green Bay Trail launches you on a tour of Chicago's swankiest North Shore suburbs of Wilmette, Kenilworth, Winnetka, Glencoe, and Highland Park.

Location: From Ronan Park, on Lawrence Ave. on Chicago's Northwest Side, the trail runs north to Highland Park.

Length: 17.7 miles one-way.

Surface: Hard-packed gravel on the northern 3 miles; asphalt and concrete on the rest.

Wheelchair access: The trails are wheelchair accessible. Sidewalks accompany nearly all the on-street sections, but some may not have ramped curbs.

Difficulty: The length may present a challenge to some trail users. Otherwise, it's easy.

Restrooms: There are portable toilets between Howard St. and Touhy Ave. and at the parking area near Dempster St.; public restrooms and water at the Metra stations in Glencoe and downtown Highland Park.

Maps: chicagocompletestreets.org.

Hazards: On a 4-mile stretch between Devon and Emerson Avenues along the North Shore Channel, you'll encounter seven busy road crossings. Since these crossings lack adequate safety infrastructure for people walking and biking, use great care at these intersections. A few on-street sections of this route follow quiet roads. The longest section by far is the 1.5 miles between the north end of the North Shore Channel Trail and the south end of the Green Bay Trail in Wilmette.

North Shore Channel and Green Bay Trails

Highland Park
Metra Station
END 🚻 🅿

🅿
Metra Station
Jens Jensen Park
Ravinia
Metra Station
Ravinia Park

🄴🄸 94

GREEN BAY TRAIL

Chicago Botanic Garden
Metra Station

🅿

LAKE MICHIGAN

🚻 🅿

Glencoe
Metra Station
Tower Road
Winnetka
Metra Station

🅿

Willow Road

🅿

43

NORTH BRANCH TRAIL

Willow Road
Metra Station

Metra Station
Lake Avenue
Wilmette
Wilmette Avenue

Chicago River North Branch

Green Bay Road

Ladd Arboretum
Golf Road
Church Street

14

Dempster Street

North Shore Sculpture Park

94   **41**   🚻 🅿

Skokie

Touhy Avenue

Lincoln Avenue

McCormick Boulevard

North Shore Channel

CHICAGO

Lincolnwood

🚻 🅿 NORTH SHORE CHANNEL TRAIL

Devon Avenue

🚻   **14**

Peterson Avenue

90

Foster Avenue

River Park

N

🅿 🚻

Lawrence Avenue

START

Ronan Park

0   1   2
Miles

Access and parking: From the corner of Western and Lawrence Avenues in Chicago, head west on Lawrence Ave. and proceed to California Ave. Turn right onto California Ave. and then left onto Argyle Ave. Park at West River Park on the right. Pick up the trail as it heads north along the North Shore Channel on the east side of the channel. UTM coordinates: 16T, 441659 E, 4646745 N.

There are several parking areas situated along McCormick Blvd. as it parallels the path. Take I-94 north to Touhy Ave. and follow Touhy east to McCormick Blvd. Turn left onto McCormick Blvd. There are three trail parking areas on the right over the next 2 miles.

The ten Metra stations along the Green Bay Trail provide many parking options. If station lots are full, consider parking on nearby side streets. Most stations are easily accessed from Green Bay Rd. Take I-94 north to Lake Ave. Head east on Lake Ave. and then turn left onto Green Bay Rd.

Transportation: The south end of the route is easily accessible from the Francisco station on the Brown Line CTA train. Metra users can start the route at one of the many Union Pacific North stations along the Green Bay Trail between Central St. and Highland Park.

Rentals: Divvy is Chicago's bikesharing program: Divvybikes.com.

Contact: Glencoe Park District, 999 Green Bay Road, Glencoe; (847) 835-3030; glencoeparkdistrict.com.

Kenilworth Park District, 419 Richmond Road, Kenilworth; (847) 251-1666; kenilworthparkdistrict.org.

Wilmette Park District, 1200 Wilmette Avenue, Wilmette; (847) 256-6100; wilmettepark.org.

Winnetka Park District, 540 Hibbard Road, Winnetka; (847) 501-2040; winpark.org.

For much of its recent history, the shores of the Chicago River's North Branch were home to steel mills, brickyards, tanneries, and soap plants. During a time when environmental regulations were nonexistent, easy access to the river simplified the waste-disposal process. Over time, though, industries discovered that the natural flow of the North Branch was not enough to carry the industrial waste downriver. The North Shore Channel was built to remedy this problem.

Constructed in 1910, the channel carried water from Wilmette Harbor south to increase the flow of the North Branch of the Chicago River. A secondary use of the 8-mile channel was to divert sewage from North Shore communities. Instead of shunting sewage into Lake Michigan, these towns sent their waste through Chicago and down to the Chicago Sanitary and Ship Canal and on to the Mississippi River. Thanks to environmental regulations and the development of sewage processing plants, the North Shore Channel is no longer a giant flushing system. In recent decades the channel has blossomed into a pleasant patch of greenery where people go to paddle, bicycle, walk, and watch wildlife.

North Shore Channel Trail

The trail starts along the North Branch of the Chicago River just south of where the North Branch and the North Shore Channel join forces. Across the river from the starting point in Ronan Park is the Lawrence Ave. Pumping Station, a large Art Deco–style building that distributes runoff during storms and sends wastewater to treatment facilities. Continuing north through River Park, the path weaves through ball diamonds, playgrounds, open grassy lawns sprinkled with trees, and a patch of restored prairie alongside the channel. The path passes under busy streets along the way.

As the path starts to run alongside the busy thoroughfare of N. McCormick Blvd., you'll pass a few outdoor sculptures along the 1-mile-long Channel Runne Park. North of Pratt Ave., the sprawling Lincolnwood Town Center mall sits to the left and the huge structures of the Winston Towers apartment complex occupy the east bank of the channel. Soon you'll pass under the high "L" tracks of the Chicago Transit Authority's Skokie Swift line.

Skokie North Shore Sculpture Park

Touhy Ave. marks the beginning of the Skokie North Shore Sculpture Park, a 2-mile-long series of sixty outdoor sculptures within a landscaped environment overlooking the North Shore Channel. The pathway weaves among artworks created by a mix of regional, national, and international contemporary artists. Large-scale pieces dominate; many are made of metal. The trees on the banks of the channel provide a pleasing background for viewing the works.

One sculpture with a strong Midwestern appeal—Hero by John Charles Cowles—looks like a piece of John Deere farm equipment designed by a space alien. Another compelling sculpture—Votive Head 2000 by Stacy Latt Savage—uses steel to create an enormous head that brings to mind the giant sculptures on Easter Island. Unfortunately this remarkable collection of outdoor art has a drawback: The persistent traffic beside the park on McCormick Blvd. tends to diminish the experience. For a quieter, less traffic-snarled experience at the sculpture park, visit early on a weekend morning.

North of Golf Rd., the trail runs through a small arboretum, which contains many dozen varieties of trees and shrubs arranged by families. Growing on small knolls alongside the trail are five varieties of pine and seven varieties of maple trees. You'll also see specimens of ginkgo, Ohio buckeye, and paper birch trees and prairie grasses growing along the banks of the channel. Several small gardens focus on prairie plants, cherry trees, nut trees, and rose bushes.

Green Bay Trail

From the arboretum, you'll travel for 1.5 miles on side streets before connecting with the Green Bay Trail in downtown Wilmette. From Wilmette the trail rises up above the street level, offering views of the surrounding the leafy neighborhoods and nearby commercial strips. To the north in Winnetka, the path drops down below street level and runs alongside the Metra Union Pacific North commuter train line. While running through this narrow thirty-foot-deep trench created for the railroad, the path ducks under numerous busy roads—out of the wind and away from street sounds. While the route is uninterrupted and peaceful, the scenery is limited to the wooded banks of the railroad ditch.

By now you've noticed that the Green Bay Trail never strays far from the commuter train tracks, and along the 9 miles of the Green Bay Trail, you'll also notice an abundance of train stations that serve this route between Chicago and Kenosha, Wisconsin. Many of these stations are attractive wood, brick, and stone structures, often located near the quaint downtown strips and sometimes set within a small park.

Many small parks decorate the sides of the Green Bay Trail. In Glencoe the path passes a small bandstand in Henry J. Kalk Park, as well as a couple of other small parks with playgrounds. Across the street from the Ravinia Metra station in Highland Park is a small park designed by Jens Jensen, the famous landscape architect responsible for some of Chicago's most well-known outdoor places, such as Garfield, Humboldt, and Columbus Parks. Some of Jensen's calling cards are evident in this tiny park, including native trees, plants, and shrubs and the circular stone bench known as a council ring. Jensen had a studio and a retreat in Highland Park from 1908 to 1934.

Before reaching Jens Jensen Park, the big brown wooden gates mark the entrance to Ravinia Park, a one-hundred-year-old outdoor live music venue. The wide-ranging music program has included such varied artists as Itzhak Perlman, Ramsey Lewis, and Frank Zappa. It's not unusual to see people bring folding chairs, a collapsible table, wine, appetizers, and a several-course meal to enjoy while listening to live music on the sprawling lawn.

The Green Bay Trail passes by the front entrance to one of the most beloved spots on Chicago's North Shore: Ravinia, a century-old outdoor concert venue.

Before the trail ends at the Highland Park Metra station, its final few miles guide you along a thin strip of land sprinkled with small community gardens. Trail users with an itch to continue north can follow the green bikeway signs through Highland Park to catch the Robert McClory Trail. From Highland Park, trail users can follow uninterrupted pathway for about 23 miles north to Kenosha, Wisconsin.

Major Milepoints

7.1 Begin this 1.5-mile on-street section of the route by turning left onto Green Bay Rd. The 0.2-mile stretch on Green Bay Rd. can be busy—if biking, consider using the sidewalk on the left.

7.3 Turn right onto Lincoln St. Pass under the railroad tracks and then turn left onto Poplar Ave., a quiet side street.

7.8 Stay on Poplar Ave. as it curves right. Immediately turn left onto Woodbine Ave.

8.0 Turn left onto Isabella St. and then resume your route north on Poplar Ave.

8.6 When Poplar Ave. ends at Wilmette Ave., continue straight to start on the Green Bay Trail.

9.6 Turn right onto Melrose St.

9.7 Turn left onto Abbotsford Rd.

9.9 Turn left onto Ivy Court and follow the green bikeway signs to resume your trip on Green Bay Trail.

Local Information

- Chicago Convention and Tourism Bureau, 2301 S. Lake Shore Drive, Chicago; (312) 567-8500; choosechicago.com.
- Chicago's North Shore Convention and Visitors Bureau, 8001 Lincoln Avenue, Suite 715, Skokie; (866) 369-0011; cnscvb.com.
- Friends of the Green Bay Trail; gbtrail.org. Local volunteer group holds events and keeps the trail in tip-top shape.

Local Events/Attractions

- Chicago Botanic Garden, 1000 Lake Cook Road, Glencoe; (847) 835-5440; chicagobotanic.org. Visitor center, café, restrooms, gift shop. A 1-mile-long trail connects the Green Bay Trail to the Botanic Garden at Lake Cook Rd.
- Ravinia Park, 418 Sheridan Road, Highland Park; (847) 266-5000; ravinia.org. For more than one hundred years, the park has hosted live summer concerts. Lawn seats are a great deal.
- Skokie North Shore Sculpture Park; (847) 679-4265; sculpturepark.org. Free public tours offered.

Restaurants

- Garden Café, 1000 Lake Cook Road, Glencoe; (847) 835-3040. At the Chicago Botanic Garden; bakery items, soups, sandwiches, salads, and snacks.
- Homers Ice Cream & Restaurant, 1237 Green Bay Road, Wilmette; (847) 251-0477; homersicecream.com. Located across Green Bay Rd. from the Green Bay Trail, Homers has been making the creamy good stuff since 1935. Allegedly Al Capone's favorite ice-cream parlor.

14 OLD PLANK ROAD TRAIL

It's for good reason this long suburban trail is one of the most popular in the state: It offers a surprising array of scenic spots. You'll see cattail-fringed ponds, patches of prairie, numerous parks, and small suburban towns with quiet, wooded neighborhoods. In the town of Frankfort, the trail's focal point, check out the historic architecture and the interesting shops before investigating several good dining options.

Location: From Logan Park in Park Forest, the trail heads west to the outskirts of Joliet.

Length: 20 miles one-way.

Surface: Asphalt.

Wheelchair access: The trail is wheelchair accessible; some parking areas are surfaced with gravel.

Difficulty: The length gives this trail a medium level of difficulty.

Restrooms: There are public restrooms at the Logan Park trailhead (water), Governors Trail Park (water), Ridgeland Ave. (portable toilet), trailside park in Frankfort, Hickory Creek Forest Preserve, Lions Den Park, and the trail's western terminus (portable toilets).

Maps: oprt.org.

Hazards: A handful of the road crossings have heavy traffic.

Access and parking: Heading south of Chicago on I-57, get off at exit 340A and head east on US 30 (Lincoln Hwy.). After passing US 54, turn right onto Orchard Dr. and then right onto North St. Park at Logan Park on the right. UTM coordinates: 16T, 442896 E, 4594085 N.

To park in Frankfort, head west from I-57 on US 30. Turn left onto La Grange Rd. (US 45) and left again onto White St. Turn right onto Kansas St. and park in the lot on the right.

To park at Hickory Creek Junction, drive east on US 30 from I-80. The parking area is on the left.

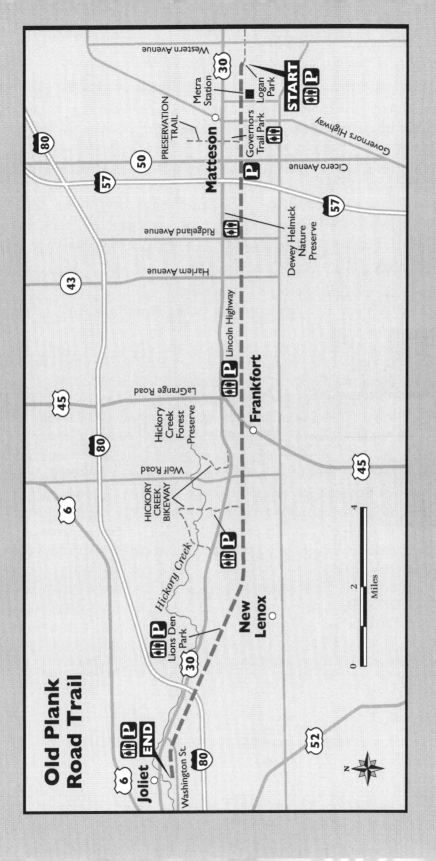

To reach the Lions Den Park parking area, take I-80 to US 30. Head east on US 30 and turn right onto Cedar Rd. Continue south after making a slight jog to the left. Lions Den Park is on the left.

To park at the lot at the trail's western terminus, drive west from I-80 on US 30. Turn left onto E. Washington St. and continue ahead for 2.5 miles. The lot is on the right.

Transportation: The Matteson station on Metra's Electric District Line is located right on the trail, not far from the eastern terminus. The Rock Island District Metra stops about six blocks north of the trail in New Lenox.

Contact: Forest Preserve District of Will County, 17540 W. Laraway Road, Joliet; (815) 727-8700; reconnectwithnature.org.

Old Plank Road Trail Management Commission, oprt.org.

The Old Plank Road Trail was never actually a plank road. A plank road is a dirt road covered with a series of planks, similar to wooden sidewalks seen in Western films. During the first half of the nineteenth century, when plank roads were wildly popular in the Northeast and Midwest, a plank road was slated to be built between Joliet and the Indiana border. But railroads began to boom, so train tracks were laid down instead. Finished in 1855, the rail line was called the Joliet Cutoff because it allowed trains to avoid going through Chicago. The Joliet Cutoff served as one of the first rail connections between Illinois and East Coast cities like Boston and New York.

During the early years of the twentieth century, the railroad right-of-way also was home to an interurban trolley line. While on the trail, look for Michigan Central Railroad concrete mile markers still in place. Etched with the letters "EG," the markers likely refer to East Gary, the dividing point on this section of the railroad.

Matteson

Heading west on the Old Plank Road Trail from the starting point at Logan Park, the first section of the trail runs through the downtown of Matteson, by a couple of parks, and through some scenic wetlands that sit behind a sprawling suburban commercial district. In Matteson the Metra station on the left and the red caboose permanently parked alongside the trail both point to the town's rich rail history.

Before crossing Cicero Ave. on the Old Plank Road Trail, the path squeezes between the former site of the huge Lincoln Mall on one side, and a series of ponds and wetlands on the other. Expect to see more of these juxtapositions between the wild and the urbanized before the route is done.

Across Cicero Ave., patches of prairie show up on the edges of the trail. One motivating factor for establishing this trail was the variety of prairie plants growing in the vicinity. Only a couple decades after the first settlers arrived in Will and Cook Counties, agencies began buying property for this right-of-way. As a result, plows never touched much of the land alongside the trail. Local botanists say there are 200 types of prairie plants identified along the trail: not only common species like goldenrod, compass plant, shooting star, and butterfly weed but also rarer specimens like scurfy pea, prairie lily, savanna blazing star, and silky aster. Pockets of prairie appear

The Old Plank Road Trail runs beside a handful of ponds and wetlands.

scattered along the trail between Cicero Ave. west all the way to New Lennox. Most, however, are located on the mile-long stretch between Cicero and Central Avenues, even under I-57.

Several nature preserves along this stretch of trail offer a surprising patch of wildness within a thoroughly built-up landscape. West of Central Ave. the trail traverses a thin strip of land that cuts through the middle of a big pond. On the left, watch for great blue herons standing like statues on the shore of a small wooded island; on the right, a cattail-fringed pond contains a graveyard of still-standing dead trees. Refocusing your eyes beyond the edges of this small wetland reveals dense housing subdivisions blanketing the surrounding landscape.

Frankfort

After crossing Harlem Ave., the trail gradually descends through a leafy landscape thick with elm, hickory, and maple—it's one of several stretches of trail that deserve a visit during fall color displays. Before entering Frankfort you'll pass a couple of small parks. In Frankfort, the first landmarks that come into view are the grain elevator, a trailside park, and a handsome iron sign for Old Plank Road Trail above the trail. Frankfort requires some exploration: A number of well-kept old buildings with interesting shops sit within the compact downtown area. Just south of the trail on White St., stop in at the trolley barn, a building that once housed the trolleys that operated on the trail, which now contains gift shops, restaurants, and a children's museum. If you have the opportunity to visit Frankfort early in the day on a Sunday between the end of April and the end of October, Frankfort's farmers market, which is held alongside the trail, will not disappoint with plenty of food options, gifts, and, of course, fresh produce.

West of Frankfort the trail mounts the appropriately named Arrowhead Bridge over LaGrange Rd. The bridge boasts an unusual design, with a pair of legs that straddle the highway and suspend the walkway with a series of four cables coming from the center of the joined struts. The struts come together at the top like the point of an arrowhead. Before the bridge, the trail passes plantings of ash trees, witch hazel, and pine.

Looking to add some extra miles to your excursion? Nearly 2 miles ahead is the turnoff for Hickory Creek Forest Preserve, which contains a picnic area, several miles of pleasantly wooded trails', and a historic one-room schoolhouse at the end of the trail.

Much of the final 7.5 miles of trail runs through the community of New Lennox. You'll pass the New Lennox Village Hall, library, police department, and a multiplex. Residential areas come and go, and many of the home-owners' backyards mingle with the path. Shortly after brushing against the backside of the sports stadium at Providence High School, you'll arrive at the end of the trail at Washington St.

Want to Add More Miles?

If you're looking to extend this route, head east of this route's starting point along the Old Plank Road Trail to the Thorn Creek Trail, which offers about 15 miles of paved trails through a string of Cook County Forest Pre-serves that follow the route of Thorn Creek. Some of the Thorn Creek trails are side paths while other stretches are heavily wooded. The most scenic section is the path to the south at Sauk Trail Woods. Visit fpdcc.com for maps. Stay tuned as the Thorn Creek Trail is extended further east in com-ing years.

Local Information

- Chicago Southland Convention and Visitors Bureau, 19900 Governors Drive, Suite 200, Olympia Fields; (708) 895-8200 or (888) 895-8233; visitchicagosouthland.com.
- Folks on Spokes, folksonspokes.com; south suburban biking and hiking club sometimes hosts rides on the trail.
- Joliet Bicycle Club; jolietbicycleclub.com; an active local riding club.

Local Events/Attractions

- During the warmer months, weekly farmers markets are held along the trail in Frankfort, Park Forest, and New Lenox.
- Joliet Area Historical Museum, 204 N. Ottawa Street, Joliet; (815) 723-5201; jolietmuseum.org. The museum provides a thorough introduction to the Joliet area.

Restaurants

- Francesca's Fortunato, 40 Kansas Street, Frankfort; (815) 464-1890; miafrancesca.com. Northern Italian upscale dining; part of the popular chain of Francesca restaurants that began with the original Mia Francesca in Chicago's Lakeview neighborhood.

15 PRAIRIE AND HEBRON TRAILS

As you follow the Prairie Trail nearly the entire north–south length of McHenry County, you'll see some of the most scenic spots in the county. In between towns such as Crystal Lake, McHenry, Ringwood, and Richmond, the trail takes you through stunning natural areas at Sterne's Woods, Glacial Park, and Nippersink North Branch Conservation Area. After finishing the Prairie Trail, the route heads west for 6.6 miles along the Hebron Trail.

Location: From Algonquin in southeast McHenry County, the trail heads north to Richmond, nearly at the Illinois–Wisconsin border, and then west to Hebron.

Length: 30.9 miles one-way.

Surface: Asphalt between Algonquin and Ringwood; crushed gravel north of Ringwood.

Wheelchair access: The trail is wheelchair accessible, but the entire route north of Ringwood is crushed gravel.

Difficulty: The trail is difficult due to the length and the long sections where trail users are fully exposed to wind and sun.

Restrooms: There are public restrooms at the Algonquin Rd. trail access, Main Street parking area in Crystal Lake, Hillside Rd. parking area, Whispering Oaks Park in McHenry, Petersen Park, Glacial Park parking area, and Nippersink North Branch parking area.

Maps: mccdistrict.org.

Hazards: Watch for traffic at busy street crossings. Use caution while following the short on-street section in Crystal Lake. Keep your eyes peeled for bike trail signs that guide you through McHenry.

Access and parking: From I-90 west of the Fox River, head north on IL 31. In Algonquin turn left onto Algonquin Rd. Turn right onto Meyer Dr. and then take a left into the Algonquin Rd. Trail access parking area. During winter,

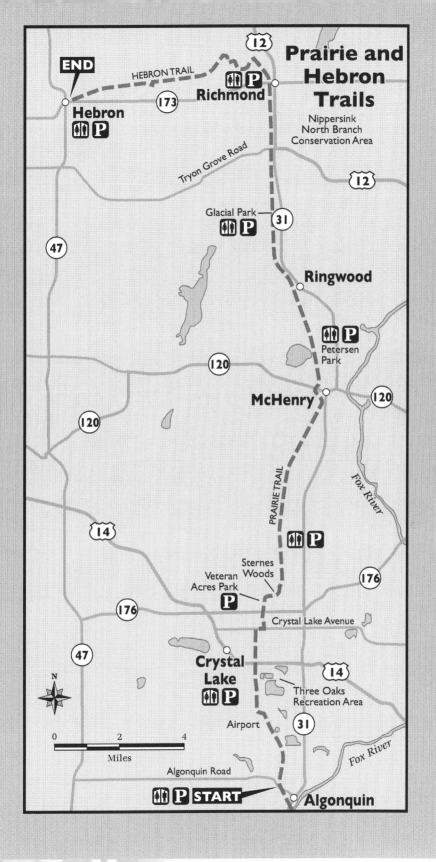

Prairie and Hebron Trails

Nippersink
North Branch
Conservation Area

END

HEBRON TRAIL

Hebron

173

Richmond

12

12

Tryon Grove Road

Glacial Park

31

47

Ringwood

Petersen
Park

120

120

McHenry

120

120

Fox River

PRAIRIE TRAIL

14

Sternes
Woods

Veteran
Acres Park

176

176

Crystal Lake Avenue

47

N

Crystal
Lake

14

Three Oaks
Recreation Area

Airport

31

0   2   4

Miles

Algonquin Road

Fox River

START

Algonquin

when this trailhead parking area is closed, use one of the parking areas listed below. UTM coordinates: 16T, 392651 E, 4669502 N.

To reach the Main St. parking area in Crystal Lake, head north on IL 31. Turn left at James Rakow Rd. and then right onto Pyott Rd. Turn left onto Berkshire Dr. and then immediately right onto Eastgate Ave.

To park at Veteran Acres Park, head north on IL 31. Turn left onto IL 176 and then right onto Lorraine Dr.

To access the trail at Petersen Park, head north on IL 31. North of McHenry turn left onto McCullom Lake Rd. and left again onto Petersen Park Rd.

To park at the Glacial Park parking area, head north on IL 31 from McHenry. North of Ringwood turn left onto Harts Rd. The parking area is on the right.

To park at the Nippersink North Branch Park parking area, head west on IL 173 from I-94. After passing Richmond, turn right onto Keystone Rd. The parking area is on the right.

To park in Hebron, keep heading west on IL 173 and turn right onto Seaman Rd. The parking area is on the right.

Transportation: The Crystal Lake Metra station on the Union Pacific/Northwest Line is less than 1 mile from the Veteran Acres parking area. The McHenry station on the same Metra line is just one block from the Prairie Trail in McHenry. Pace buses 550 and 806 serve Crystal Lake and McHenry.

Contact: McHenry County Conservation District, 18410 US 14, Woodstock; (815) 338-6223; mccdistrict.org.

The first few miles of this trail will answer the burning question you probably never had: Where does Chicagoland get its gravel for making all this concrete? The answer is McHenry County, and as you travel from Algonquin to Crystal Lake, the trail leads you by a series of gravel pits, some currently active, some not. In many spots residential developments have been built on top of the former gravel pits. Thanks to the stone and sand left by receding glaciers, McHenry County is the top gravel producer in the state and one of the biggest in the Midwest. As you pass the long conveyer belts and industrial buildings that are part of an active gravel mining operation, you'll see some ponds as well a couple of small creeks flowing on either side of the trail.

Crystal Lake and McHenry

On the way into Crystal Lake, you'll pass Lake of the Hills Airport followed by Three Oaks Recreation Area, a former gravel pit that has been transformed into a large city park offering trails, boat rentals, a swimming beach, and a restaurant. Continuing ahead, the trail slices through a buzzing commercial district, complete with shopping malls and big box stores.

Once you've left the bustle of Crystal Lake behind and completed the 1-mile-long on-street section of the route, Sternes Woods will take you by surprise. The trail wriggles like a snake over steep hills and underneath arthritic limbs of big oak trees. Even though this hilly section is brief, those on bicycles should ride the steep, curving downhill sections with care—wipeouts sometimes happen at the bottom of these steep hills. A tiny stream runs through a small ravine on the right; benches along the path invite you to sit down to admire the hills and fragrant groves of pine.

Continuing north toward McHenry, the trail shadows a set of railroad tracks through a wide-open landscape that leans strongly toward agriculture.

Glacial Park

After passing through McHenry, the trail brushes against Petersen Park, which contains some fine picnicking spots on the shore of McCullom Lake. For those with an interest in learning the ways that glaciers sculpted the landscape in northeastern Illinois, be sure to visit Glacial Park, which you'll encounter at 19.2 miles. The park is chock-full of kames—essentially mounds—which are formed when glacial meltwater deposits heaps of sand and gravel in depressions in the ice or at the edge of the glacier. More than 5 miles of hiking trails allow you to explore the kames, dry and wet prairie, woodland, and a creek.

Between Glacial Park and Richmond, the gently rolling terrain surrounding the trail contains swaths of attractive wetland. In some spots, ravines rise up on the sides of the trail, but most often you're granted long views of the surrounding landscape. On the way into Richmond, duck under a one-hundred-year-old wooden railroad bridge. The main drag in Richmond is lined with a collection of buildings from the turn of the twentieth century containing a small assortment of shops focused on items such as jewelry, handmade crafts, and antiques. Further explorations of the village will reveal attractively restored Victorian homes and several Sears Catalog homes.

The Hebron Trail

After Richmond you'll cross the North Branch of Nippersink Creek and then encounter more sprawling wetlands. One-third mile before the end of the Prairie Trail, turn left onto the crushed gravel path that leads into Nippersink North Branch Conservation Area. This winding trail runs through many acres of rolling terrain covered with restored prairie and

About one-half mile south of the Wisconsin border, the trail connection between the Hebron and Prairie Trails crosses over the North Branch of Nippersink Creek in the North Branch Conservation Area.

stands of hardwood. You'll cross the Nippersink North Branch again as it winds through the prairie.

The first mile or so on the 6.6-mile Hebron Trail is dominated by cropland with patches of intermittent woodland alongside the trail. After a very short on-street section, you'll know you're approaching wetlands when you hear the rattly honking of sandhill cranes, a large gray waterbird becoming more common in Illinois. Streets Lake offers a trailside viewing platform where you can survey a collection of muskrat lodges, big stands of sedge grasses and cattails, and rafts of waterbirds. The trail ends on the outskirts of the tiny town of Hebron.

Major Milepoints

5.1 Start the 0.8-mile-long on-street section by turning right onto Crystal Lake Rd. This road is busy; take the side path.

5.4 Turn left onto East St. and then bear left on Prairie St.

5.7 Turn right onto Glenn Ave.

5.9 Turn right onto Terra Cotta Ave.

6.0 Turn left onto Lorraine Dr.

6.1 Resume the Prairie Trail from the parking area.

24.1 Leave the Prairie Trail and start the Hebron Trail by turning left into Nippersink North Branch Conservation Area.

Local Information

- Fox Valley Bicycle and Ski Club, fvbsc.org. Recreation club that organizes local bike rides.
- Naturally McHenry County, 11879 E. Main Street, Huntley; (815) 893-6280; visitmchenry county.com

Local Events/Attractions

- Visit Lake Geneva, 201 Wrigley Drive, Lake Geneva, Wisconsin; (800) 345-1020; visitlakegeneva. com. Lake Geneva is a charming—if somewhat touristy—town situated on a beautiful lake just across the Wisconsin border about 10 miles north of the trail.
- Royal Oak Orchard, 15908 Hebron Road, Harvard; (815) 648-4141; royaloakfarmorchard.com. In addition to the orchard, there's a bakery, a gift shop, and a restaurant; located west of Hebron.
- City of Woodstock, 121 W. Calhoun Street, Woodstock; (815) 338-4300; woodstockil.gov. Woodstock claims one of the most attractive town squares in all Illinois; plenty of shopping and eating opportunities.

Restaurants

- Doyle's Pub and Eatery, 5604 Mill Street, Richmond; (815) 678-3623; doylespub.net. Located in the former mill next to the trail in Richmond.
- Quarry Cable Park and Grille, 5517 Northwest Highway, Crystal Lake; (815) 893-0036; thequarrycablepark.com. Located near the trail within the Three Oaks Recreation Area in Crystal Lake.

Accommodations

- Marengo Ridge Conservation Area, 2411 IL-23, Marengo; (815) 338-6223; mccdistrict.org. One of the best small campgrounds in northern Illinois, located about 15 miles west of the trail.

16 | ROBERT MCCLORY TRAIL

This trail introduces you to a string of active North Shore towns: Lake Forest, Lake Bluff, North Chicago, Waukegan, Zion, and Kenosha. You'll pass the nation's largest Navy training center, parks such as Lyons Woods Forest Preserve, and historic communities like Fort Sheridan and Zion.

Location: From the Fort Sheridan Metra station, located at Old Elm and Sheridan Roads 25 miles north of downtown Chicago, head north to Kenosha, Wisconsin.

Length: 23.2 miles one-way.

Surface: Paved south of Waukegan; crushed gravel the remainder of the trail.

Wheelchair access: The trail is wheelchair accessible. There are, however, many street crossings and a fair number of them have heavy traffic.

Difficulty: Be ready for a medium level of difficulty due to the length and the stretches where trail users are fully exposed to the elements.

Restrooms: There are public restrooms and water at the Fort Sheridan, Lake Bluff, and Great Lakes Metra stations, and at Anderson Park (at the northern end of the trail in Kenosha).

Maps: www.lakecountyil.gov.

Hazards: Watch for cars pulling in and out of parking spaces as the trail cuts through Metra station parking lots. The trail crosses busy roads in a number of places.

Access and parking: From I-94 north of Chicago, head north on US 41 (the Skokie Hwy.). Turn right onto Old Elm Rd. Park in the lot on the north side of Old Elm Rd. at the Fort Sheridan Metra station. UTM coordinates: 16T, 432212 E, 4674134 N.

To park at the Lake Bluff station, take US 41 north from I-94. Turn right onto IL 176/Rockland Rd. Turn left onto Sheridan Rd. and park in the station on the left.

In North Chicago and Waukegan, on-street parking options are frequently available alongside the trail. Follow Sheridan Rd. north and then take any major street west to reach the trail.

To park at Lyons Woods Forest Preserve, exit from I-94 on IL 120 heading east. Turn left onto Sheridan Rd./IL 137. Turn left on Blanchard Rd. and look for the parking area on the right. Stay left on the Lyons Woods Trail to reach the Robert McClory Trail.

To park at Anderson Park, located at the northern end of the trail, take I-94 north into Wisconsin. Exit at 104th St. and head east. Turn left at 39th Ave. and then right onto 89th St. Turn left onto 30th Ave. and then right onto 87th Place. Park in the lot between the high school and Anderson Park. Catch the trail heading south from the intersection of 30th Ave. and 89th St.

Transportation: Take a Union Pacific District North Metra train to the Fort Sheridan station. The Union Pacific North Line runs parallel to this entire route. The first 7 miles of the trail run next to four Metra stations. Continuing north, another five Metra stations are within 1 to 2 miles east of the trail. The Kenosha Metra station is a few miles north of the northern end of the trail.

Pace buses 472, 563, 564, 572, 566, 569, 571, 573 also connect with the trail.

Rentals: George Garner Cyclery, 1111 Waukegan Rd., Northbrook; (847) 272-2100; also located at 740 N. Milwaukee Ave., Libertyville; (847) 362-6030; georgegarnercyclery.com

Contact: Kenosha County Division of Parks manages the Kenosha County Bike Trail; 19600 75th St., Bristol, WI; (262) 857-1869.

Lake County Division of Transportation manages the Robert McClory Trail; 600 W. Winchester Rd., Libertyville 60048; (847) 377-7400; lakecountyil.gov/transportation. A side path will take you 1.6 miles south of the starting point; further south, link up with the Green Bay Trail in Highland Park.

||||||||||||||||||||||||||||||||||||||||||||||||||||||||||||||||||||||||||||||||||||||||||||||||||||||

Across the street from the starting point of this trail stands Fort Sheridan and its centerpiece, a 227-foot-tall brick water tower, originally the tallest structure in the Chicago area when it was built in 1889. The long, squat row of buildings on each side of the tower served as troop barracks for this Army base established on the shore of Lake Michigan. The fort was built not because of the threat of foreign invaders, but to respond to worker uprisings. The military built the fort at the urging of North Shore businessmen so that troops could respond quickly to labor protests in Chicago and prevent turmoil from reaching the more affluent communities north of Chicago.

An Army Reserve base continues to occupy some of the land, but the majority of it is now privately owned. Fort Sheridan was a busy place while it served as a training and administrative center from the Spanish American War through World War II, when over 500,000 military men and women were processed at the fort. The attractive grounds are well worth a tour, and if you want to visit Lake Michigan, this is the easiest place to do so along the Robert McClory Trail (look for signs pointing to the Fort Sheridan Forest Preserve).

Sheridan Road

The first 7 miles of the trail follows the route of the Metra Union Pacific North commuter train line that runs between Ogilvie Station in Chicago's Loop and Kenosha, Wisconsin. In between the three train stations you'll pass, much of the trail accompanies Sheridan Rd., one of the busier roads in the area.

Peeking through the trees on the right at about 3.5 miles is Lake Forest High School, where the 1980 Academy Award–winning film Ordinary People was filmed. The school claims a handful of alumni involved in creative pursuits, such as musician Andrew Bird, writer Dave Eggers, and actor Vince Vaughn.

Before arriving at the Lake Bluff Metra station, you'll see the North Shore Bike Path branching to the left alongside IL 176/Rockland Rd. The North Shore Bike Path intersects the Des Plaines River Trail about 4 miles to the west.

Lake Bluff was one of the communities represented by the trail's namesake, Robert McClory, a member of the U.S. House of Representatives for twenty years. The national spotlight shone on the Republican congressman when he served on the House Judiciary Committee and became a key figure in the impeachment proceedings against President Richard Nixon.

Next up along the trail is the Great Lakes Naval Training Center, the largest Navy training center in the nation. The eighty-year-old naval base has more than 1,000 buildings throughout 1,600 acres. In the Great Lakes Metra station that sits alongside the trail, you'll likely see some train passengers sporting brush cuts and bright white sailor hats.

Far North Shore

As the route follows a perfectly straight course through North Chicago, the trailside scenery offers a mix of industrial developments and working-class neighborhoods. Vegetable gardens planted alongside the trail add vitality to the open, grassy right-of-way. Continuing through North Chicago and entering Waukegan reveals more of the bustling industry for which these North Shore cities are known.

As the pockets of industry retreat, suburban residential neighborhoods take over and several community parks appear alongside the trail. At about 13 miles into the trail, a sign marks the entrance to Lyons Woods Forest Preserve, which contains 3 miles of trails that wind through savanna, oak woodland, and restored prairie.

North of Lyons Woods, residential neighborhoods come and go; small parks offer spots to take a break. The path gets lush and leafy before reaching Zion and then becomes open and grassy again once you've entered the city.

Zion and Kenosha

In Zion the McClory Trail meets up with a couple other trails that allow you to explore this community founded in 1890 by Scottish faith healer John Alexander Dowie. The church owned the town's commercial establishments and forbade liquor, playing cards, pork, clams, and tan shoes, among other proscribed items. The community collapsed financially in 1939, and private individuals began acquiring the property that belonged to the church. The streets in the town are all named after people or places in the Bible.

After entering the Badger State at Russell Rd., all that remains is 3.5 miles to the trail's northern terminus in Kenosha, Wisconsin. As you travel these final few miles—now along the Kenosha County Bike Trail—the greenery becomes more prominent as you pass the occasional housing development and agricultural field. The trail ends at 89th St., across the road from Anderson Park.

Local Information

- Bicycle Club of Lake County, PO Box 521, Libertyville; bikebclc.com. Hosts rides around the county.
- Lake County Convention and Visitors Bureau, 5465 W. Grand Avenue, Suite 100; Gurnee; (847) 662-2700; lakecounty.org.

Local Events/Attractions

- Fort Sheridan Forest Preserve, 1275 Gilgare Lane, Lake Forest; (847) 367-6640; lcfpd.org/fort-sheridan. Features several miles of hiking trails on the shore of Lake Michigan.
- Shiloh House, 1300 Shiloh Boulevard, Zion; (847) 746-2427; zionhistoricalsociety.weebly.com. Elegant twenty-five-room mansion built by Zion's founder, John Alexander Dowie; limited hours.

Restaurants

- The Silo, 625 Rockland Road, Lake Bluff; (847) 234-6660; silopizza.com. Known for its deep-dish pizza.
- Bluffington's Café, 113 E. Scranton Avenue, Lake Bluff; (847) 295-3344. Good sandwiches and salads.

Accommodations

- Adeline Jay Geo-Karis Illinois Beach State Park, Zion; (847) 662-4811; bit.ly/ilbeach. Popular beach and campground; located 2.5 miles from the trail.
- Sunset Motel, 511 Rockland Road, Lake Bluff; (847) 234-4669; sunsetmotelroute41.com. Affordable motel accessible from the North Shore Trail.

17 SALT CREEK TRAIL

The Salt Creek Trail is a fun, winding route that passes through a series of forest preserves straddling Cook and DuPage Counties. While much of the route closely follows the arboreal banks of Salt Creek, you'll frequently meander through the adjoining floodplain among tangles of deadfall and stands of shrubs. The final leg of the route introduces you to the islands, high banks, and dense woodlands of Fullersburg Forest Preserve, one of the most eye-catching parks in DuPage County.

Location: Start across the street from the Brookfield Zoo and head west along Salt Creek to Fullersburg Forest Preserve in Oak Brook.

Length: 10.6 miles one-way.

Surface: Asphalt on the Salt Creek Trail and the bike path along York Rd.; crushed gravel on the trail through Fullersburg Woods.

Wheelchair access: The trail is wheelchair accessible. The half-mile trip on Canterberry Ln. does not have sidewalks, but has very light traffic.

Difficulty: Despite the occasionally rolling terrain, the trail is mostly easy.

Restrooms: There are public restrooms at the Brookfield Woods parking area, 26th St. Woods, Brezina Woods, Bemis Woods North, the Dean Nature Sanctuary, and near the Fullersburg Forest Preserve Visitor Center (water).

Maps: epd.org.

Hazards: This route crosses five major streets. Use caution while crossing.

Access and parking: Driving from Chicago, take I-290 to IL 171 (First Ave.). Head south on IL 171 and then turn right onto 31st St. Look for Brookfield Woods Forest Preserve on the right. Park at the far back of the lot, where the trail starts. UTM coordinates: 16T, 430147 E, 4631718 N.

To park at Brezina Woods Forest Preserve, take I-290 from Chicago to US 12/45 (Mannheim Rd.). Follow US 12 south. The entrance to the forest preserve is on the left. The trail crosses the park road just before the parking area.

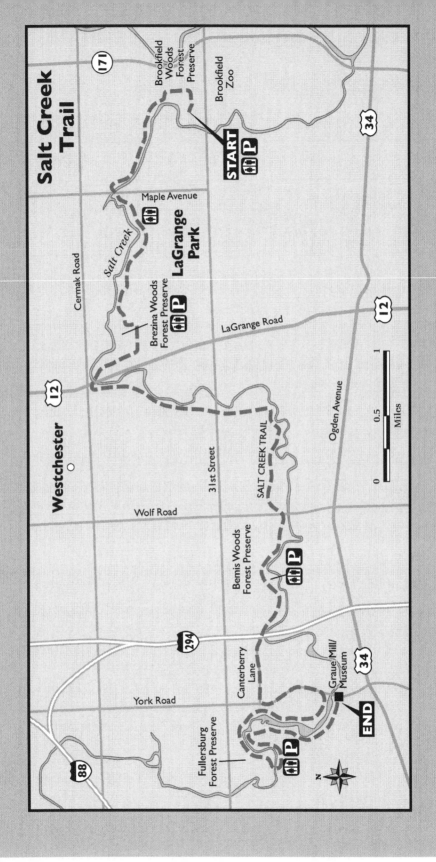

To park at Fullersburg Forest Preserve, take I-290 west from Chicago to I-88. Follow I-88 until reaching IL 83 (Kingery Hwy.). Follow IL 83 south. Turn left onto 31st St. and then right onto Spring Rd. Turn left at the sign for Fullersburg Park.

Transportation: The BNSF Metra line stops in Brookfield about 1 mile from the trail. You can also access the trail with Pace buses 331 and 330.

Rentals: The Wheel Thing, 15 S. La Grange Rd., La Grange; (708) 352-3822; thewheelthing.net.

Contact: Forest Preserve District of Cook County, 536 N. Harlem Ave., River Forest; (800) 870-3666; fpdcc.com.

DuPage County Forest Preserve District, 3S580 Naperville Rd., Wheaton; (630) 933-7200; dupageforest.com.

F or most of its 50-mile-long route, Salt Creek winds through a series of densely populated western Chicago suburbs. The section of the creek that you'll see on the Salt Creek Trail, however, flows through a handful of county-operated forest preserves that feature gently rolling topography, thick bottomland woods, and plenty of spots to sit and enjoy the meandering creek.

As the story goes, Salt Creek got its name when a nineteenth-century farmer's wagon was stuck in the creek while hauling a barrel of salt. Leaving the wagon in the creek overnight, the farmer returned the next morning and found the salt had dissolved. Even though early maps labeled the waterway the Little Des Plaines River, the name Salt Creek eventually took hold.

Wooded Floodplain

Starting at the east end of the Salt Creek Trail in Brookfield Woods, the path takes you on a curving route through a small savanna before meeting up with Salt Creek. As you trace the riverbank, you'll notice that this thirty-foot-wide creek occupies a shallow ravine that is wide in some places, narrow in others. After the first road crossing (Maple Ave.), you'll see one of Salt Creek's only major tributaries, Addison Creek, merging from the north.

Now on the south side of the creek, the trail wiggles back and forth between the creek bank and the nearby floodplain strewn with woody vegetation. Closer to the creek, the landscape tends to undulate gently. Away from the creek, the landscape is flat bottomland dense with shrubs, deadfall, and small trees.

Bluffs and a Small Dam

After an awkward crossing of La Grange Rd., the trail shoots straight alongside the creek and passes by a riffled shallow spot where the creek bed is bisected by a set of old bridge supports made from limestone blocks. Not far ahead, look for the one-foot-high dam that provides one of many pleasant spots along the trail to sit and enjoy the creek's swirling eddies.

Between 31st St. and Wolf Rd., the trail mounts a few small bluffs overlooking bends in the creek. From these small bluffs, look for the sharp turns where this portion of the creek is in the process of getting cut off from the rest. (A couple of small islands have been created by the creek's changing course.)

The final leg of the Salt Creek Trail cuts through Bemis Woods Forest Preserve, where you'll see a couple of tiny streams that feed into Salt Creek and a trailside golf course. Also, you'll pass a footbridge leading to the Bemis Woods South, where there's a treetop adventure park with ziplines and an aerial pathway.

After passing under I-294, you'll leave the Salt Creek Trail and take a short trip on a low traffic road to reach a side path on York Rd., which will lead you to Fullersburg Forest Preserve. At Fullersburg Forest Preserve, Salt Creek meanders beneath more small bluffs and around more islands on its way to the historic watermill at the south tip of the park. While following the creek through the park, you'll pass a series of impressive stone picnic shelters with benches and a fireplace. Many of the Fullersburg picnic shelters, as well as the log visitor center and the Graue Mill, were built or restored by the Civilian Conservation Corps, which had a camp here in the 1930s.

The Graue Mill

Originally built in 1852, the Graue Mill in Fullersburg Forest Preserve is one of only a few remaining "stations" that served the Underground Railroad in DuPage County. An exhibit in the basement of the mill explains how it was part of the clandestine network of places where former enslaved people could rest and be fed on their way to Chicago and then to Canada. The mill also features a grain milling exhibit as well as room settings, farm implements, and a recreated general store from the late 1800s.

Major Milepoints

7.2 After passing under I-294, continue straight ahead on Canterberry Ln.

7.7 Turn left onto York Rd. Follow the bike path on the right side of the road. The bike path soon switches to the other side of the road.

8.3 Turn right before crossing Salt Creek on the crushed gravel path into Fullersburg Forest Preserve.

9.7 In Fullersburg cross the Salt Creek on the second bridge to the left. Stay to the left to reach the visitor center.

Local Information

- DuPage County Convention and Visitors Bureau, 915 Harger Road, Suite 240, Oak Brook; (630) 575-8070; dupagecvb.com.
- Salt Creek Greenway; epd.org/salt-creek-greenway-trail; obparks.org/bike-trail-maps. The Salt Creek Trail is part of a nearly 25-mile system of trails and on-street biking connections between the Brookfield Zoo and the Busse Woods Forest Preserve in Elk Grove Village. Beware, the route is not well marked.

Local Events/Attractions

- Brookfield Zoo, First Ave. and 31st St., Brookfield; (708) 485-2200; brookfieldzoo.org. One of the largest zoos in the world; more than 2,500 animals. The east end of the trail starts across the street from the zoo's north entrance.

- Dean Nature Sanctuary, 115 Canterberry Lane, Oak Brook; (630) 990-4233; bit.ly/deannc. Located at the west end of the trail; has an apiary, several different gardens, and access to Salt Creek.
- Fullersburg Forest Preserve Visitor Center, 3609 Spring Road, Oak Brook; (630) 850-8110; dupageforest.com. The visitor center has on display a 13,000-year-old woolly mammoth skeleton uncovered locally in 1977. At the south entrance to the park is the Graue Mill and Museum; grauemill.org.
- Riverside Historic District. Enjoy winding streets, many parks, and attractive historic neighborhoods and public buildings in this community designed by Frederick Law Olmstead. Start your visit at the Riverside Historical Museum; 10 Pine Avenue, Riverside; (708) 447-2574. Located 2 miles from the east end of the trail.

Restaurants

- York Tavern, 3702 York Road, Oak Brook; (630) 323-5090; yorktavernoakbrook.com. Reliable spot for burgers and beer; located next to Fullersburg Forest Preserve.
- Benjarong Thai Restaurant, 2138 Mannheim Road, Westchester; (708) 449-9291; benjarongwestchester.com. Well-regarded Thai restaurant located yards from the trail near the La Grange Rd. crossing.

Accommodations

- Hyatt House Chicago/Oak Brook, 210 22nd Street, Oak Brook; (630) 590-1200; hyatt.com. One of a cluster of hotels located very close to the west end of the trail.

18 VIRGIL GILMAN TRAIL

This trail offers a perfect chance to get to know Aurora and its nearby environs. West of the city, the trail repeatedly crosses Blackberry Creek and occasionally runs alongside its wooded banks. After crossing a 100-yard-long trestle bridge over IL 56, and passing the popular Blackberry Farm park, the trail bobs and weaves through stunning woodland at Bliss Woods Forest Preserve.

Location: From Hill Ave. just south of Aurora, the trail runs northwest to Waubonsee Community College in Sugar Grove.

Length: 11.3 miles one-way, with options for extending the trip.

Surface: Asphalt.

Wheelchair access: The trail is wheelchair accessible, but there is no sidewalk for a portion of the on-street section. This is also where there's a bit of heavy industry and truck traffic.

Difficulty: The trail is easy.

Restrooms: There are public restrooms at Lebanon Park, Copley Park (water), and Bliss Woods Forest Preserve (water).

Maps: foxvalleyparkdistrict.org.

Hazards: Watch for traffic—especially trucks—while following the brief on-street section.

Access and parking: Head south on IL 31 from I-88. In downtown Aurora turn left onto Galena Blvd. Continue ahead on Galena Blvd. as the street curves right and becomes Hill Ave. Look for the parking area on the right. UTM coordinates: 16T, 393130 E, 4619671 N.

To park at Copley Park, head south on IL 31 (Lake St.) from I-88. After passing Aurora's central downtown area, look for the park on the right.

To park at the Blackberry Farm parking area, head south on Orchard Rd. from I-88. Turn right onto Galena Blvd. and then left onto Barnes Rd. There's a trailhead parking area on the right.

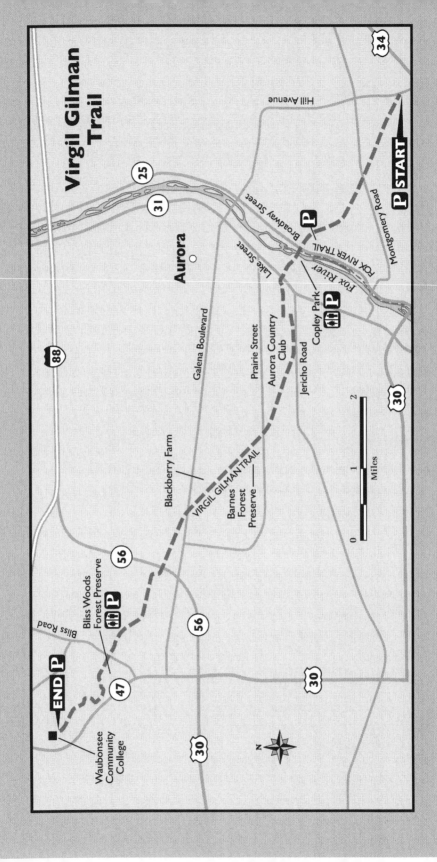

To park at the Merrill Rd. parking area at the west end of the trail, take I-88 west from Aurora. Exit at IL 56 and follow IL 56 to IL 47. Take IL 47 north to Waubonsee Dr., the entrance for Waubonsee Community College. Turn right onto Waubonsee Dr. and then turn right on Circle Dr. Park near the trail on the right.

Transportation: The BNSF Metra line stops in Aurora a mile or so north of the trail. Pace bus routes 597 and 524 connect with the trail.

Rentals: Several bike-sharing stations are available in downtown Aurora; the station closest to the trail is at the Aurora Public Library, 101 S. River Street, Aurora; aurora-il.org.

Contact: Fox Valley Park District, 101 W. Illinois Avenue, Aurora; (630) 897-0516; foxvalleyparkdistrict.org.

The Virgil Gilman Trail provides a chance to get to know the second largest city in Illinois. The trail, named after the man who led the city's parks department through thirty years of intense growth, gives you a taste of both the city and the outlying suburban and rural areas. One of the highlights of the trail is crossing the Fox River on an old train bridge from 1897. This is also the place where you'll have an opportunity to add some miles to your excursion and explore some of the islands in the river that Aurora is known for.

The Fox River

The first few miles of this trail guide you through the modest leafy neighborhoods on the east side of Aurora. After an initial stretch where the trail traces an embankment that rises about six feet above the surrounding cropland and bottomland woods, residential neighborhoods take over.

At 2.7 miles the trail crosses the Fox River on an old latticed train bridge, last used by a train in 1977. Before taking in fine views of the Fox from the high bridge, you may consider a side trip south on the Fox River Trail as it passes through several parks, the best of which is South Island

Park, a long, thin island in the river. In addition to taking the Fox River Trail south for 4.7 miles to Oswego, you can also take the trail north for 1 mile on the west bank of the river to Hurds Island.

Continuing west on the Virgil Gilman Trail, you'll duck under several bridges and skirt the edge of Copley Park. After passing the park, watch for trucks on Rathbone St. as the trail drops you off in the middle of a not-too-welcoming industrial area for a few blocks of on-street travel.

Blackberry Farm

The beginning of the next section of the trail is marked by a handsome limestone sign and concrete benches. As the trail parallels a swath of bottomland woods, you'll see occasional small ponds and you'll catch glimpses of the Aurora Country Club through the trees on the right. After crossing Orchard Rd., look for waterbirds as the trail passes a lake and a couple more ponds at Barnes Forest Preserve. If you enjoy exploring grassland, turn left onto the trail near the ponds for a quick loop through the adjoining prairie and savanna.

After crossing Blackberry Creek on an old steel bridge, you'll arrive at Blackberry Farm, a county park that offers kiddie rides, paddle boats, and several museum exhibits. One exhibit displays forty carriages, sleighs, and vintage commercial vehicles. Another exhibit contains a display of eleven late Victorian-era stores. There's also a walking/biking trail that circles a small lake and follows the route of the park's railroad ride. The water park across the street from Blackberry Farm is another popular stop for local families.

Bliss Woods

A mile or so west of Blackberry Farm, the ramp of a steel bridge spanning IL 56 gradually rises from the prairie in front of you. After crossing IL 56, the trail crosses Blackberry Creek again and then runs beside the creek as it cuts a straight course northwest.

At Bliss Woods Forest Preserve, the path runs through a lovely swath of state-protected woodland thick with sugar maple and basswood trees. In early spring you'll see flowers such as hepatica, bloodroot, and rue anemone. On the left, you'll pass a hill called an esker—a winding ridge

The west end of the Virgil Gilman Trail winds through enchanting woodland at Bliss Woods Forest Preserve.

of gravel deposited by a subglacial river. Crossing Bliss Rd. takes you into a grove of bottomland woods largely comprised of oak and maple.

The final section of the trail takes you through a large prairie on the campus of Waubonsee Community College. The college operates several campuses in the area, but this is the main one, open since 1967. At the end of the trail, if you feel like exploring the campus, you'll find a pleasant little pond behind the first set of buildings.

Major Milepoints

3.4   On-street section: Start brief on-street section by turning right onto Rathbone St.

3.8   Turn left onto Terry Ave.

3.9   Pick up the trail on the right.

Local Information

- Aurora Area Convention and Visitors Bureau, 43 W. Galena Boulevard, Aurora; (630) 256-3190; enjoyaurora.com.
- Kane County Forest Preserve District, 1996 S. Kirk Road, Suite 320, Geneva; (630) 232-5980; kaneforest.com.

Local Events/Attractions

- Aurora Regional Fire Museum, 53 N. Broadway, Aurora; (630) 256-4140; auroraregionalfiremuseum.org. Vintage firefighting equipment; located in downtown Aurora, across the street from the trailhead for the Aurora Branch of the Prairie Path.
- Blackberry Farm, 100 S. Barnes Road, Aurora; (630) 892-1550; foxvalleyparkdistrict.org. Farm animal exhibits, rides, picnic areas, concessions, and many historical exhibits featuring live demonstrations.

Restaurants

- La Quebrada Restaurant, 723 S. Broadway, Aurora; (630) 229-0057; quebradarestaurant.com. Authentic Mexican food, located right on the trail at the Fox River.
- Two Brothers Roundhouse, 205 N. Broadway, Aurora; (630) 264-2739; twobrothersbrewing. com. A local favorite brewpub located 1.5 miles north of the trail.

Accommodations

- Big Rock Forest Preserve, 46W499 Granart Road, Big Rock; (630) 444-1200; https://bit.ly/bigrockcg. Offers tent camping sites tucked away in a wooded area; located a few miles west of the trail.
- Holiday Inn Express, 111 N. Broadway Ave., Aurora; (630) 896-2800. Located in downtown Aurora, one block from the Hollywood Casino.

19 WAUPONSEE GLACIAL TRAIL

The Wauponsee Glacial Trail runs from Joliet south to the Kanka-kee River, mostly through wide-open farmland. After passing the town of Manhattan, the trail skirts the eastern edge of the sprawling Midewin National Tallgrass Prairie, formerly the largest ammunition-production plant in the world. At the Kankakee River you'll enjoy long views from a former railroad bridge.

Location: From Rowell Rd. on the south side of Joliet, the trail runs south to the Kankakee River.

Length: 22.3 miles one-way.

Surface: Paved surface for first several miles; crushed gravel for the remainder.

Wheelchair access: The trail is wheelchair accessible.

Difficulty: The trail borders on the difficult category because of the length, lack of trail amenities, and lack of protection from the wind and sun.

Restrooms: There are public restrooms at Sugar River Forest Preserve (water), the Hoff Rd. parking area, the trail parking areas in Manhattan and Symerton, and at the Forked Creek Preserve on Ballou Rd.

Maps: reconnectwithnature.org.

Hazards: Bring plenty of water; there is no drinking water available on the trail south of Manhattan.

Access and parking: From I-80 go south on Briggs St. (exit 134). Imme-diately turn right onto New Lenox Rd. and right again onto Rowell Ave. Look for the beginning of the trail on the left. There is no parking lot at the trailhead—you must park on the road's ample shoulder. (The closest access spot with off-street parking is the Sugar Creek Forest Preserve—see below.) UTM coordinates: 16T, 411360 E, 4595923 N.

To catch the trail at Sugar Creek Forest Preserve, take Briggs St. (exit 134) south from I-80. Continue ahead as Briggs St. merges with US 52. Turn right onto Laraway Rd.; the entrance to the forest preserve is on the right.

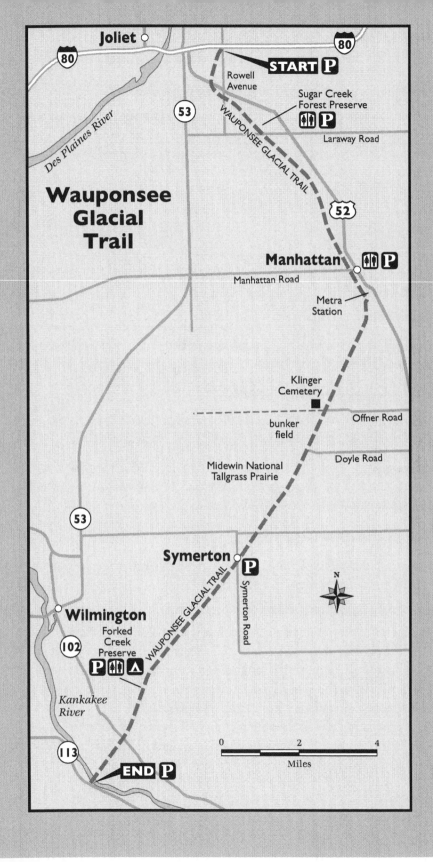

To park at the Manhattan Rd. parking area in Manhattan, continue south on US 52 and then right onto Manhattan Rd. The trail parking area is on the left.

To reach the parking area in Symerton, head south on I-55. Exit east on River Rd. (exit 241). Turn right onto IL 53 and then left onto Peotone Rd. Turn left onto Symerton Rd. and right onto Commercial St. Look for the trail parking area two blocks ahead.

To park at the Forked Creek Preserve on Ballou Rd., take I-57 south from Chicago to Wilmington Rd. Head west on Wilmington Rd., and then turn left on Old Chicago Rd. Turn right on Ballou Rd. The entrance to the preserve is on the left.

To park at the south end of the trail, take IL 53 south to IL 102. Turn left onto IL 102 in Wilmington. Turn right onto Rivals Rd. Park on the side of the road near the trail crossing.

Transportation: Metra's Southwest Service goes to Manhattan, but service is very limited. The Rock Island District and Heritage Corridor Metra lines serve Joliet. Both train lines are located a few miles north of the trailhead. Pace Bus's 504 route provides access to the trail along US 52 and Mills Rd.

Rentals: No bike rental options in the area.

Contact: Will County Forest Preserve District, 17540 W. Laraway Road, Joliet; (815) 727-8700; fpdwc.org.

This trail is named for a glacial lake that covered much of the local terrain some 16,000 years ago. Lake Wauponsee reached a depth of 100 feet but lasted for a relatively short period of time before draining away into the Illinois River Valley. The glacial lake takes its name from Chief Waubonsee, an influential Potawatomi chief who lived near Aurora in the early 1800s.

South of Joliet

Leafy residential neighborhoods and a dash of light industry show up on the first few miles of the trail. At Mills Rd. you'll pass the manufacturing facility and retail store for the Mancuso Cheese Company, local purveyors of mozzarella and ricotta since 1907. After crossing Sugar Creek, the trail briefly accompanies the creek through adjoining bottomland woods.

The Will County Forest Preserve administration building sits alongside the trail at Sugar Creek Forest Preserve. This environmentally friendly structure was built using recycled materials and has solar energy panels mounted on the roof. Southwest of the Sugar Creek Preserve, the 47,000-seat Chicagoland Speedway rises from the cropland. Across the road from the speedway is another smaller car racing venue, the Route 66 Raceway, with seating for around 30,000.

Manhattan

With a few exceptions, farmland dominates the landscape for the remainder of the trail. Farmhouses, silos, and barns often appear in the distance. Patches of trees sometimes offer shade, and small creeks regularly meander underneath the trail, flowing from one field to another. New housing developments spring up as you enter the town of Manhattan. The trail angles southwest as you leave Manhattan and pass the local commuter train station and a cluster of oil storage tanks.

South of Hoff Rd., the Wauponsee Trail intersects the Bailey Bridge Trail at the edge of the Midewin National Tallgrass Prairie, containing 22 miles of biking trails. If you take a quick side trip on the Bailey Bridge Trail, you'll immediately pass a small pioneer cemetery established 1877 by a local homesteader from Pennsylvania. Just after the cemetery you'll enter a swath of land containing many dozens of the earth-covered bunkers, remnants from when Midewin was an ammunition plant.

Forked Creek Preserve

Before and after the tiny village of Symerton, shade trees thin out along the trail and a carpet of cropland unrolls for miles in every direction. At Ballou Rd., take a break within the picnic area at the pleasant Forked Creek Preserve, which also contains a dog run a couple of campsites. For the final few miles of the trail south of Ballou Rd., the trail becomes more wooded as it hops over Forked Creek and crosses IL 102.

Midewin Nation Tallgrass Prairie

Formerly the largest ammunition-production plant in the world, Midewin National Tallgrass Prairie is now the biggest—and perhaps the most tranquil—piece of protected land in northeastern Illinois. The park contains woodland, savanna, prairie, and many remnants of the former arsenal, but mostly it's composed of farmland that is slowly being converted back to prairie and woodland. About half of the park's 15,000 acres are open to the public; among the highlights are a herd of bison and 34 miles of trails, most of which are open to bikes. (One of the hikes at Midewin is described in my book *60 Hikes within 60 Miles: Chicago*.) At its peak, the arsenal employed some 14,000 people and produced 5.5 million tons of TNT a week. In operation from World War II through the Korean and Vietnam Wars, it was shut down in 1975, leaving some 1,300 structures, including 392 concrete bunkers that were used to store the TNT.

Just before reaching the Kankakee River, you'll brush against a sizable wetland on the right. As you cross the Kankakee River on a rehabbed railroad bridge, breathtaking views of the wide river and its wooded banks open up on each side. The trail ends on the south bank of the Kankakee River.

Local Information

- Chicago Southland Convention and Visitors Bureau, 19900 Governors Drive, Suite 200, Olympia Fields; (708) 895-8200 or (888) 895-8233; visitchicagosouthland.com.
- Heritage Corridor Convention and Visitors Bureau, 2701 Black Road, Suite 201, Joliet; (844) 944-2282; heritagecorridorcvb.com.

Local Events/Attractions

- Joliet Area Historical Museum, 204 N. Ottawa Street, Joliet; (815) 723-5201; jolietmuseum.org. Offers a thorough introduction to the history of the Joliet area.

The rural setting along the Wauponsee Trail attracts equestrians.

- Joliet-area rail trails; reconnectwithnature.org. Three other long rail trails can be accessed in Joliet. Check the website for route advice and on-street connections.
- Midewin National Tallgrass Prairie, 30239 Highway 53, Wilmington; (815) 423-6370; fs.fed.us/mntp. The visitor center has exhibits, maps of the park, and plenty of programs.

Restaurants

- Creamery, 525 W. North Street, Manhattan; (815) 478-0345; ourcreamery.com. Local ice cream chain with some fast food options; close to the trail.
- Kat's Café, 340 W. North Street, Manhattan; (815) 680-6092; katscafemanhattan.com. Basic diner fare close to the trail.

Accommodations

- Forked Creek Forest Preserve—Ballou Rd. Access, located on Ballou Rd. east of IL 102 in Wilmington; (815) 727-8700; bit.ly/goodenowcg. Two shaded campsites located right off the trail in a wooded area; permit required.
- Kankakee River State Park, 5314 Highway 102, Bourbonnais; (815) 933-1383; bit.ly/kankcg. The park contains a couple of campgrounds, hiking trails, and a 10-mile-long multi-use trail close to the south end of the Wauponsee Glacial Trail (see Honorable Mention trails in the back of this book).

Northern Illinois

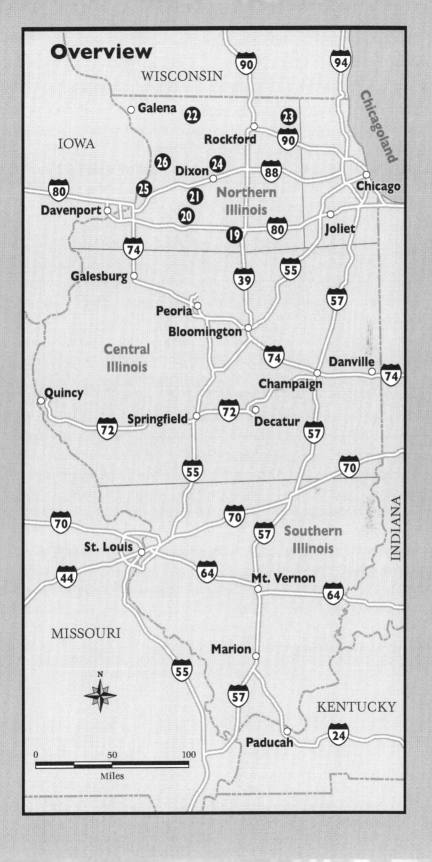

In northwest Illinois, the dominant natural feature is the Mississippi River. This upper portion of the river contains many square miles of wetlands, bottomland woods, and open water sprinkled with islands. Ambitious trail users can voyage upstream for 30 miles along the Mississippi River Trail. Starting in the Quad Cities, the trail runs north through a string of river towns and ends in Albany, where you'll encounter one of the largest collections of American Indian mounds in the nation.

East of the Quad Cities, the 60-mile-long Hennepin Canal Trail runs through the rural landscape between the Mississippi and Illinois Rivers. At its halfway point, the Hennepin Feeder Canal Trail comes down from the north to join up with the main Hennepin Canal Trail. Similar to the I&M Canal on the other side of the state, the Hennepin Canal stopped serving as a transportation route many years ago.

In addition to these longer trails, there are a handful of shorter but no less interesting rail trails in the area. As the Jane Addams Trail runs north from Freeport to the Wisconsin state line, it parallels the route of a creek that once powered mills in several small towns along the way. In the town of Dixon, the Lowell Parkway Trail takes you by the shore of the lovely Rock River on the way to a park situated on a high bluff above the river. The Long Prairie and Stone Bridge Trails offer unlimited solitude as you tour a landscape containing small farm towns, open cropland, and gently rolling woodland.

A rural landscape generally dominates north-central and northwest Illinois. While exploring the rail trails in this region, you'll find that the towns tend to be spread apart. Amenities such as restaurants and convenience stores are sometimes hard to come by. This part of the state often feels remote and out of the way, but you're never terribly far from population centers like Freeport, Rockford, and the Quad Cities. Nor are you far from the interesting historic towns of Galena or Bishop Hill or breathtaking natural areas like Mississippi Palisades State Park or Starved Rock State Park.

20 HENNEPIN CANAL TRAIL

While following the former towpath alongside the Hennepin Canal, you'll encounter many miles of open space and agricultural land, as well as patches of woodland and prairie. Since the route runs through only one town, cultural attractions are limited, but there are old railroad bridges, thirty-two locks (many with the original mechanical hardware intact), and six aqueducts that carry the canal over streams and rivers.

Location: From Bureau Junction, located about 40 miles north of Peoria, the trail runs west to the Rock River and the outskirts of the Quad Cities.

Length: 60.3 miles one-way.

Surface: Crushed gravel on much of the trail; some sections have "tar and chip"—tar base covered with very small rocks.

Wheelchair access: The route is wheelchair accessible.

Difficulty: This trail sits solidly in the difficult category: It's incredibly long, with a dearth of amenities and frequent exposure to wind and sun.

Restrooms: There are public restrooms at the trailhead, Lock 6, Lock 11, Lock 17, Lock 21 (water), Hennepin Canal State Park Visitor Center (water), Lock 22 (water), boat launch, Lock 23, Lock 24, Lock 26 alongside the trail in Colona, and at the end of the trail at Rock River.

Maps: bit.ly/hcanltrail.

Hazards: Large portions of the route are wide open, leaving trail users exposed to wind and sun. Restaurants and stores are nonexistent on the first half of the trail; they're few and far between on the second half.

Access and parking: From I-180 west of Princeton, take IL 26 south. In Bureau look for the trailhead parking area on the right. UTM coordinates: 16T, 301117 E, 4573188 N.

Parking is abundant all along the trail. Among the dozens of road crossings, only a few do not have parking spots for trail users. Following are a few of the picnic areas along the trail:

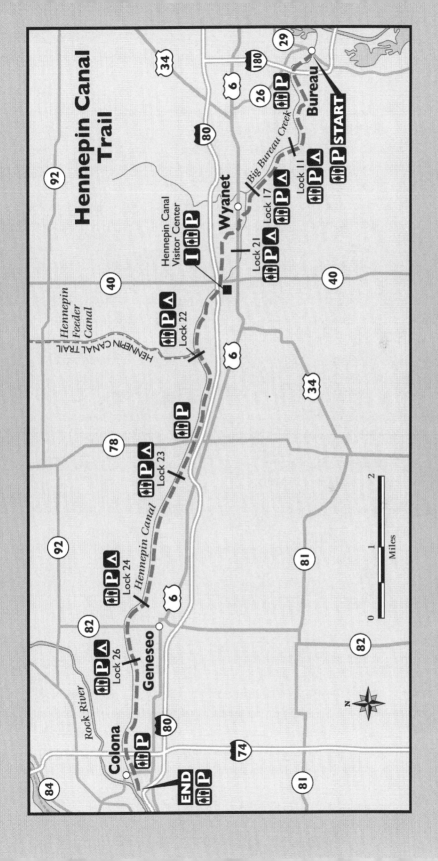

To park at Lock 11, head south on IL 26 from I-80. Follow IL 26 as it curves left, becomes Main St., and then becomes Tiskilwa Bottom Rd. Turn right onto Princeton-Tiskilwa Rd. (CR 1250 N).

To park at Lock 17, go south on IL 40 from I-80. Turn left onto US 34/6. In Wyanet, turn right onto Wyanet-Walnut Rd. (CR 8). Turn left onto Canal St. (CR 1410 N). Turn right onto CR 1550 E.

To park at Lock 21, go south on IL 40 from I-80. Turn left onto US 34/6. After crossing the canal, look for the entrance to the camping/picnic area on the right.

To park at Hennepin Canal State Park, go south on IL 40 from I-80. Follow the sign on the right to the visitor center.

To park at Lock 22, exit south on IL 78 from I-80. Turn left onto US 6. After passing through Mineral, turn left onto 1550 North Ave. and then right onto 300 East St.

To park at lock 23, go north on IL 78 from I-80 and turn left onto CR 22 (Baker School Rd.).

To park at the west end of the trail in Colona, exit I-80 west on Cleveland Rd. just north of Colona. Turn right onto IL 84 and then left onto Sixth St. Follow the park road out to the boat launch on the Rock River.

Transportation: Amtrak trains stop in Princeton, located about 5 miles north of the east end of the trail.

Rentals: Quad Cities Convention and Visitors Bureau rents bikes, 1601 River Dr., Suite 110, Moline, (309) 277-0937; visitquadcities.com.

Contact: Hennepin Canal Visitor Center, 16006 875 East St., Sheffield; (815) 454-2328; bit.ly/hcstrail.

||||||||||||||||||||||||||||||||||||||||||||||||||||||||||||||||||||||||||||||||||||||||||||||||||||||||||

In the late nineteenth and early twentieth centuries, the I&M and Hennepin Canals were dug in northern Illinois to speed up transportation between Lake Michigan and the Mississippi River. The Hennepin Canal, which runs from the Illinois River nearly to the Mississippi, is the lesser known of the two. Long closed to barge traffic, the canal now is essentially a long, narrow pond that stretches nearly halfway across the state.

Big Bureau Creek and Wyanet

Starting the trail in Bureau Junction (usually called simply "Bureau"), the first few miles reveal intermittent stretches of Big Bureau Creek as it winds through a considerable plot of bottomland woods. Shortly after passing under I-180, wooded bluffs rise up from the Bureau Creek floodplain on the north side of the canal. Woods continue to sprawl to the south. In the first 6 miles of the canal, you'll encounter nine locks that raised and lowered boats nearly forty-five feet as they traveled the canal. After Lock 10, Bureau Creek closely parallels the canal for a long stretch. At Lock 11 sycamore and fir trees provide shade for the pleasant picnic grounds that sit at the foot of an old trestle bridge.

Between Lock 15 and US 34, the trail runs through a 4.2-mile stretch where you'll encounter an aqueduct and six locks, many with the original mechanical devices still intact. At Lock 17 you'll see another old trestle bridge and the remains of a bridge built on a system of rollers so that it could be moved aside for canal boats. After Lock 18 a railroad bridge—now a pedestrian bridge—takes you over the canal toward Wyanet. (A

Many iron bridges and mechanical features of the Hennepin Canal remain, offering a glimpse of what canal transportation was like more than 100 years ago.

convenience store and diner are located in Wyanet, nearly 1 mile north of the trail.) Another mile up the trail, near US 34, Lock 21 has a large, shaded picnic area, areas for tent and equestrian camping, and one of several lift bridges left along the canal. The lines of concrete blocks near the camping area are the remnants of a canal boat repair shop.

Feeder Basin and Wildlife

Nearly 21 miles along the trail, you'll reach the rolling grassy lawn of the Hennepin Canal Visitor Center. The visitor center contains a few exhibits focusing on the history of the canal, including a model of a lock and an aqueduct and a display of tools used to build the canal. Take a breather from your life on the trail by visiting the park's small wildflower prairie, the wooded hiking trails, and wetlands.

Once you've racked up some miles on this trail, you'll likely realize that at its heart, the canal is basically a pond immeasurably stretched. As with any area pond, observers will see great blue herons, white egrets, kingfishers, and red-winged blackbirds. You may see hawks loitering in the top branches of the huge cottonwood trees at the edge of the canal. If good fortune allows, you may catch a glimpse of a beaver or muskrat moving through the water before ducking out of sight. On summer evenings you'll likely see swallows careening over the surface of the canal in search of insects.

The slender canal widens into a lake-size basin at the point where the Hennepin Feeder Canal and its accompanying trail join from the north. As the largest expanse of open water along the canal, the Feeder Basin, as it's called, often hosts local anglers casting from their boats. From the basin the feeder canal and its trail shoot north for 28.9 miles to the Rock River in the town of Rock Falls (learn about the Hennepin Feeder Canal Trail in the next chapter).

Big Open Spaces

Lock 22 is one of the few locks that are largely intact, with wooden gates, metal gears, pulleys, and counterweights that lifted the small drawbridge over the canal. At the edge of the canal, a picnic area offers an inviting spot to take a break. Paddlers like to put in at Lock 22 because they can travel nearly 10 miles west to Lock 23 with no portages.

For such a long trail, there are surprisingly few traces of civilization. The best opportunity in the trail's midsection to patronize a convenience store, a restaurant, or a hotel rears up near Annawan at 32.9 miles. (Turn left at IL 78; the amenities are just 0.5 mile south of the trail.)

Beyond Lock 23, it can feel as though you're piling up some long and lonely miles on the windswept prairie. A veil of trailside trees restricts the scenery for long stretches. Periodically, the greenery drops away revealing vast tracts of corn and soy plants occasionally interrupted by farmhouses and small patches of woodland. Every mile or so you're shuttled under a road and through a short metal tunnel about 6 feet in diameter. Also along this stretch, keep watch for the equestrians using the mowed path on the opposite side of the canal.

Green and Rock Rivers

Anglers often launch their boats near Geneseo, where the canal grows wide and the shores are thick with woodland. Nearby you'll catch glimpses of the Green River, which has been channelized with levees. West of

The Canal That Arrived Too Late

Finished in 1907, the Hennepin Canal was envisioned as a shortcut between Lake Michigan and the Upper Mississippi, specifically the Quad Cities. Supporters of the canal hoped to replicate the success of the I&M Canal, which turned Chicago into a transportation epicenter. But as the last long-distance canal built in the United States, the Hennepin Canal arrived too late in the game to find success. Riverboat traffic was already on the decline, and railroads had become the preferred method of transportation. In addition, a widening of the locks on both the Illinois and Mississippi Rivers made larger riverboats the standard of the day. With lock chambers much narrower than the rivers it connected, the canal was obsolete almost immediately. By the 1930s, the Hennepin was already used primarily for recreation.

Geneseo, near Lock 25, the trail follows an embankment that offers views of the surrounding countryside. A few houses sit along the road on the opposite side of the canal. Beyond Lock 26, thicker woodland continues after crossing over the Green River. The aqueduct over the Green River was one of a handful of aqueducts along the canal that were removed.

In the town of Colona, residential neighborhoods border the canal, as do a series of pleasant community parks with benches, picnic tables, and pavilions. A row of big cottonwood trees escorts you along the final stretch of canal to its confluence with the Rock River.

Local Information

- Friends of the Hennepin Canal, c/o Gary Wagle, President, 1639 N. Cherry Street, Galesburg; friends-hennepin-canal.org. Local advocacy group holds regular hikes and other activities on the trail.
- Bureau County Tourism, 205 S. 5th Street, Princeton (815) 866-3606; bureaucounty-il.com.

Local Events/Attractions

- Bishop Hill Museum State Historic Site, 304 Bishop Hill Street, Bishop Hill; (309) 927-3345; visit-bishophill.com. This well-preserved village once hosted a religious commune in the mid-1800s. It now contains interesting shops, galleries, and several historic structures.
- Owen Lovejoy Homestead, 905 E. Peru Street, Princeton; owenlovejoyhomestead.com. Former home and now a museum that was one of the most important stations on the Underground Railroad in Illinois; located about 5 miles north of the trail.

Restaurants

- Geneseo Brewing Co., 102 S State Street, Geneseo; (309) 945-1422; geneseobrewing.com. Pleasant atmosphere with sandwiches and pizza; located a couple miles from the trail.
- Lavender Crest Winery, 5401 US 6, Colona; (309) 949-2565; lavendercrest.com. Good selection of sandwiches, salads, and wine; lunch only.

Accommodations

- Best Western Annawan, 315 N. Canal Street, Annawan; (309) 935-6565; bestwestern.com. Pool and a spacious lounging/breakfast area; located 0.5 mile south of the trail.
- The Tiskilwa Inn, 155 High Street, Tiskilwa; (815) 646-1300; thetiskilwainn.com. Handsome Italianate mansion located less than 1 mile from the trail. Bike rentals available.
- Camping along the canal is available at Locks 11, 17, 22, 23, and 26 and at Bridges 14, 23, and 37; bit.ly/hcanltrail. While the camping areas are typically quiet and rural, it's rustic and privacy is often limited.

21 HENNEPIN FEEDER CANAL TRAIL

Shooting south from Rock Falls, this historic towpath attracts cyclists, hikers, and anglers who come to enjoy the stocked waters, the peaceful wooded banks, and the canal's abundant birdlife. Swallows are often seen wheeling above the surface of the water, and great blue herons stand in the shade of giant cottonwood trees. As the trail takes a series of gentle turns heading south through rural countryside, the number of visitors dwindles, allowing you to have many miles of trail all to yourself.

Location: From the Rock River in Rock Falls, the trail runs south to where it meets up with the main Hennepin Canal Trail.

Length: 28.9 miles one-way.

Surface: The first 3.6 miles of the trail is paved before it becomes smooth, hard-packed gravel. At 17.2 miles the surface becomes "tar and chip"—tar base covered with very small rocks.

Wheelchair access: The trail is wheelchair accessible.

Difficulty: This trail is inching toward the difficult category due to its length, lack of amenities, and lack of shade.

Restrooms: There are public restrooms at the Jim Arduini Boat Launch next to the trailhead parking area, Centennial Park (water), Bridge 50 (crossing for IL 172), Bridge 52 (Hahnaman Rd.), and Bridge 64 (crossing for 1945 Ave. N.).

Maps: https://bit.ly/hcanltrail.

Hazards: Bring plenty of water: After the first mile, there is no drinking water along the way—no stores or restaurants, either. The path becomes very narrow when it passes under many of the bridges. Approach these underpasses slowly.

Access and parking: Exit I-88 on IL 40, heading north. In Rock Falls turn right onto E. 2nd Ave. UTM coordinates: 16T, 0277544 E, 4629588 N.

Trail users can choose from numerous places to park and pick up the trail. Nearly all twenty-four bridges along the trail have small parking

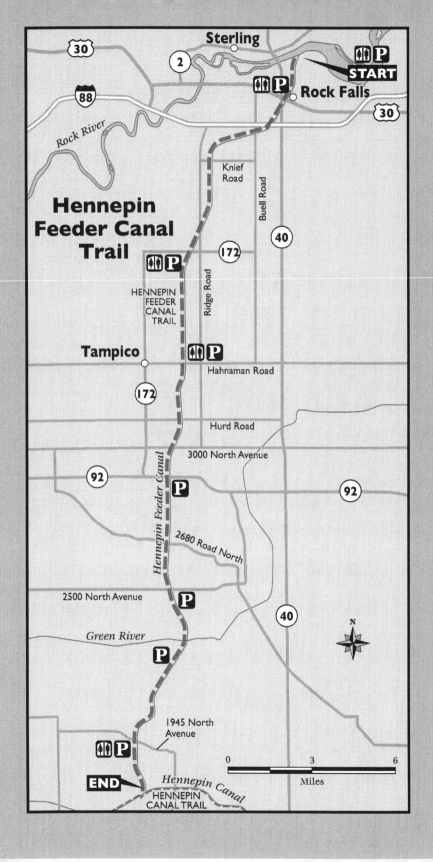

areas. You may still park if there is no official parking area, but do not block car traffic or the trail. To reach the IL 172 and the Hahnaman Rd. parking areas (both with restrooms), follow these roads west from IL 40, which runs parallel to the trail.

To park at Bridge 64, the southernmost parking area with restrooms, head west on 2000 North Ave. from IL 40. After curving to the left onto 675 East Ave., turn onto 1950 North Ave. Go left onto 450 St. East and right onto 1900 North Ave.

Transportation: The closest Amtrak stations are in Mendota, Princeton, and Kewanee.

Rentals: Rock Falls has a bike sharing options at the RB&W Riverfront Park; visitrockfalls.com.

Contact: Hennepin Canal State Park and Visitor Center, 16006 875 East Street, Sheffield; (815) 454-2328; bit.ly/hcstrail. Located on the main Hennepin Canal Trail about 6 miles east of the Feeder Basin.

U nlike the rest of the Hennepin Canal, the Hennepin Feeder Canal was not built for boat traffic. Instead its main purpose was to harness water from the Rock River to fill the 60-mile-long expanse of the main canal. The feeder canal was originally slated to take water from the Rock River in the town of Dixon, about 10 miles northeast of Rock Falls. But local citizens changed the route of the canal by raising money for a survey to show that building the mouth of the feeder canal in Rock Falls would be 6 miles shorter, require one less bridge, and eliminate the need for a lock.

After it was finished in 1907, the Hennepin Canal never grew to become the prominent shipping route it was expected to be. The exponential growth of railroads, the widening of locks in the Illinois and Mississippi Rivers, and the dredging of the Illinois River all conspired to minimize the boat traffic on the canal. In the 1960s state and federal agencies began a lengthy process to transform the entire canal and the path alongside it into a long, narrow recreation area.

Leaving Rock Falls

The trail starts on the Rock River, next to a hydroelectric plant and a newly constructed pedestrian bridge over the river. The first 5 miles on the trail heading out of Rock Falls brings you under ten bridges. Not far from Rock Falls, a bright red train caboose appears through the trees on the right, marking Centennial Park, which contains a lagoon where you can rent paddleboats.

Enormous cottonwood trees grow on both sides of the canal as the trail takes you farther from Rock Falls. Many of these trees—typically with branches fanning out toward the top—tower 100 feet above the canal. In early spring, the trees' cottony seeds coat the surface of the canal.

It doesn't take long to figure out that birds love the canal: Cardinals, orioles, kingbirds, red-winged blackbirds, red-tailed hawks, and great blue herons are just a few of the birds commonly seen along the way. Keep watch for beavers and muskrats, as well as such reptiles as water snakes, painted turtles, and the much larger softshell turtles—often with shells larger than dinner plates.

The Hennepin Feeder Canal Trail takes you into a remote landscape with many miles of peaceful, scenic views.

A Presidential Birthplace

If presidential birthplaces give you a thrill, and you're riding a bike, consider a short side trip to the birthplace of Ronald Reagan. At Bridge 52, Hahnaman Rd. will take you 1.6 miles west to the tiny town of Tampico, where there's a small museum and gift shop located next to the building where the fortieth U.S. president was born. For the first ten years of Reagan's life, his family lived in an apartment above a restaurant on Main St.

Continuing south, patches of wetland occasionally break up the scenery. Intermittently, the banks on either side of the canal drop down to reveal long views of the rural landscape speckled with garnet-colored barns in the distance.

Green River Aqueduct

The highlight of the second half of the trail appears when the canal is funneled over an aqueduct about forty feet above the Green River. (Of the nine aqueducts on the Hennepin Canal, only one was built on the feeder canal.) This impressive piece of early-twentieth-century engineering occurs in a pleasant spot with views up and down the sandy-bottomed river. Swallows make their nests underneath the aqueduct and are frequently twirling through the trees and above the river in search of bugs.

The small lake that appears where the Feeder Canal meets with the main Hennepin Canal is called the Feeder Basin. From here you can turn around and head back to Rock Falls or extend the trip with a visit to the Hennepin Canal Visitor Center, about 6 miles to the east along the main canal.

Local Information

- Blackhawk Waterways Convention and Visitors Bureau, 201 N. Franklin Avenue, Polo; (800) 678-2108; visitnorthwestillinois.com.
- Friends of the Hennepin Canal, c/o Gary Wagle, President, 1639 N. Cherry Street, Galesburg; friends-hennepin-canal.org. Local advocacy group holds regular hikes and other activities on the trail.
- Rock Falls Tourism, 603 W. 10th Street, Rock Falls; (815) 622-1106; visitrockfalls.com.

Local Events/Attractions

- Dillon Home/Sterling Rock Falls Historical Society, 1005 E. Third Street; (815) 622-6202; sterlingparks.org. Check out this lavish historic home as well a history museum on the grounds; take the walking/biking bridge across the Rock River from the trailhead parking area.
- Ronald Reagan Birthplace, 111 S. Main Street, Tampico; (815) 622-8705; tampicohistoricalsociety.com. The family apartment has been restored to its original 1900s style. Next door is a small gift store and museum. To reach Tampico take Hahnaman Rd. to the right from the trail at Bridge 52. Traffic is mellow on the 1.6-mile route into town.

Restaurants

- Arthurs Garden Deli, 1405 First Avenue, Rock Falls; (815) 625-0011; arthursgardendeli.com. Close to the trail as you pass Centennial Park.
- Candlelight Inn, 2200 First Avenue, Rock Falls; (815) 626-1897; candlelightinnrestaurant.com. Sandwiches and steaks.

Accommodations

- Holiday Inn Express, 301 E. 2nd Street, Rock Falls; (815) 622-4000; ihg.com. Located blocks from the trail on the Rock River.
- Camping options are abundant along the main Hennepin Canal Trail, but not the feeder canal. Closest camping options on main canal trail is at Lock 22 and at Bridge 14.

22 JANE ADDAMS TRAIL

The Jane Addams Trail offers a satisfying ramble through wetlands, prairie, wooded landscapes, and farmland north of Freeport. While following the Richland Creek floodplain, the trail crosses twenty-one wooden bridges and cuts through a handful of small towns and hamlets. An optional side trip to Jane Addams's hometown allows visitors to learn more about this important figure in U.S. history.

Location: From Wes Block trailhead on US 20, located several miles north of Freeport, head north to the Wisconsin border.

Length: 13.0 miles one-way. Extend the trip on the north end by following the 40-mile-long Badger State Trail. You can also extend the trip by a few miles on the south end.

Surface: Smooth crushed gravel.

Wheelchair access: The route is wheelchair accessible.

Difficulty: The trail is easy.

Restrooms: There are public restrooms at the Wes Block trailhead (water), at the trail parking area in Red Oak, and at a trailside park in Orangeville (water).

Maps: janeaddamstrail.com.

Hazards: No hazards other than a few semi-busy roads that must be crossed.

Access and parking: From I-39 south of Rockford, take US 20 west. Exit US 20 at IL 26, heading south. Turn right on N. Riverside Dr. Turn right on Heine Rd. and the trailhead parking is at the end of the road on the right. UTM coordinates: 16T, 280345 E, 4689694 N.

To reach the parking area in Red Oak, take IL 26 north from Freeport. In Cedarville turn left on W. Washington St. and then right on N. Mill St. Continue ahead on W. Red Oak Rd. and then bear left on W. Beaver Rd. The trailhead is on the right.

To park in Buena Vista, take IL 26 north and then turn left on W. McConnell Rd. Park on the left just before the trail crosses the road. Immediately turn left on Ewing St. and park on the right.

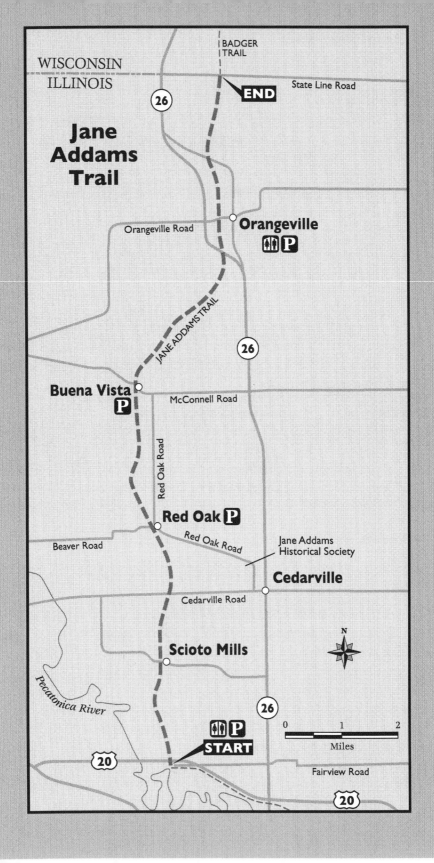

Transportation: The closest Amtrak station is in Rockford.

Rentals: No bike rental options in the area.

Contact: Freeport Park District, 1122 S. Burchard Avenue, P.O. Box 417, Freeport; (815) 235-6114; freeportparkdistrict.org.

||||||||||||||||||||||||||||||||||||||||||||||||||||||||||||||||||||||||||||||||

The Jane Addams Trail follows the route of the Illinois Central Railroad as it runs through the floodplain of Richland Creek. Once the tracks were laid down in the area in 1887, a handful of small railroad towns sprouted up in their wake: Scioto Mills, Buena Vista, Red Oak, and Orangeville. The towns also benefited from a series of mills that were built along the creek. As happened in so many other places, the towns shrank as the need for water-powered mills dried up and the use of the railroad declined.

Small Towns

Less than 2 miles into the trail, before reaching the hamlet of Scioto Mills, the first glimpses of Richland Creek appear, zigzagging through the bottomland on the left. Scioto Mills was built in the early 1850s around a sawmill and a gristmill. The gristmill, powered by Richland Creek, reportedly did brisk business grinding feed and flour with three millstones. At Cedarville Rd., if you're biking consider a short detour to the Cedarville Historical Society, where you can learn about the trail's namesake—the person President Theodore Roosevelt called "America's most useful citizen." It's 2 miles to the historical society from the trail; Cedarville Rd. is not terribly busy but has no shoulder and may not be comfortable for less experienced riders. (Follow Cedarville Rd. east and then turn left on N. Mill St., passing by Jane Addams childhood home. The historical society is to the right on 2nd St.)

Heading north from Cedarville Rd. brings you through wetlands and bottomlands galore. Along this section you'll pass through the sleepy hamlets of Red Oak and Buena Vista, both of which had mills along Richland Creek.

Richland Creek

At about 7 miles into the trail, just north of McConnell Rd., the route cuts through a rocky embankment before crossing a bridge over Richland Creek. For the rest of trail, Richland Creek and most of its accompanying wetlands move from the west side of the trail to the east.

While many of the bridges offer pleasant views of the surrounding wetlands and prairie, the bridges just before and after Brush Creek Rd. allow for particularly eye-catching views of Richland Creek as it winds through swaying grasslands.

Orangeville and Beyond

On the way into Orangeville, you'll see a quarry to the left and then pass a small pond surrounded by grassland. From Orangeville it's just a short trip up to the state line, where the Jane Addams Trail becomes the Badger State Trail.

The Badger State Trail extends 40 miles north from the Illinois border to Madison. (Bicyclists, cross-country skiers, and equestrians age sixteen and older must have a Wisconsin state trail pass.) About 8 miles north of

Near the Jane Addams Trail's halfway mark, it cuts through a rocky bluff.

Jane Addams, a Local Hero

Born and raised in Cedarville, Jane Addams is best known for founding and operating the Hull House, an institution on Chicago's near west side that was once recognized around the world. The Hull House spearheaded what was called the settlement house movement, which provided services to people in need—many who were recent immigrants. The complex eventually expanded to include thirteen buildings. Later in Addams's life, she helped found numerous organizations and advocacy groups that worked on behalf of children, families, and workers. She also became involved in the peace movement. In 1931 Addams was the first woman to receive the Nobel Peace Prize.

the Illinois border is the town of Monroe, the self-proclaimed Swiss cheese capital of the nation. In the center of the square is an impressive courthouse. In the town of Exeter between Monticello and Belleville, the trail enters a 1,200-foot-long, century-old tunnel.

The Badger State Trail connects with the 40-mile-long Military Ridge State Trail, the 24-mile Sugar River State Trail, and the 17-mile-long Capital City Trail in Madison.

Local Information

- **Greater Freeport Partnership, 110 W. Main Street, Freeport; (815) 233-1350; greaterfreeport.com.**

Local Events/Attractions

- Cedarville Historical Society, 450 W. Second Street, Cedarville; (815) 990-0417; cedarvilleareahistoricalsociety.org. Contains photos, letters, and personal items that belonged to Jane Addams. Located 2 miles from the trail: turn right onto Cedarville Rd. and follow the blue signs to the museum.
- Stephenson County Historical Museum, 1440 S. Carroll Avenue, Freeport; (815) 232-8419; stephcohs.org. Features local toy manufacturers and industries, as well as a historic schoolhouse and cabin.

Restaurants

- The Muse on Cedar Creek, 395 W. Cedarville Road, Freeport; (779) 994-6873; museoncedar-creek.com. Restaurant located about 2.5 miles east of the trail in Cedarville.
- The Union Dairy, 126 E. Douglas, Freeport; (815) 232-7099; theuniondairy.com. Old-fashioned ice-cream parlor located in downtown Freeport; sandwiches and sides, as well.
- The Wagner House, 1 E. Spring Street, Freeport; (815) 232-4408; wagnerhouseil.com. Bar and restaurant in large warehouse in downtown Freeport.

Accommodations

- Baymont Hotel, 1060 N. Riverside Drive, Freeport; (815) 656-4632; wyndhamhotels.com. The Jane Addams Trail runs by the hotel.
- Lake Le-Aqua-Na State Park, 854 N. Lake Road, Lena; (815) 369-4282; bit.ly./leaquasp. Pleasant campground located 8 miles west of the trail in Buena Vista.

23 LONG PRAIRIE AND STONE BRIDGE TRAILS

As you travel these two connected trails, you'll encounter little winding creeks, a few small railroad towns, and big expanses of farmland. Proceeding west toward the northern suburbs of Rockford, the greenery grows thick and the landscape becomes more rolling. Toward the end of the route, a short trip off-trail brings you to a picturesque landmark—an old double-arched limestone bridge straddling a rocky creek.

Location: From the County Line Rd. parking area, located about 5 miles west of Harvard, head west to Roscoe, a northern suburb of Rockford.

Length: 19.4 miles one-way.

Surface: Asphalt on the 14.1-mile Long Prairie Trail; crushed gravel on the 5.3-mile Stone Bridge Trail.

Wheelchair access: The route is wheelchair accessible.

Difficulty: The route offers a medium level of difficulty. Some sections leave you exposed to sun and wind.

Restrooms: There are public restrooms at the parking area on the east end of the trail, Poplar Grove parking area, Caledonia parking area, the Brown Conservation Park (water), and Roland Olson Forest Preserve on CR 7 (water).

Maps: bit.ly/lpsbtrail.

Hazards: Watch for traffic while crossing the busier roads.

Access and parking: From I-90 west of Elgin, exit north onto US 20. In Marengo turn right onto IL 23. South of Harvard turn left onto US 14 and left again onto IL 173. Turn right onto County Line Rd. The parking area is on the left. UTM coordinates: 16T, 359598 E, 4696263 N.

Parking lots are provided in all three villages along the route:

To park in Poplar Grove, head west on IL 173 from Harvard. Turn left onto State St. and look for the trail as it crosses the road.

To park in Caledonia head west on IL 173 from Harvard. Turn left onto Front St.

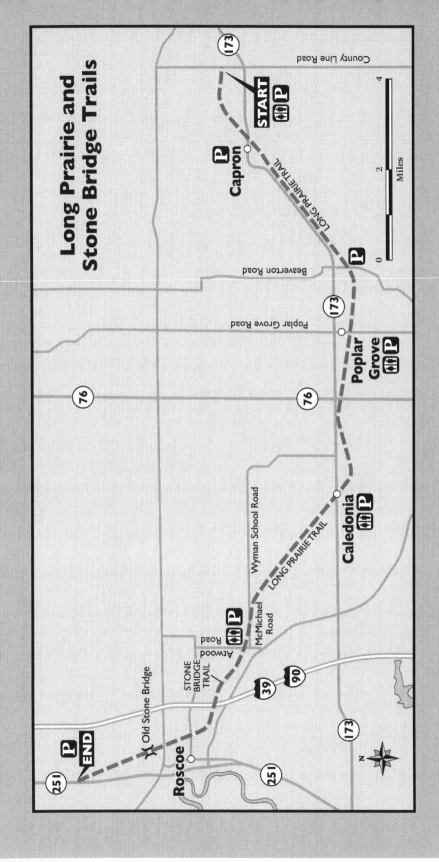

To park at the Roland Olson Forest Preserve, head east IL 173 from I-90. Turn left onto Belvidere Rd. Turn right on Atwood Rd. The forest preserve entrance is on the right. To park at the west end of the trail, take I-90 north of Rockford. Exit at Rockton Rd. and head west. The parking area is on the left just before passing under IL 251.

Transportation: Amtrak trains serve Rockford and Metra trains serve Harvard.

Rentals: No bike rentals in the area.

Contact: Boone County Conservation District, 603 Appleton Road, Belvidere; (815) 547-7935; bccdil.org; maintains the Long Prairie Trail.

Village of Roscoe, 5792 Elevator Road, Roscoe; (815) 623-7323; villageofroscoe.com; maintains the Stone Bridge Trail.

The Long Prairie Trail originally served a railroad that the Kenosha, Rockford, and Rock Island Railroad Company started operating in 1858. The company that built the railroad soon sold it to the Chicago and Northwestern Railroad, which maintained it as an active line for nearly a century. As the story goes, the railroad was abandoned when a train crossing Beaverton Rd. (trail mile 5.6) derailed, leaving behind a torn-up railbed, broken ties, and twisted tracks. In lieu of making costly repairs, the railroad was mothballed. A gouge in the railbed remains today.

Capron

As you start toward Capron from the east end of the Long Prairie Trail, the route immediately reaches across an arm of Picasaw Creek. Not far ahead, Picasaw Creek brushes against the trail in a couple of spots, resulting in lush greenery and grassy wetlands fringed with willows. When the number of big oaks leaning over the trail start to dwindle, you're allowed glimpses of horse pastures and the gently rolling agricultural landscape of the surrounding area.

The small town of Capron has been adorned with several different names. Originally called Helgesaw in honor of the many Scandinavians in the area, it was later renamed Long Prairie due to a sizable swath of nearby prairie. Then, like so many other towns in Illinois, it acquired the name of a manager with the local railroad.

Embankments and Ravines

South of Capron the trail hugs IL 173 for 2.5 miles. This largely unshaded strip of trail follows a small embankment and crosses a couple of minor streams. Look for Queen Anne's lace, black-eyed Susans, and goldenrod growing alongside the trail. After crossing Beaverton Rd. on the way into Poplar Grove, look for the gouge caused by the train derailment on the side of the trail. After the gouge, you'll pass over Beaver Creek and then follow a ten-foot embankment above the surrounding landscape. Poplar Grove announces its arrival with a grain elevator and big storage silos alongside the trail. The small park in Poplar Grove offers a pleasant spot to catch your breath.

Outside of Poplar Grove, the golf fairways alongside the trail are part of a housing community called Candlewick Lake. After Caledonia, oak-hickory woods grow thick and the landscape becomes more textured. At one point the trail mounts an embankment thirty feet high; in another, thirty-five-foot-high ravines rise up on the sides of the trail. When the greenery opens, farms appear in the distance, but rarely are there structures near the trail. The lack of nearby development, combined with a small number of trail users, lends the trail a distinctly remote feel.

The Old Stone Bridge

Leaving Boone County and entering Winnebago County at 14.1 miles signals the beginning of the Stone Bridge Trail. In Winnebago County the landscape becomes more rolling and wooded. Long views grow more frequent, and the ravines and embankments built for the railroad multiply.

As the trail passes over North Kinnikinnick Creek, the surrounding shrubs and grasses disguise the fact that you're high up on a bridge. The only features that give away your location are the wooded fencing on the sides of the trail and gurgle of the creek below. A walking path leads you on a series of switchbacks down the ravine to a wooden platform overlooking the creek, adjoining wetlands, and the trail's namesake—a double-arched limestone bridge built in 1882. Local engineers say the bridge (now on the National Register of Historic Places) is unique for its date of construction and its design, which includes an internal drainage system.

The trail's namesake, a double-arched stone bridge, is on the National Register of Historic Places.

For the final couple of miles, the railroad right-of-way carves a straight, level path through open savanna and prairie. Houses speckle the landscape. The views are wide, but shade is thin. Shortly after crossing the final bridge, which spans Dry Creek, you'll reach the parking area at the end of the trail.

Local Information

- Rockford Area Convention and Visitors Bureau, 102 N. Main Street, Rockford; (800) 521-0849; gorockford.com.

Local Events/Attractions

- Edwards Apple Orchard, 7061 Centerville Road, Poplar Grove; (815) 765-2234; edwardsorchard. farm. Donuts, cider, sandwiches, and U-pick apples, located a couple miles off the trail.
- McEachran Homestead Winery, 1917 Wyman School Road, Caledonia; (815) 978-5120; mceachranhomestead.com. Grape and fruit wines, and snacks, located 1.5 miles from the trail.

Restaurants

- Arturo's Mexican Restaurant, 107 W. Main Street, Poplar Grove; (815) 765-1144; arturosmexicanfood.com. Standard Mexican fare located steps from the trail.
- Poplar Grind, 100–104 W. Main Street, Poplar Grove; (815) 519-0651. Coffee, breakfast items, and baked goods right on the trail.

Accommodations

- Hononegah Forest Preserve, 80 Hononegah Road, Rockton; (815) 877-6100; winnebagoforest. org. Camping close to the Rock River; located a couple of miles from the west end of the Stone Bridge Trail.
- Ironworks Hotel Beloit, 500 Pleasant Street, Beloit, Wisconsin, (608) 362-5500; ironworkshotelbeloit.com. Boutique hotel on the Rock River, located a few miles north of the west end of the Stone Bridge Trail.

24 LOWELL PARKWAY TRAIL

Lowell Park has been a cherished landmark in the Dixon area for the past one hundred years. The park's high wooded bluffs, scenic shoreline along the Rock River, and collection of rustic rock shelters have drawn people for generations. On the way to the park from Dixon, you'll take a mile-long ramble along the Rock River and then explore an attractive wooded landscape.

Location: From the corner of Bradshaw St. and Washington Ave. in Dixon, the trail runs northwest to Lowell Park.

Length: 8.5 miles one-way.

Surface: The route includes paved path, quiet park road, and a 3.3-mile segment on gravel path. The gravel path is not a well-compacted surface, which is great for hiking but not so great for bikes with skinny tires. Medium to wide tires will work best. If you don't have wider tires, this section is easily skipped.

Wheelchair access: The Lowell Parkway Trail is wheelchair accessible; the gravel path and the route through Lowell Park would not be good for wheelchair use.

Difficulty: The route is easy until reaching Lowell Park, where you must go up and down a high bluff.

Restrooms: There are public restrooms at the 0.8-mile trail junction (portable toilet) and the Lowell Park boat ramp (water). There is a trailside water fountain at 0.5 mile.

Maps: bit.ly/lowellpky.

Hazards: While traffic is very light in Lowell Park, be careful on the winding, shoulderless park road, particularly if walking or running the route.

Access and parking: From I-88 exit to Dixon on IL 26. A half mile after crossing the Rock River in Dixon, turn right onto Bradshaw St. The parking area for the trailhead is 0.5 mile ahead on the right at the intersection with Washington Ave. UTM coordinates: 16T, 294277 E, 4636554 N.

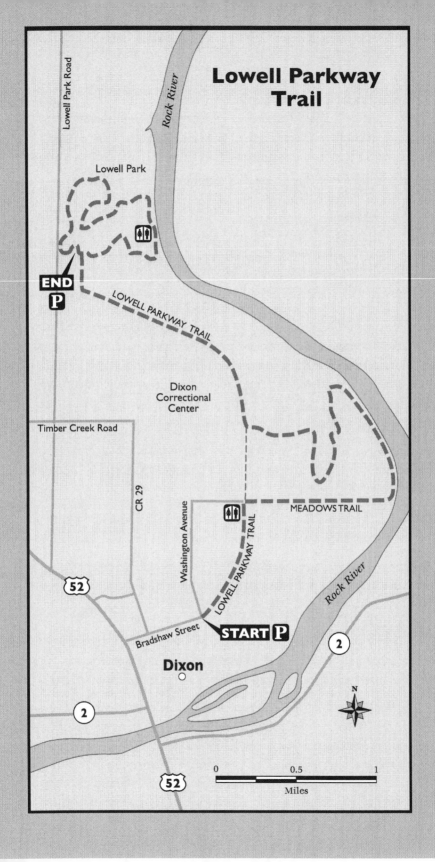

To reach Lowell Park follow IL 26/US 52 northwest of Dixon. On the way out of Dixon, turn right onto Lowell Park Rd. The park entrance is on the right. Park either by the nature center or down by the river.

Transportation: The closest Amtrak stations are in Mendota, Princeton, and Kewanee.

Rentals: No nearby bike rentals are available.

Contact: Dixon Park District, 804 Palmyra Street, Dixon 61021; (815) 284-3306.

The Lowell Parkway Trail—running from Dixon to Lowell Park—was once part of the Illinois Central Railroad, which initially traveled from Galena in the northwest corner of the state to the southern tip of Illinois. When completed in 1856, it was the longest rail line in the world. This section of the former rail line runs through an attractive, leafy landscape that likely hasn't changed much in the past 150 years.

The Rock River

Nearly 1 mile out from the trailhead in Dixon, turn off the Lowell Parkway and follow the gravel-surfaced Meadows Trail (the first path on the right) through the agricultural fields and down to the bank of the Rock River. As the path parallels the river for nearly 1 mile, the benches scattered along the way offer inviting places to rest and admire the intermittently wooded and grassy riverbanks.

The trail eventually curls away from the river and takes a sinuous route through wooded areas, savanna, and patches of cropland back up to the Lowell Parkway. Occasionally the main trail intersects grassy mowed trails used for horseback riding.

Back on the Lowell Parkway, the Dixon Correctional Center, Illinois's largest medium-security prison, peeks through the greenery on the left. Soon, on the right, you'll see bluffs tumbling steeply down toward the Rock River.

Lowell Park

Once in Lowell Park, the route immediately follows an exhilarating descent of the bluff on a squiggly road, cutting through a tunnel of trees. This century-old park was once a popular destination for some of Chicago's upper crust. Dixon's most famous former resident, Ronald Reagan, spent thirteen years of his youth in Dixon and served as a lifeguard at Lowell Park for six summers. On the way down the bluff, an overlook located across from the stone picnic shelter offers an expansive view of the Rock River Valley. Descending from the viewing spot, a rocky limestone wall accompanies the road on the right.

At the bottom of the bluff, follow the park road along the wooded shore of the river. If you've brought a picnic, pull up a bench at one of the old stone picnic shelters and enjoy the river view. You'll be glad to know that the route up the bluff isn't excessively steep. Returning to the top of the bluff, take the first right for a quick tour of the north section of the park. Completing the north leaf of the circuitous park road, continue past the nature center for the final leaf that runs through the park's pine plantation. Stay to the right and follow the signs leading back to the Lowell Parkway Trail, which you'll follow back to Dixon.

If you've got energy to burn, you can extend your trip another 0.8 mile north along the Lowell Parkway Trail beyond the turnoff for Lowell Park. Also, a few miles northwest of Lowell Park is the Joe Stengel Trail, which runs for 5.5 miles between the towns of Woosung and Polo. If you're on a bike, wider tires will be useful since the trail surface is grass and hard-packed dirt rather than asphalt or crushed gravel.

Major Milepoints

0.8   Turn right on the gravel path leading down to the Rock River. The path is unmarked but is easy to identify—it's the first path you'll encounter on the right.

4.1   Turn right when you return to the paved Lowell Parkway.

5.5   Turn right to enter Lowell Park (follow the sign).

5.7   Turn right onto the park road.

7.3   Turn right onto the park road at the top of the bluff.

8.1   Continue straight ahead through the pine plantation.

8.5   Turn right onto the park road (follow signs for the bike trail).

Local Information

- Lee County Tourism, 37 S. East Avenue, Amboy; (815) 288-1840; leecountyfun.com.
- Blackhawk Waterways Convention and Visitors Bureau, 201 N. Franklin Avenue, Polo; (815) 946-2108 or (800) 678-2108; visitnorthwestillinois.com.

Local Events/Attractions

- John Deere historic site, 8393 S. Main Street, Grand Detour; (815) 652-4551; bit.ly/jdhsite. Located a few minutes north of Dixon; historic buildings and recreation of Deere's famous shop.
- Nachusa Grasslands Preserve, 2075 S. Lowden Road, Franklin Grove; (815) 456-2340; nachusa-grasslands.org. Large native prairie and wetland area; hiking trails and a herd of bison.
- Ronald Reagan Boyhood Home and Visitor Center, 816 Hennepin Avenue, Dixon; (815) 288-5176; bit.ly/rrbhcenter.

Restaurants

- Baker Street, 111 W. First Street, Dixon; (815) 285-2253; bakerstreetcafeandcatering.com. Coffee, baked goods, soups, and sandwiches.
- Basil Tree Ristorante, 123 E. 1st Street, Dixon; (815) 288-7555; basiltree2008.com. Quality Italian fare in downtown Dixon.
- Salamandra Restaurant, 105 W. First Street, Dixon; (815) 285-0874. Features dishes from various regions of Mexico. Located on main downtown strip.

Accommodations

- Lincoln Way Inn, 409 N. State Street, Franklin Grove; (815) 456-7700; lincolnwayinn.com. Upscale environmentally friendly B&B, featuring inventive breakfasts. About 10 miles east of the trail.
- White Pines Inn/White Pines Forest State Park, 6712 W. Pines Road, Mt. Morris; (815) 946-3817; whitepinesinn.com. One of Illinois's oldest state parks; camping, cabins, and a restaurant.

25 MISSISSIPPI RIVER TRAIL—QUAD CITIES TO ALBANY

Starting in the cities of Rock Island and Moline, the trail hugs the bank of the river as it leads you through parks, industrial areas, and the downtown business districts. Continuing north, a series of small river towns are lined up like pearls on a string: Hampton, Rapids City, Port Byron, and Cordova. The trail ends at a park containing one of the largest collections of Native American burial mounds in the nation.

Location: From Sunset Park, located in Rock Island at the convergence of the Rock and Mississippi Rivers, the trail runs north along the Mississippi River to Albany.

Length: 35.6 miles one-way.

Surface: Asphalt.

Wheelchair access: While much of the route is wheelchair accessible, there are plenty of on-street sections in the towns of Hampton, Port Byron, and Cordova that are not wheelchair friendly.

Difficulty: The trail is difficult because of the lack of shade on many portions, the length, and the long stretch where it accompanies traffic on IL 84.

Restrooms: There are public restrooms and water at Sunset Community Park, the south trailhead in downtown Moline, and at the Schwiebert Riverfront Park in Moline, Empire Park, Illiniwek Forest Preserve, the riverside park in Rapids City, the boat launch in Port Byron, and Albany Mounds State Historic Site.

Maps: qctrails.org; greatrivertrail.org.

Hazards: Occasionally the trail crosses busy streets; watch for traffic at these crossings and when traveling along the on-street sections in Hampton, Port Byron, and Cordova. North of the Quad Cities, 10 or so miles of trail stick close to Hwy. 84, a fairly busy thoroughfare. Sometimes the trail is right alongside the highway or it may be ten to twenty feet away.

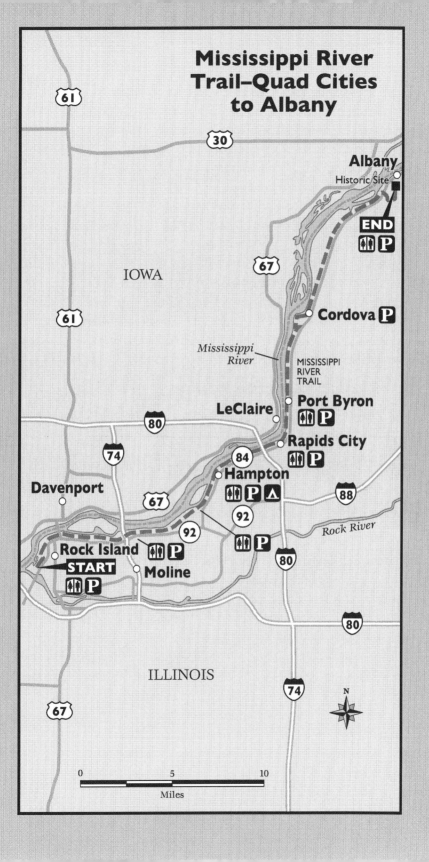

Access and parking: From I-280 south of Rock Island, head north on IL 92. Exit at Sunset Ln. and turn left. Enter Sunset Park and park in the first lot on the right. UTM coordinates: 15T, 700168 E, 4595169 N.

Heading north on I-74 into Moline, exit at Seventh Ave. and go northeast. Bear left on 23rd Ave. Turn right on River Dr. The park on the left contains a couple of large parking areas.

To park at Illiniwek Forest Preserve, go north on I-80. Just before crossing the Mississippi River, exit onto IL 84 and head south. The park is several miles ahead on the right.

To park in Port Byron, go north on IL 84 from I-80. In Port Byron turn left onto Cherry St. and look for the parking area near the boat launch.

To park at the Albany Mounds State Historic Site, take I-88 to the Albany Rd. exit northeast of the Quad Cities. Head northwest on Albany Rd. As you enter the town of Albany, turn left onto Cherry St. The parking area is at the end of the road.

Transportation: Amtrak trains stop in Galesburg.

Rentals: Quad Cities Convention and Visitors Bureau rents bikes; 1601 River Drive, Suite 110, Moline; (309) 277-0937; visitquadcities.com.

Contact: The Great River Trail Guide; (309) 277-0937; greatrivertrail.com.

||||||||||||||||||||||||||||||||||||||||||||||||||||||||||||||||||||||||||||||||||||||||||||

Old river towns are one of the treasures of the backroads of Illinois. When you visit them, you can count on intriguing history, plenty of scenic views, and unusual attractions—like Port Byron's Tug Fest, an annual tug-of-war competition held across the Mississippi River. The first 10 miles of the trail features a tour of the Illinois side of the Quad Cities—Rock Island and Moline (on the Iowa side is Davenport and Bettendorf). Leaving the Quad Cities, you'll start racking up the miles as you head upstream through riverside parks, agricultural land, and pleasant small towns.

As the trail strikes out north from Sunset Park in Rock Island, you'll scoot alongside Lake Potter, a backwater lake that hosts a marina. Getting closer to downtown Rock Island, the trail mounts the river levee and passes numerous industrial areas. Up on the levee, you'll catch fine views up and down the river. The first bridge along the way, an old latticed train bridge, has a midsection that rotates to allow river barges to pass. Farther north, the newer Centennial Bridge calls your attention to its series of arched, latticed support sections.

Following the River through the Quad Cities

Downtown Rock Island offers a choice of watering holes and restaurants within blocks of the trail. Like Moline to the east, Rock Island has its roots in manufacturing agriculture implements for Midwestern farms. John Deere in Moline, and International Harvester was located in Rock Island.

Just after passing the bridge to Arsenal Island, a historic military base, you won't miss the seventy-foot-tall glass structure of the Quad City Botanical Center on the right. Inside is a tropical garden with a fifteen-foot waterfall set amid palm trees, orchids, and bromeliads.

Continuing on, the path passes a smattering of industrial sites while following a levee that puts you about forty feet above the surface of the river. Tucked among the industrial sites is a pedestrian bridge that leads out to Sylvan Island. Once host to a steel mill and a rock-crushing operation, the thirty-six-acre island now is a wooded park laced with hiking trails.

In downtown Moline the trail brushes against the backside of a 12,000-seat entertainment venue and home rink for the local minor league hockey team, the Quad City Storm. After passing a sprawling John Deere manufacturing plant, the atmosphere becomes quieter, greener, and more scenic as the trail winds through a few parks.

Hampton and Rapids City

Just north of Hampton, you can break out the picnic basket at the Illiniwek Forest Preserve and have lunch at the edge of the river looking out at Lock and Dam 14. Illiniwek provides a perfect spot to watch the progression of river barges moving up and down the 0.5-mile-wide waterway (watch for coal going upriver and grain coming down).

A couple miles upstream from Hampton is Rapids City, named for the rapids that once existed on this stretch of river. Before the rapids were removed with dynamite, riverboats had to unload cargo onto a train, transport it north, and then load it on another boat upstream. In Rapids City the path cuts through a small riverside park overlooking river wetlands.

Port Byron and Cordova

In Port Byron the river narrows, offering views of LeClaire, Iowa, located on a bluff across the river. Each August the atmosphere heats up between these two towns. This is when boat traffic on the river shuts down and the townspeople stretch a 2,400-foot, 680-pound rope from one shore to the other for an interstate tug-of-war. Multiple teams compete, and whichever town chalks up the most wins during the day is the winner for the year.

Another few miles upstream, on-street bike route signs guide you from one end of the town of Cordova to the other. Cordova once served as a shipping point for grain grown by local farmers. The main shipping storage facility was eventually turned into a site for manufacturing clamshell buttons.

Expansive views of the Mississippi River are abundant on many sections of the Mississippi River Trail.

Arsenal Island's Long History

Located on the Mississippi River between Davenport, Iowa, and Rock Island, Illinois, Arsenal Island was previously a summer camp for the Sauk Native Americans. During the Civil War, it served as a Confederate prison camp. Not long after the Civil War, an armory was established on the island. The island now hosts a museum displaying various types of weapons and firepower. (Note: Photo identification is required to access the island, and guards are notorious for being very strict about who gets access.)

North of Cordova, you'll enjoy the sprawling Mississippi backwater and thick bottomland woods that are a part of the Upper Mississippi River National Fish and Wildlife Refuge. This section of the trail features big swaths of farmland peppered with occasional heavy industry sites.

When the trail ends at Meredosia Rd., turn right for a few hundred yards of on-street travel. At Bunker Hill Rd. take the trail left and enter the Albany Mounds State Historic Site. Within the rolling prairie and woodland of this small park are nearly one hundred American Indian mounds—one of the largest collections of such mounds in the nation. A sizable community of Hopewell Indians lived in the area about 2,000 years ago, using the mounds as burial sites for their dead.

Major Milepoints

12.6 On-street section: To start the 0.8-mile-long on-street section in Hampton, keep straight ahead on First Ave.

13.0 Turn right on Eighth St.

13.4 Resume the trail on the left.

23.8 **On-street section:** Turn left on Thirteenth Ave. and quickly turn right on Third St. to start a 2.3-mile-long on-street section in Cordova.

24.5 Turn right on Third Ave.

24.9 Turn left on Ninth St.

25.4 Turn left on River Rd.

26.1 Turn right on 171st Ave. and resume the Mississippi River Trail.

33.5   On-street section: Turn right on Meredosia Rd. to reach Albany Mounds State
       Historic Site.

33.7   Enter the park via the trail on the left. The parking lot is about 1 mile ahead.

Local Information

- Mississippi River Visitors Center, overlooking Lock and Dam 15; (309) 782-1337; bit.ly/mrvs15.
  Operated by the U.S. Army Corps of Engineers at the west end of Arsenal Island, Rock Island.
- Quad Cities Convention and Visitors Bureau, 1601 River Drive, Suite 110, Moline; (800)
  747-7800; visitquadcities.com.

Local Events/Attractions

- Albany State Historic Site, P.O. Box 184, Albany; albanymounds.com. A couple miles of hiking
  trails lead you through an area with dozens of mounds; interpretive signs highlight the history.
- Celebration River Cruises, 2501 River Drive, Moline; (309) 764-1952; celebrationbelle.com.
  The 800-passenger *Celebration Belle* is one of the largest functioning riverboats on the Upper
  Mississippi. The trail passes the boarding area.
- Rock Island Arsenal Museum, Rock Island Arsenal, Rock Island, Building 60, 3500 N. Avenue;
  (309) 782-5021; arsenalhistoricalsociety.org/. Focuses on firearms and arsenal history.
- **Port Byron Great River** Tug Fest; tugfest.org. Interstate tug-of-war is part of several-day-
  long festival in Port Byron, usually in August.

Restaurants

- Bier Stube, 415 15th Street, Moline; (309) 797-3049; bier-stube.com. German food served in
  comfortable atmosphere.
- Blue Cat Brew Pub, 113 18th Street, Rock Island; (309) 788-8247; bluecatbrewpub.com. One
  block away from the trail.

Accommodations

- Illiniwek Forest Preserve, IL 84 north of Hampton; (309) 496-2620. Pitch a tent on the
  river's edge.
- Stony Creek Hotel, 101 18th Street, Moline; (855) 213-0582; bit.ly/schqc. Outdoors-themed
  hotel in downtown Moline, right alongside the path.
- Leisure Harbor Inn Bed and Breakfast, 701 Main Avenue, Cordova; (309) 654-2233; leisurehar-
  borinn.com. Located close to the route on the Mississippi River.

26 MISSISSIPPI RIVER TRAIL—THOMSON TO FULTON

This short trip between the two Mississippi River towns of Thomson and Fulton offers a pleasing collection of scenic riverside spots. Near Thomson the trail brushes against a beautiful, bird-laden wetland area and an unusual sand prairie. In Fulton the river levee guides you to the town's main attraction, a traditional Dutch windmill located on the bank of the river.

Location: From Thomson Causeway Recreation Area along the Mississippi River in Thomson, the trail runs south along the Mississippi River to Fulton.

Length: 10.3 miles one-way, with a couple of on-road options for extending the route.

Surface: Crushed gravel for the first couple of miles, followed by paved path.

Wheelchair access: There are a couple of on-streets sections which may be difficult for wheelchair users.

Difficulty: The trail is easy.

Restrooms: There are public restrooms at the Thomson Causeway Recreation Area's main picnic area (water here and at trail's starting point) and the windmill in Fulton (water).

Maps: greatrivertrail.org.

Hazards: None.

Access and parking: On I-88 west of Rock Falls take exit 36 (Como Rd.) north. Keep straight as Como Rd. merges with US 30 heading west. Turn right onto IL 78 and follow it for nearly 10 miles before turning left onto Thomson Rd. After Thomson, turn left onto Lewis Ave. and enter Thomson Causeway Recreation Area. Once past the gatehouse, stay to the right. Park in the small lot on the right next to the bike path. UTM coordinates: 15T, 739401 E, 4648577 N.

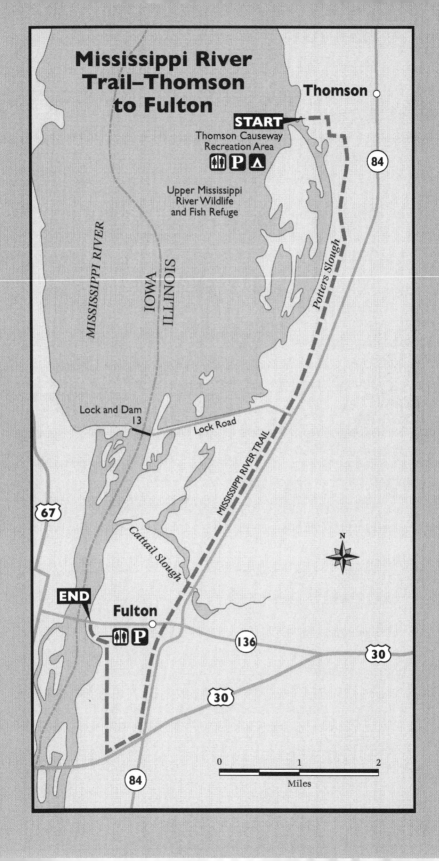

The Dutch windmill in Fulton offers parking and access to the trail. From the intersection of IL 84 and IL 136, follow IL 136 east toward the river. Turn right onto Fourth St. and then left onto 10th Ave.

Transportation: Amtrak trains stop in Galesburg.

Rentals: A bike sharing program is available in Clinton, Iowa, across the Mississippi from Fulton; clintoniowatourism.com.

Contact: City of Fulton, 415 11th Avenue, Fulton; cityoffulton.us; (815) 589-2616.
The Great River Trail Guide; (309) 277-0937; greatrivertrail.com.

As you reach the end of this route, you'll come across an odd sight: a traditional Dutch windmill on the banks of the Mississippi. But getting a better look, it seems like a natural spot for the hundred-foot-tall windmill. The windmill is perched on the flood-control dike in Fulton, a town where Dutch heritage runs deep and wide. While this fully operational windmill looks old, it's not: It was built in 2000 by Dutch craftsmen using traditional methods.

Grasslands and Wetlands

Start the trip from Thomson, located a few miles upriver from Fulton. From the trailhead, the crushed-rock trail winds through grassland managed by the U.S. Fish and Wildlife Service. The sandy soil supports plants unusual for the area, such as prickly pear cactus, visible on the side of the trail. At about 1.75 miles the trail rises just enough to provide striking views of the lush wetlands known as Potters Marsh and Potters Slough. With the help of field glasses, you'll likely see ducks, pelicans, and wading birds such as great blue herons and white egrets.

After the trail drops you off on a narrow, very quiet paved road, the route accompanies gently rolling grassland dotted with the occasional pine trees. Like the grassland earlier, an unusual sandy soil is prevalent here. This sand prairie, as it's called, has been designated as a state preserve. At the stop sign, consider taking a side trip to Lock and Dam 13, where you can enjoy views of the widest pool on the Upper Mississippi River. (This will add about 4 miles to the route; traffic on Lock Rd. is very sparse. There are picnic areas, restrooms, water, and great views of the lock and dam, and nearby wetlands.)

Into Fulton

Continuing toward Fulton you'll cross Johnson Creek just before pulling alongside IL 84. Farther ahead, the route passes a small municipal park and the Fulton Industrial Park.

The parkland along the river in Fulton offers many spots to linger. Kiwanis Park is where the path mounts the levee that keeps back the river's floodwaters. Grab a bench to sit and watch the waterbirds, or just enjoy the view of the huge steel-truss bridge rising sixty-five feet above the water, connecting Fulton with Clinton, Iowa. The river is only 0.3 mile across here; upstream by Lock and Dam 13 it swells to about 3 miles across.

This bridge over the Mississippi River connects Fulton, Illinois, with Clinton, Iowa.

Continuing under the bridge along the levee brings you to the Dutch windmill. On street level, you can enter the windmill and drop in to the gift shop and see the mill in action. Inside, you'll see that the grinding machinery takes up three floors and uses a set of blue basalt millstones that produce flours from buckwheat, corn, rye, and wheat.

After completing the trail, consider visiting some of the old storefront buildings that line the town's nearby shopping district.

In addition to this section of the Mississippi River Trail and a much longer 52-mile segment between Quad Cities and Albany that's also described in this book, there's a lovely trail segment that runs for about 5 miles south of Savanna. That trail starts about 6 miles north of this trail's trailhead and is easily accessed on quiet rural roads from Thomson.

Major Milepoints

2.0   On-street section: Turn right onto the paved road. Follow Railroad Ln. for the next 2 miles. This is a narrow, extremely low-traffic road.

7.1   On-street section: In Fulton the signs direct you to perform a quick zigzag on streets for 0.2 mile. Turn right onto 14th Ave. (IL 136) and then immediately left onto 14th St. At 16th Ave., turn left and then resume the trail on the right.

Local Information

- Blackhawk Waterways Convention and Visitors Bureau, 201 N. Franklin Ave., Polo; (800) 678-2108; visitnorthwestillinois.com.

Local Events/Attractions

- The Dutch Windmill and Windmill Cultural Center, 10th Avenue and First St., Fulton; (815) 589-4033; cityoffulton.us. Milling demonstrations, a gift shop, and a visitor center featuring twenty-two windmill models.
- Heritage Canyon, 515 N. Fourth St., Fulton; (815) 589-4545; cityoffulton.us. Recreated historic village within a rock quarry near the Mississippi River.
- Clinton, Iowa; clintoniowatourism.com; consider extending your trip a few miles by crossing Fulton's 14th Street Bridge into Iowa to enjoy a multi-use path along the Mississippi in Clinton. There's a museum and several parks along the way, including Eagle Point Park that has a lodge that looks like a medieval castle.

Restaurants

- Steam Anchor Coffee & Café, 1310 17th Street, Fulton; (815) 208-7074; steamanchor.com. Coffee and sandwiches right on the trail.

Accommodations

- AmericInn, 1301 17th Street (corner of IL 84 and IL 136), Fulton; (815) 589-3333.
- Thomson Causeway Recreation Area; (815) 259-2353. Campground at the northern trailhead has 131 campsites that draw in the RV crowd.

Central Illinois

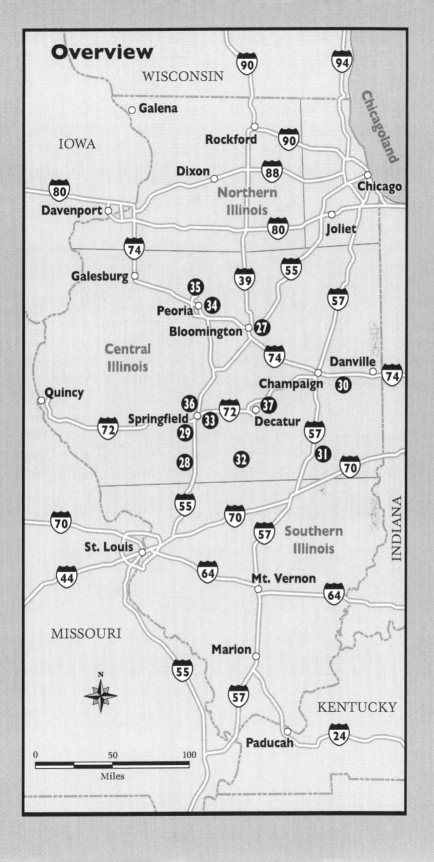

Contrary to popular belief, central Illinois is not one great expanse of farmland. Sure, there's plenty of corn and soy, but there are also great parks, interesting towns and cities, and a nice collection of rail trails that run through a mix of urban and rural settings. A handful of the rail trails in central Illinois are located in the vicinity of Bloomington, Decatur, Springfield, and Peoria. If you've never visited, now's your chance to get to know these cities that sprouted up on the central Illinois prairie. Expect to see leafy parks, pleasant neighborhoods, and historic downtowns.

The highlight among central Illinois rail trails is the Rock Island Trail, which runs north from Peoria. Along this 34-mile-long trail, you'll encounter a few small towns, wetlands, woods, and plenty of wide-open farmland before crossing the Spoon River on an old train bridge. In the late nineteenth century, trains used this route for transporting grains to the distilleries of Peoria, cementing it's the city's status as the whiskey capital of the world. Another feature of the Rock Island Trail: There's an excellent campground alongside the trail specifically for trail users.

Given that two of the trails in central Illinois have the words "Lincoln" and "Prairie" in their names, it's difficult to miss the local historic connections. While the big prairies are mostly gone, the legacy of the sixteenth U.S. president remains vibrant. Tourism bureaus throughout the area are grateful that Lincoln visited so many local courthouses as an itinerate lawyer. And of course the state capital of Springfield contains museums and a roster of historic landmarks relating to Lincoln's career as a state politician.

27 CONSTITUTION TRAIL

There's nary a better way to get to know the cities of Bloomington and Normal than following this section of the Constitution Trail as it runs through the center of each town. The tree-lined north section of the trail takes you through Normal's new residential areas, public parks, and downtown. To the south in Bloomington, you'll see the town's old warehouse district and pleasant residential neighborhoods before heading west into the outlying countryside.

Location: Starting from the Kerrick Rd. parking area, north of Bloomington-Normal, the trail runs south and then west to the western edge of Bloomington.

Length: 11 miles one-way.

Surface: Asphalt.

Wheelchair access: The entire path is wheelchair accessible.

Difficulty: The trail is easy.

Restrooms: There are public restrooms at Rosa Parks Commons (water), Hidden Creek Nature Sanctuary (water), Allers Shelter Wayside (water), Atwood Wayside Herb Garden (water), and the Route 9 Wayside (portable toilet).

Maps: normal.org; bloomingtonparks.org.

Hazards: During the warmer months, the main section of the trail in Normal can be busy with walkers and cyclists.

Access and parking: From Bloomington-Normal, follow I-55 north to I-39. Continue north on I-39 and then exit south onto US 51. Turn left onto Kerrick Rd. The parking area is on the right. Coming from the northeast, take I-55 south to I-39 and follow the directions above. UTM coordinates: 16T, 331640 E, 4490919 N.

To catch the trail in downtown Normal, head south on Linden St. at College Ave. in downtown Normal. Cross the tracks and enter the parking area on the right. (The path runs by the Amtrak station.)

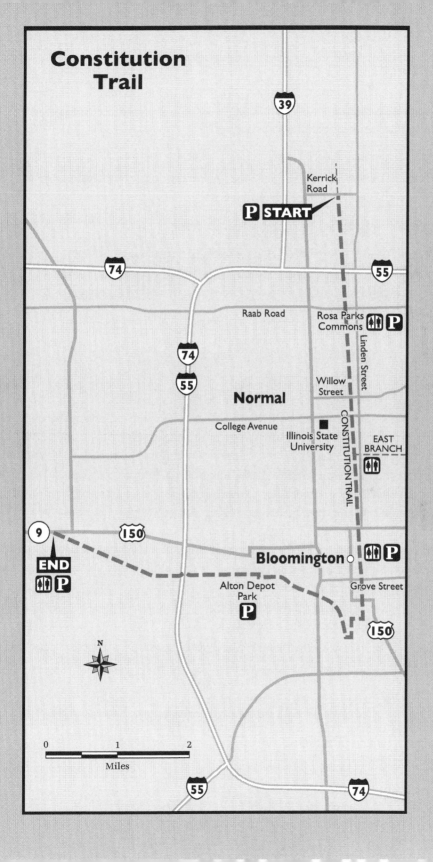

To reach the Route 9 Wayside (the endpoint for this route), head west from Bloomington on Market St. (IL 9/US 150). The wayside is on the left just after passing the Rivian Motorway.

Transportation: Amtrak serves Bloomington/Normal. Nearly all fifteen bus routes operated by the Bloomington/Normal public transit system intersect with the trail. Visit connect-transit.com.

Rentals: No nearby bike rentals are available.

Contact: Bloomington Parks, Recreation and Cultural Arts; 115 E. Washington St, Bloomington; (309) 434-2260; bloomingtonparks.org.

Town of Normal, 11 Uptown Circle., P.O. Box 589; Normal; (309) 454-2444; normal.org.

|||||||||||||||||||||||||||||||||||||||||||||||||||||||||||||||||||||||||||||||||||||

Set within the most fertile farmland in Illinois, the twin cities of Bloomington and Normal both claim rich histories and an intriguing mix of people. Farmers of course come to the cities to pick up supplies and unload their harvest. Teachers, students, and administrators come to the sprawling campus of Illinois State University in Normal and Illinois Wesleyan University in Bloomington. And workers come for jobs at companies such as State Farm Insurance, Rivian, and Beer Nuts . . . yes, Beer Nuts. (More on that later.)

Dedicated in September 1987 in celebration of the 200th anniversary of the U.S. Constitution, the Constitution Trail now includes a half dozen trail segments within the two cities. This route comprises the main north–south stem and the longer and more scenic of the branches. A couple of the more notable branches of the main stem are mentioned below; learn about the shorter disconnected segments by getting a copy of the Constitution Trail map.

Parks and Greenery

The parking area on Kerrick Rd., where this route starts, sits beside a series of monolithic grain silos that look vaguely like silver spaceships ready for liftoff. Heading south along the trail, you'll see the agricultural fields and light industry that adorn the outskirts of every medium-size Illinois city. After the I-55 underpass, you can survey a long progression of residential backyards. Continuing ahead, the trail passes a collection of sports fields at Rosa Parks Commons and a side path that heads 1.3 miles east alongside Raab Rd.

Getting closer to downtown Normal, the tree-lined trail corridor passes Hidden Creek Nature Sanctuary, decorated with wildflowers, prairie grasses, and groves of hardwood. In downtown Normal, things get busy as the trail crosses College Ave., the town's main business strip, and then runs by the Amtrak station and Normal City Hall. Keep an eye on the route in downtown Normal. It gets fuzzy at times but is easy to figure out.

The Camelback Bridge

South of downtown Normal, consider a side trip on the first half of 4.4-mile eastern arm of the Constitution Trail as it runs beside pleasant residential backyards, past two small public gardens, and alongside Sugar Creek (the fun dissipates for the final 2.4 miles of this route as it accompanies the heavy traffic on General Electric Rd.).

Back on the main stem of the Constitution Trail, the trail mounts an embankment built for the railroad and then passes beneath a historic bridge. The bridge, listed on the National Register of Historic Places, is the only surviving camelback-style bridge in Illinois. Built with wood in 1904, it was constructed with a distinctive high arch that allowed steam locomotives to pass underneath. During its restoration, the bridge's hump was lowered to allow vehicles easier passage on Virginia St. above the trail. Continuing south, the camelback theme continues as the trail crosses two newly constructed arched pedestrian bridges. The first provides a view of Sugar Creek down below; the second passes over Emerson Ave.

Bloomington's Industrial Districts, Old and New

Emerging from the short tunnel under Washington St., you'll see the one and only Beer Nuts factory to the right. This family-owned company has been producing nut snacks under various names since 1937. In the 1950s

The Constitution Trail is popular with the students at Illinois State University in Normal.

the company changed its name to Beer Nuts when it was trying to get local bar owners to stock the salty, thirst-inducing treats.

After a brief on-street section, the trail takes you through Bloomington's old industrial district. Interpretive signs along the path explain that many businesses once operated warehouses along this stretch of railroad. An old brown-brick building on the left was built by Illinois's own

John Deere Company in 1847. Also operating in the area was a foundry and a National Guard armory, both located close to the tracks for easy transportation.

Leaving the industrial area, you'll see the high steeple of St. Mary's Church, built in 1886 by German immigrants who lived in the neighborhood. After passing through tiny Allen Depot Park, the trail descends a hill and then accompanies Washington St. through a more recently built industrial area.

After passing under I-55/74, the path breaks away from Washington St. and suddenly transports you into the Illinois countryside. The final couple of miles of trail lead you through wooded and grassy stretches with cropland always in the background.

Major Milepoints

5.9   Turn right onto Croxton Ave. to begin the 0.4-mile on-street segment.

6.0   Turn left onto Bunn St.

6.3   At Lincoln St. turn right. Pick up the path before the cemetery on the right.

Local Information

- Bloomington-Normal Area Convention and Visitors Bureau, 101 S. Madison St., Bloomington; (309) 665-0033 or (800) 433-8226; visitbn.org.
- Friends of the Constitution Trail, PO Box 525, Bloomington; constitutiontrail.org. Local advocacy group that supports the trail.
- McLean County Wheelers Bicycle Club, PO Box 1162, Bloomington; mcleancountywheelers.com. A very active local biking club that often organizes rides on the trail.

Local Events/Attractions

- Beer Nuts Plant and Company Store, 103 N. Robinson Street, Bloomington; (309) 585-6159; beernuts.com.
- David Davis Mansion State Historic Site, 1000 E. Monroe Drive, Bloomington; (309) 828-1084; daviddavismansion.org. Take a tour of this posh historic home once owned by a U.S. Supreme Court judge. Located a few blocks off the trail.
- Illinois Shakespeare Festival, Campus Box 5700, Normal; (309) 438-2535; illinoisshakes.com. Runs much of the summer at the Ewing Manor.

Restaurants

- Keg Grove Brewing Company, 712 E. Empire Street, Bloomington; (309) 585-2021; keggrove-brewing.com. Innovative beers located right on the trail.
- The Rock Restaurant, 203 W. North Street, Normal; (309)-451-4976; therockrestaurant.net. Mediterranean and American food, one block from the trail in downtown Normal.

Accommodations

- Comlara County Park, 13001 Recreation Area Drive, Hudson; (309) 434-6770; mcleancountyil. gov. The best camping in the area. Located fifteen minutes north of Bloomington.
- Vrooman Mansion Bed and Breakfast, 701 E. Taylor Street; (309) 828-8816; vroomanmansion. com. Impressive Victorian home with thirty-six rooms over three floors. The trail runs close to the mansion.

28 GREEN DIAMOND TRAIL

Expect wide-ranging views of the surrounding farmland as you follow this short trail between two small rural towns about 25 miles south of Springfield. You'll cross Maucopin Creek and its wooded banks on the north end of the trail. At the south end of the trail, you may want to take a side trip to a shrine intended to protect travelers along former Route 66.

Location: From Veterans Park in Farmersville, located about 25 miles south of Springfield, the trail runs south to the tiny town of Wagonner.

Length: 4.4 miles one-way.

Surface: Small rock chips applied over a tar surface.

Wheelchair access: The trail is wheelchair accessible.

Difficulty: The route is easy.

Restrooms: There are no public restrooms on this route.

Maps: bit.ly/grdtrail.

Hazards: None.

Access and parking: From I-55 exit west to Farmersville on Main St. Turn left onto S. Cleveland Ave. Park in the trailhead parking lot at the end of S. Cleveland St. UTM coordinates: 16S, 0271810 E, 4368483 N.

To park at the south end of the trail, exit I-55 heading west in Farmersville on IL 48. Immediately turn left onto Frontage Rd. Turn left on County Rd. 2600 N. and park next to the old train depot.

Transportation: The closest Amtrak station is in Carlinville, located about 15 miles southwest of Waggoner.

Rentals: No nearby bike rentals are available.

Contact: Montgomery County Offices, 120 N. Main Street, Hillsboro; (217) 532-9530; montgomeryco.com.

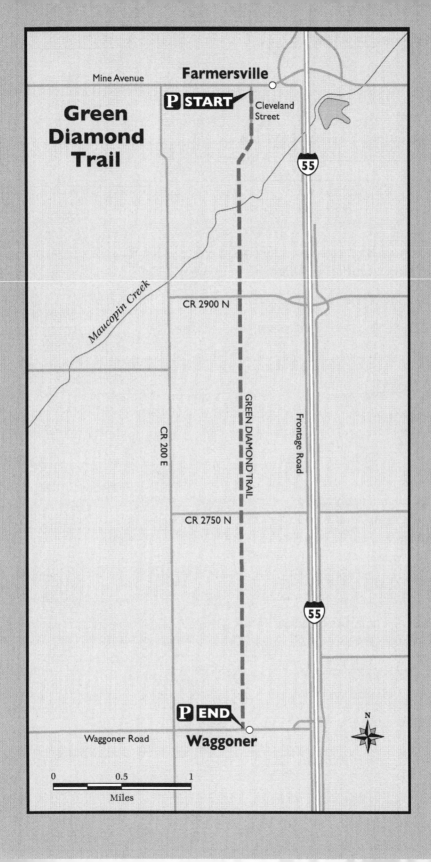

|||||||||||||||||||||||||||||||||||||||||||||||||||||||||||||||||||||||||||||||||||||||||||||||

The Green Diamond was the Illinois Central Railroad's fastest of several trains that ran between Chicago, Springfield, and St. Louis. The train, in operation until 1968, was painted in a two-tone green that led to its nickname, "Tobacco Worm." The train made seven stops during a journey of nearly five hours. This trail follows a short section of the Green Diamond Line as it ran through farm country between Farmersville and Waggoner.

Maucopin Creek

After picking up the minimally marked trailhead on the south edge of the village of Farmersville, you'll pass through a grove of cottonwoods and then cross a small tributary to Maucopin Creek. Once you get on the straight-as-an-arrow railroad right-of-way, dense woodland appears on the left as you cross over the creek's main branch. The 70-mile-long creek is named for a yellow pond lily—historically a favorite food source of local Native Americans. The maucopin has a large root that was baked in a fire pit.

After the creek, the big trees dwindle and the shrubs and smaller trees take over. Prairie flowers such as goldenrod, Queen Anne's lace, and phlox decorate the sides of the trail. A half mile to the east is the constantly buzzing I-55. Frontage Rd.—which served as Route 66 from 1940 to 1977—sits beside the interstate. You'll catch glimpses of these roads now and then, but for the most part the landscape is dominated by agricultural land with a sprinkling of farms in the distance.

Waggoner

At the south end of the trail in the hamlet of Waggoner sits a tiny historic train depot within a small park. Before heading back to Farmersville, take a break on the bench within the park's little wooden gazebo.

If you're interested in Route 66 history, you may want to visit Shrine of Our Lady of the Highways a few miles south of Waggoner. Erected by schoolchildren in 1959 along the former Route 66, the shrine's statue of the Virgin Mother is meant to watch over travelers along the Mother Road.

(To reach the shrine, head east on Main St. in Waggoner. Turn right onto Frontage Rd. as it runs on the west side of I-55. The shrine is located south of Goby Rd. [N. 23rd Rd.] at 22353 W. Frontage Rd.)

The Shrine of Our Lady of Highways is one of a few Route 66 landmarks found in the area. Litchfield, a dozen miles south of Waggoner, hosts Route 66 attractions like the Ariston Café, a diner open since 1924, and the still-operating Skyview Drive-In Theatre.

Local Information

- City of Litchfield Office of Tourism, 120 E. Ryder Street, Litchfield; (217) 324-5253; cityoflitchfieldil.com.
- Visit Springfield, 109 N. Seventh Street, Springfield; (217) 789-2360; visitspringfieldillinois.com

Local Events/Attractions

- Litchfield Museum & Route 66 Welcome Center, 334 Old Route 66 N., Litchfield; (217) 324-3510; litchfieldmuseum.org. Local history and the history of Route 66.

This old wooden train depot sits at the south end of the Green Diamond Trail in Waggoner.

- Sky View Drive-In Theatre, 150 N. Historic Old Route 66, Litchfield; (217) 324-2533; litchfield-skyview.com. Last surviving drive-in along the historic roadway.

Restaurants

- Ariston Café, 413 Old Route 66 N. Road, Litchfield; (217) 324-2023; ariston-cafe.com. Originally opened in 1924 but relocated when Route 66 was rerouted. Still owned by same family, it is said to be the oldest café on Route 66.
- Jubelt's Bakery & Restaurant; 303 N. Old Route 66 S., Litchfield; (217) 324-5314; jubelts.com. In business since 1922.

Accommodations

- Holiday Inn Express & Suites, 4 Thunderbird Circle, Litchfield; (217) 324-4556; bit.ly/hixlitch. Indoor pool; located about 15 miles south of the trail.
- Sangchris Lake State Park, 9898 Cascade Road, Rochester; (217) 498-9208; bit.ly/sanglsp. Two large campgrounds and one small walk-in camping area.

29 INTERURBAN TRAIL

While exploring this route between southwest Springfield and the nearby town of Chatham, you'll see suburban neighborhoods, attractive woodlands, and the occasional agricultural field. Near Chatham the trail runs for a stretch alongside a lovely section of Lake Springfield and its adjoining wetlands.

Location: From the trailhead in southwest Springfield, follow the trail east and then south to the town of Chatham.

Length: 10.8 miles one-way.

Surface: Asphalt.

Wheelchair access: The entire trail is wheelchair accessible.

Difficulty: The route is easy.

Restrooms: There are portable toilets at Vredenburg Park.

Maps: bit.ly/springbikemap.

Hazards: Use caution while crossing a handful of busy streets.

Access and parking: Head west on I-72 south of Springfield and exit north on Veterans Parkway (IL 4). Turn left onto Lindbergh Blvd. and right onto Robbins Rd. The trailhead parking area shares the salon parking lot on the right. UTM coordinates: 16S, 267630 E, 4403907 N.

To park at the trailhead on Park Ave., head east on Wabash Ave. from IL 4. Turn right onto Park Ave.; the parking area is to the right on Park Ave.

To park at the south end of the trail in Chatham, follow IL 4 south from I-72. Turn left on E. Walnut St. and the parking area is on the right at the corner of N. State St.

Transportation: Amtrak serves Springfield.

Visit ride.smtd.org for local bus access.

Rentals: No nearby bike rentals are available, but keep watch for a bike-sharing program that is to launch in Springfield.

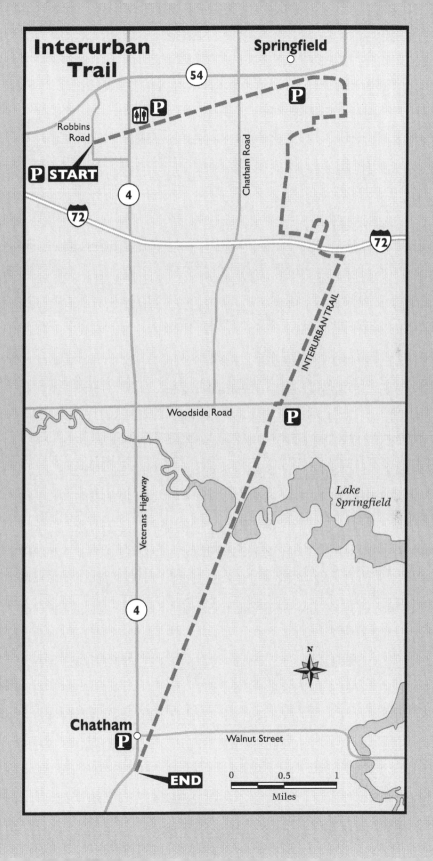

Contact: Springfield Park District, 2500 S. 11th Street, Springfield; (217) 544-1751; springfieldparks.org.

IIIIIIIIIIIIIIIIIIIIIIIIIIIIIIIIIIIIIIIIIIIIIIIIIIIIIIIIIIIIIIIIIIIIIIIIIIIIIIIIIIIIIIIIIIIIIIIIIIIIII

The Interurban Trail is one of a half dozen rail trails in Illinois built on the former routes of electric passenger trains that stitched together communities in central and southern Illinois. The largest of these interurban train operations was the Illinois Terminal Company. At its peak, the company operated trains on more than 550 miles of tracks. Before the widespread demise of passenger train service in the mid-1950s, Springfield hosted four different railroad depots that served as stops for the interurban trains.

The Wabash Trail

The first section of this route, along what is called the Wabash Trail, starts off by offering a tour of Springfield backyards, some adorned with flower gardens. After the trail brushes against the commercial strip on Wabash and then crosses a couple of busy roads, you'll be heading south alongside McArthur Rd. between a residential area on the right and agricultural land on the left.

After taking a circuitous route around a new development, going under MacArthur Blvd., and then ducking under I-72, the trail begins shadowing the Union Pacific Railroad. This is the route of higher-speed Amtrak trains that run between Chicago and St. Louis, Missouri. As you accompany the railroad, chokecherry and hickory trees provide leafy curtains on both sides of the trail.

Lake Springfield

The best part of the trail appears as you cross the west arm of Lake Springfield and then take an extended ramble alongside the lake's wetlands. Near the lake, check out the signs featuring photos of the old interurban rail line and its trains. As you cross the pedestrian bridge, big views open up of the lake's wooded shores and hills that slope down toward the water. You're looking at the west end of the 9-mile-long artificial lake that was created in 1935 by damming Sugar Creek.

Continuing south for nearly 0.5 mile, the trail traces an embankment about twenty feet above the open water and wetlands laden with cattails. On the way into Chatham, the trail scoots alongside several golfing fairways and a swath of newly planted subdivisions.

Once in Chatham, be sure to peek into the Chatham Railroad Museum, located in the old train depot alongside the trail. Since the hours are extremely limited, you probably won't find the museum open, but no matter; you can see most of the historic exhibits through the windows. The office contains a potbelly stove, a safe, an early typewriter, and a table-top printing press and looks like you would imagine the interior of a small train depot to appear when the building was constructed in 1902.

Local Information

- Visit Springfield, 109 N. Seventh Street, Springfield; (217) 789-2360; visit-springfieldillinois.com.
- Springfield Bicycle Club; (217)720-1568; spfldcycling.org. A local biking advocacy group.

The Interurban Trail spans the west arm of Lake Springfield.

Local Events/Attractions

* Chatham Railroad Museum, 100 N. State Street, Chatham; (217) 483-7792; chathamil.gov/railroadmuseum.

* Old State Capitol State Historic Site, 1 Old State Capitol Plaza, Springfield; (217) 785-7960; old-statecapitol.org/osc.htm. Restored with period furnishings.

Restaurants

* Mariah's Steakhouse and Pasta, 3317 Robbins Road, Springfield; (217) 793-1900; mariahssteak-house.com. Conveniently located across the street from the north end of the trail.

* Engrained Brewing Company, 1120 W. Lincolnshire Boulevard, Springfield; (217) 546-3054; engrainedbrewery.com. Sandwiches, salads, and a brewery located steps from the trail.

Accommodations

* Carpenter Street Hotel, 525 N. Sixth Street, Springfield; (217) 789-9100; carpenterstreethotel.com. Affordable; located north of downtown.

30 KICKAPOO RAIL TRAIL

Located on the outskirts of Urbana, the Kickapoo Rail Trail's peaceful, rural atmosphere makes you feel like you're taking a trip back in time. Top it off with views from a high bridge over a scenic river and a visit to a pleasant little town with some good eating (and drinking) options, and you've got a nearly perfect rail trail ramble.

Location: From the western edge of Urbana at the corner of University Ave. and S. Highcross Rd., the trail runs east to St. Joseph.

Length: 6.7 miles one-way.

Surface: Crushed gravel.

Wheelchair access: The trail is wheelchair accessible.

Difficulty: Easy, but the open landscape leaves you vulnerable to wind and to the sun.

Restrooms: No public restrooms along the trail, but you can use the Walmart at the west trailhead.

Maps: onekrt.org.

Hazards: Traffic is light in the area, but if it's harvest time, watch for big trucks and farm equipment while crossing multiple farm roads.

Access and parking: If heading south on I-57 into Champaign/Urbana, head east on I-74 at exit 237A. After 6 miles, take exit 185 and follow IL 130 south (E. University Ave.). Turn left on US 150 and follow it for 1 mile to S. High Cross Rd., where you'll turn right. Park in the northwest corner of the Walmart parking lot. UTM coordinates: 16T, 0400963 E, 4440900 N.

To park in St. Joseph at the east trailhead, continue east from Urbana on US 150 for 6 miles. Turn right on N. Fourth St. and park in the trail parking area in back of Casey's.

Transportation: The Champaign-Urbana Mass Transit's Grey line will take you from downtown Urbana to the western trailhead at the Urbana Walmart. Bikes can be transported on the buses' front-mounted bike racks.

Amtrak trains serve Urbana.

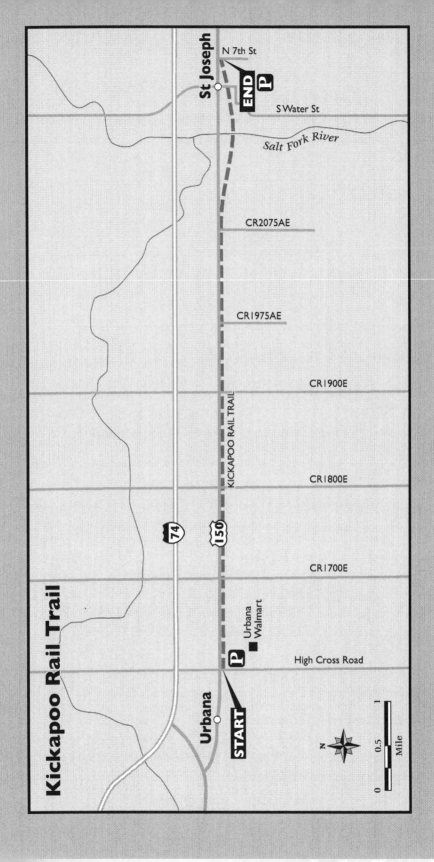

Rentals: Neutral Cycle, 624 S. Fifth St., Champaign; (312) 834-3560.

VeoRide is Urbana's app-based dockless bike-sharing service, veoride. com/uiuc.

Contact: Champaign County Forest Preserve District; ccfpd.org; onekrt. org.

Plans are afoot to extend both ends of this trail—to Urbana on the east and to Danville on the west, for a total of 24.5 miles. Stay tuned to onekrt.org as new segments open up.

||||||||||||||||||||||||||||||||||||||||||||||||||||||||||||||||||||||||||||||||||||||||||

If you're starting at the western end of this trail, don't let the bustling atmosphere of the trailhead scare you off. The heavy car traffic in the area combined with the fact that the trail parking area is in the corner of a Walmart parking lot may seem to indicate a less-than-tranquil experience in front of you. Fortunately, this is not at all the case.

Open Space Galore

The commotion fades fast once you get going. Before you know it, fields of corn unfurl for miles on either side of you. Old wooden barns stand in the distance. Alongside the trail, clusters of trees and small patches of wetlands come and go. In the open areas, you'll likely see a sparrow hawk or two perched patiently on nearby power lines, waiting for prey to appear.

As the trail parallels US 150, you'll be pleased to see that the road has minimal traffic and a shrubby buffer between you and the road muffles the traffic sounds.

After 2 miles, the farmland is interrupted by a well maintained cemetery from the early 1870s on the other side of US 150, and beyond the cemetery, you'll see I-74 nearly a half mile away. As the trail runs through the hamlet of Mayfield, keep an eye out for an old wooden church that was transformed into a home.

Continuing beyond Mayfield, an enormous grain elevator—multiple silos made of concrete and steel—rises in the distance. If it's harvest time, you'll see big trucks lined up dropping off their harvest. Of course it's no accident that the elevator exists alongside this railroad, which was once called the Indianapolis, Bloomington, and Western Railway. Putting the grain elevator alongside the train line allowed the farmers to easily move grain to market.

After following a course as straight as an airplane runway for 5 miles, the trail finally curves to the right while passing a sprawling Pioneer agricultural facility across the highway.

Crossing the Salt Fork into St. Joseph

Approaching the town of St. Joseph, you'll encounter Meier Field, a baseball field that looks like it means business. It's the home to the local high school team as well as the Royal Giants, which plays in the Eastern Illinois Baseball League. Since it started in 1933, the league has groomed a number of players who have gone on to play professionally.

Just before reaching the tiny town of St. Joseph, you'll cross the Salt Fork River on a bridge with glorious views. Standing high above the sandy-bottomed creek, the wooden bridge offers a perfect spot to linger while scouting for herons, kingfishers, and (reportedly) otters. All you hear are the birds and the sound of breeze blowing through the leaves.

After crossing the bridge, you're suddenly among the yards and houses and streets of St. Joseph. You'll pass under a water tower as well as more grain silos that once served the railroad. Like so many other small towns in Illinois, St. Joseph owes its existence to the railroad. But in St. Joseph this relationship has an added dimension because the town was actually moved to this spot because of the railroad. Originally located 1.5 miles to the south, the town pulled up stakes and settled beside the tracks in 1870 when the railroad came through.

After reaching the end of the trail and taking a quick tour of the St. Joseph's handsome brick storefront buildings, pull up a chair for a bite or a drink at one of several eateries just steps from the trail.

Local Information

- 2nd Wind Running club; secondwindrunningclub.org. Hosts runs on the trail.
- Champaign County Bikes; P.O. Box 2373, Champaign; champaigncountybikes.org. A local biking advocacy group that has campaigned for this trail and others.

Rail Trails Help Preserve Prairies

Once covering two-thirds of the Prairie State's landscape, tallgrass prairie now, sadly, makes up only one-tenth of one percent of the land. The tiny parcels of prairie in Illinois that remain often appear alongside railroad tracks (or a former railroad like the Kickapoo Rail Trail). Since the land immediately alongside tracks was largely spared from development and the plow, plants like milkweed, goldenrod, and big bluestem grass continued to grow. Transforming an unused rail line to a trail helps preserve these prairie remnants, which in turn provides food and refuge for local animals, birds, and insects.

- Prairie Cycle Club; P.O. Box 115 Urbana; prairiecycleclub.org. A local recreational bicycling club.
- Visit Champaign County, 17 E. Taylor Street, Champaign; (217) 351-4133; visitchampaign-county.org

Local Events/Attractions

- Geschenk Coffee Haus, 228 E. Lincoln Street, St. Joseph; 217-469-6034. Gifts, coffee, and teas in downtown St. Joseph.
- Wyldewood Cellars, 218 E. Lincoln Street, St. Joseph; (217) 469-9463; wyldewoodillinois.com. Wine retailer and tasting room known for its elderberry products; located steps from the trail.

Restaurants

- Crane Alley, 115 W. Main Street, Urbana; (217) 384-7526; crane-alley.com. Good food with plenty of vegetarian options; outdoor seating in downtown Urbana.
- The Ribcage, 208 N. Main Street, St Joseph; theribcagesjo.com. A meat lover's delight; located one block from the trail.
- The Wheelhouse, 109 N. Main Street, St. Joseph; (217) 469-6252; atthewheelhouse.com. Bicycle-themed restaurant located on the trail; farm-to-table offerings with an impressive beer selection.

Accommodations

- Middle Fork River Forest Preserve Campground, 3485 CR 2700 E., Penfield; (217) 595-5432; bit.ly/middleforkcg. A quiet, scenic county campground, one of the best in the area; located about 20 miles north of Champaign/Urbana.

Grain was loaded on rail cars at this grain elevator outside of Urbana before the railroad was transformed into the Kickapoo Rail Trail.

- Radisson Hotel & Conference Center Champaign-Urbana; 1001 W. Killarney Street, Urbana; radissonhotelsamericas.com. Pool, bar, and pleasant modern rooms; one of the upscale options among the dozen chain hotels in the immediate area.
- Sylvia's Irish Inn, 312 W. Green Street, Urbana; sylviasirishinn.net. Victorian house in convenient location close to downtown Urbana.

31 LINCOLN PRAIRIE GRASS TRAIL

Starting out in Mattoon, the west half of this trail runs through sprawling tracts of farmland that are interrupted now and then with ravines, ponds, creeks, and patches of prairie and woods. In Charleston the eastern part of the trail borders several historic points of interest, including the oldest fairground in the state.

Location: Starting from Mattoon, which is located south of Champaign, the trail runs east to Charleston.

Length: 12.1 miles one-way.

Surface: The entire trail is paved.

Wheelchair access: The trail is wheelchair accessible.

Difficulty: This trail is easy; however, if the sun is hot or the wind is strong, this trail could become more difficult because of the lack of shade and wind protection.

Restrooms: There are public restrooms just south of the starting point at Mattoon Peterson Park and at the Douglas-Hart Nature Center (water fountain at trailhead).

Maps: bit.ly/lpgtrail.

Hazards: None.

Access and parking: From I-57 head west on IL 16 at exit 190B. Turn right onto N. 10th St. in Mattoon. The trailhead parking area is at the corner of 10th St. and Richmond Ave. at the Ninth St. baseball/softball fields. UTM coordinates: 16T, 382585 E, 4371285 N.

To park at the Loxa Rd. parking area, take IL 16 east from I-57. About halfway between Charleston and Mattoon, go north on Loxa Rd. (CR N. 1100 E.). Park on the right where the trail crosses the road.

The easternmost parking area is at North Park in Charleston. From IL 16 in Charleston head north on Division Street. After passing the trail, park at the ball diamonds.

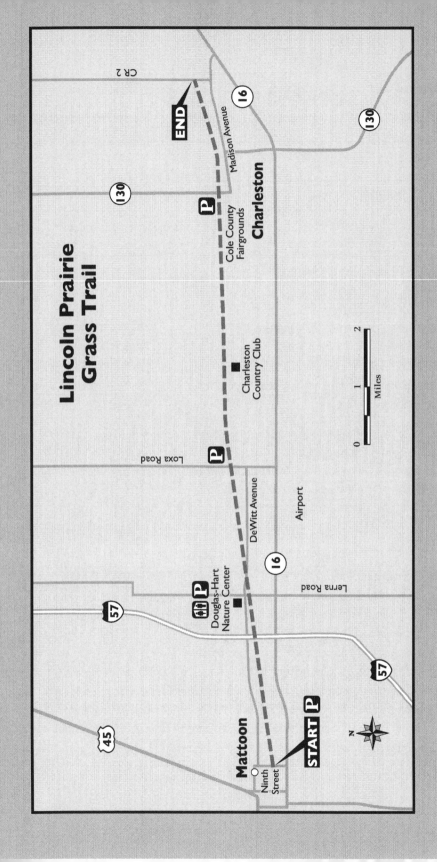

Transportation: Amtrak trains stop in Mattoon. There are plans to extend the trail 0.5 mile to the Mattoon Amtrak station.

Contact: Charleston Parks and Recreation Department (maintains the east half of the trail), 520 Jackson Avenue, Charleston; (217) 345-6897; charlestonillinois.org.

Mattoon Public Works Department (maintains the west half of the trail), 208 N. 19th Street, Mattoon; (217) 234-3611; mattoon.illinois.gov.

||||||||||||||||||||||||||||||||||||||||||||||||||||||||||||||||||||||||||||||||||||||||

Illinois history buffs will enjoy this trail as it makes its way between the two east central Illinois towns of Mattoon and Charleston. In Charleston, the trail brushes against the town's historic fairgrounds and you'll see a shoe factory from the early 1900s. In addition to the history is plenty of natural scenery to enjoy.

Mattoon

On the way out of Mattoon, the trail runs by the town's water tower and a few light industrial buildings before it ducks under I-57. The next road after I-57, Lerna Rd., provides access to the Douglas-Hart Nature Center, where you'll find a picnic spot, a collection of nature exhibits, and 1.5 miles of foot trails that wind through prairie, woodland, and wetland.

Back on the trail, you may notice that prairie restoration is underway on the land alongside the trail. Indeed, the goldenrod, milkweed, compass plants, black-eyed Susans, morning glories, and trumpet vines provide a welcome buffer to the seemingly endless expanse of corn and soy. But don't get too distracted by trailside prairie plants on this stretch of trail: Every thirty yards or so, the trail squeezes between dual telephone poles. The poles positioned on each side of the trail create the curious effect of a continuous gateway, as if you're constantly entering some new territory.

Charleston

At the trail's halfway point, more trees start to appear on the side of the trail, and soon the route cuts through the middle of the Charleston

Country Club's golf course. You'll see fairways and access trails on either side of the trail. After passing the golf course pond on the right, the trail dips below the surrounding landscape and then rises to mount a small embankment within a rural residential area. From the embankment, look through the walnut and maple trees on the right to see Riley Creek flowing at the bottom of a sixty- to seventy-foot ravine.

Getting farther into Charleston brings you past the grandstand, the track, and the exhibit buildings of the Coles County Fairgrounds, which has been hosting county fairs since 1854—making it the oldest county fair in the state. In its early years, the fairgrounds hosted popular speakers such as William Jennings Bryan and the evangelist preacher Billy Sunday, and it hosted one of the famous Lincoln-Douglas debates in 1858. Not far ahead on the trail you'll see faded lettering on the side of long, squat brick building that once served as a plant for the Brown Shoe Company. If you look closely, you'll make out the huge letters bragging that workers here made "2,000 pairs daily." In the early 1900s the Brown Shoe Company (now owner of brands such as Famous Footwear and Naturalizer) branched out from its headquarters in St. Louis to build many plants such as this one in small Illinois towns that were beyond the reach of the large urban labor unions.

Approaching IL 130 on the left brings you by a large grain elevator and a couple of old train depots. Leaving Olive Ave./IL 130 behind, you'll immediately return to the rural landscape that you saw before entering Charleston. The trail ends at CR 2, nearly 1.5 miles past Olive Ave.

While in Charleston, be sure to check out its charming downtown area, located 0.25 mile south of where the trail intersects IL 130. And a little further south in town is a landmark gothic revival style Old Main building on the campus of Eastern Illinois University.

Local Information

- Charleston Tourism Office, 520 Jackson Avenue, Charleston; (217) 348-0430; charlestontourism. org. Check out the courthouse and murals depicting the community's history in Charleston's historic downtown.
- Mattoon Tourism and Arts Department, 208 N. 19th Street, Mattoon; (800) 500-6286; mattoon. illinois.gov

‖‖‖

Lincoln and the Coles County Fairgrounds

In 1858 about 10,000 people showed up at the fairgrounds in Charleston for one of the seven debates between Abraham Lincoln and Stephen Douglas in a campaign for one of the state's U.S. Senate seats. Although Lincoln lost the election, these debates launched him into national prominence that eventually led to his election as president. A small museum on the fairgrounds explores the debates through film, audio, artifacts, and photos. In the museum you'll learn that Lincoln was a regular visitor to the area—his parents lived south of Charleston at what is now Lincoln Log Cabin State Historic Site.

‖‖‖

Local Events/Attractions

- Douglas-Hart Nature Center, 2204 Dewitt Avenue E., Mattoon; (217) 235-4644; dhnature.org. Located one block from the trail.
- Lincoln-Douglas Debate Museum, 126 E. Street, Charleston; (217) 348-0430. Located at the Coles County Fairgrounds.

Restaurants

- Bangkok Thai, 1140 Lincoln Avenue, Charleston; (217) 348-1232; t-garden-thai.business.site. Standard Thai fare in a pleasant atmosphere.
- Jackson Avenue Coffee, 708 Jackson Avenue, Charleston; (217) 345-5283; jacksonavenuecoffee. com. Serves up the good stuff in a great downtown location.

Accommodations

- Days Inn Charleston, 810 W. Lincoln Avenue, Charleston; (217) 345-7689. Clean and affordable.
- Fox Ridge State Park, 18175 State Park Road, Charleston; (217) 345-6416; bit.ly/foxrsp. Occupies a beautiful spot south of Charleston along the Embarras River. Plenty of campsites and several small cabins.

32 LINCOLN PRAIRIE TRAIL

The best part of this trail is the north section that runs through bottomland woods, over the Sangamon River, and beside Lake Taylorville. The rest of the trail takes you through a couple of small towns and the wide-open farmland of Central Illinois.

Location: From the western edge of Taylorville, which is located southeast of Springfield, the trail follows IL 29 southeast to Pana.

Length: 14.5 miles one-way.

Surface: Asphalt.

Wheelchair access: The route is wheelchair accessible.

Difficulty: The trail presents a medium level of difficulty because of the minimal amount of shade along the way.

Restrooms: There are portable toilets and water at Lake Taylorville's Jaycee Park.

Maps: bit.ly/lptrail.

Hazards: Watch for traffic as the trail crosses multiple side roads.

Access and parking: Head southeast of Springfield on IL 29. As IL 29 turns left in Taylorville, continue straight on Webster St. Turn left onto Main Cross St. and right onto Paw St. There are no signs and only a few parking spaces near the trailhead on the left. UTM coordinates: 16T, 303722 E, 4379995 N.

Coming from the south on I-55, head northeast on IL 48. Outside Taylorville, turn left onto Shumway St. Turn right onto Main Cross St. and then right onto Paw St.

Since the trail shadows IL 29 for nearly the entire distance, it's easy to find access points. The many road crossings along the way typically offer a small grassy spot for parking. One dedicated parking area exists at Lake Taylorville. Turn right on Il 29 at Lake Dr. and then turn right on E. Lake Shore Dr.

The parking area at the south end of the trail is just north of Pana on IL 29, at the junction with E. 350 N. Rd.

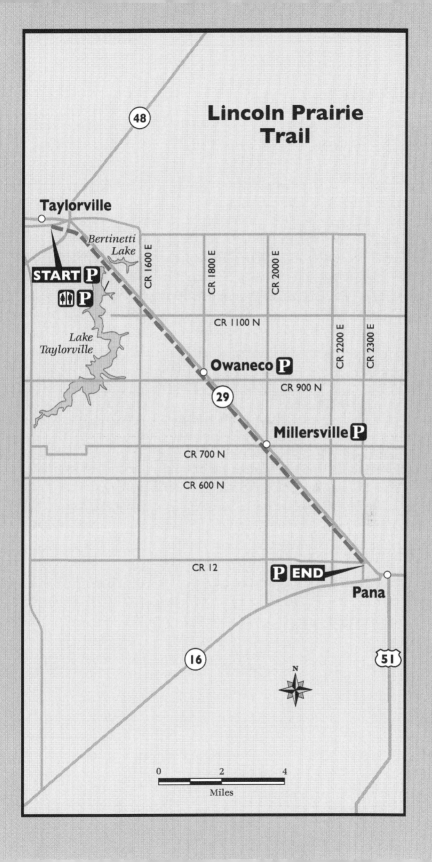

Lincoln Prairie Trail

48

Taylorville

Bertinetti Lake

START P

P

CR 1600 E

CR 1800 E

CR 2000 E

CR 1100 N

Lake Taylorville

Owaneco P

CR 900 N

CR 2200 E

CR 2300 E

29

Millersville P

CR 700 N

CR 600 N

CR 12

P **END**

Pana

16

51

N

0   2   4
Miles

Transportation: Amtrak trains serve Springfield.

Contact: Visit Springfield, 109 N. Seventh Street, Springfield; (217) 789-2360; visitspringfieldillinois.com.

||||||||||||||||||||||||||||||||||||||||||||||||||||||||||||||||||||||||||||||||||||||||||||||||||||

Given that most of the trails in Central Illinois are in cities like Springfield, Decatur, Urbana, and Bloomington, the Lincoln Prairie Trail is unique for this part of the state because it runs between two smaller towns, Taylorville and Pana. As the trail cuts diagonally through an agricultural checkerboard, most of it runs shoulder to shoulder with IL 29. Sometimes there's a buffer of greenery between the trail and the highway, but often there's not. Although IL 29 isn't overly busy or noisy, it usually hosts a steady flow of traffic.

Lake Taylorville

The most interesting part of the trail is the north section, which crosses the Flat Branch of the Sangamon River and brushes against Lake Taylorville. First, though, you'll go through Taylorville residential areas, cross IL 48 (very busy, with fast-moving traffic), and then mount an embankment. The embankment leads you through a heavily wooded bottomland. Look for jewelweed and vine-covered hickories as the trail drops from the embankment and the walls of a ravine start to rise on both sides of the trail.

After the second bridge, which spans a waterway connecting Bertinetti Lake with the Sangamon River, look left for a view of Lake Taylorville and its spillway. There are a couple of nearby parks and a marina that occupy the rolling grassy hills bordering the lake. The parking area near the trail overlooks the dam and a thirty-foot-high spillway that shunts water toward the Sangamon River.

South of Lake Taylorville, the landscape smooths out as corn and soybeans take center stage. The slight embankment under the trail, combined with the lack of trees along much of the route, allows for long views of cropland and distant farms. A variety of prairie grasses grow beside the trail, including flowers such as phlox, compass plants, Queen Anne's lace, morning glory, and chicory.

Owaneco and Pana

There are occasional interruptions of the vast agricultural fields. One of these is the Taylorville Prison—a minimum-security state facility surrounded by fortified walls topped with razor wire. In Owaneco, bike route signs direct trail users briefly along a couple of side streets and by grain elevators. After passing more grain elevators in Millersville, you'll cross Locust Creek and a research farm operated by the University of Illinois.

Wrap up at the trailhead parking area just north of Pana. While visiting Pana, keep watch for a few downtown murals depicting the history of the town. Some murals show Pana's history as a major coal producer in the area. Oddly enough, this small town also was a major Midwest flower grower. At one time the town hosted five different companies that shipped fifteen million roses annually. Pana still considers itself the City of Roses.

Local Information

- City of Pana, 120 E. Third Street, Pana; (217) 562-3626; cityofpana.org/attractions. Town has a collection of Victorian homes; walking tour maps available.
- City of Taylorville, 115 N. Main Street, Taylorville; (217) 824-2101; taylorville.net.
- Lincoln Prairie Trails Conservancy, PO Box 392, Taylorville; (217) 820-0849; lincolnprairietrailsconservancy.com. Advocacy group working to improve the trail.

Events/Attractions

- Christian County Coal Mine Museum, 1324 E. Park Street, Taylorville; (217) 823-1819. Features history of local coal mining.
- Christian County Historical Society Museum, E. Route 29, Taylorville; (217) 824-6922; cchistoricalsociety.blogspot.com/. Contains an 1820 log house and the 1839 courthouse where Lincoln argued cases.

Restaurants

- Florinda's Pizza Ristorante Italiano, 114 S. Main Street, Taylorville, (217) 287-2226; florindaspizza.com. Located downtown.

Accommodations

- The Inn at Oak Terrace Resort, 100 Beyers Lake Road; (800) 577-7598; oakterraceresort.com. Lodging, golf course, spa, and a restaurant.
- Market Street Inn Bed and Breakfast, 220 E. Market Street, Taylorville; (217) 824-7220; marketstreetinn.com. Lodging in an 1892 Queen Anne Victorian house.

A stone sign outside Pana marks the south trailhead of the Lincoln Prairie Trail.

33 LOST BRIDGE TRAIL

This well-used trail on the west side of Springfield takes you through a wooded landscape, over a couple bridges, and alongside a handsome community park. In the community of Rochester at the south end of the trail, you'll learn about a historic meeting between a former president and Abraham Lincoln when he served in the Illinois legislature.

Location: From the east side of Springfield, the trail heads southeast to Rochester.

Length: 6.1 miles one-way.

Surface: Asphalt.

Wheelchair access: This trail is wheelchair accessible.

Difficulty: This trail is easy.

Restrooms: There are portable toilets and water at the trailhead and at the trail parking area in Rochester on Main St.

Maps: bit.ly/springbikemap.

Hazards: None.

Access and parking: From I-55 on the east side of Springfield, exit heading west on IL 29. Turn left onto the Dirkson Parkway. Turn into the parking area for the Illinois Department of Transportation. Follow signs to the trailhead. UTM coordinates: 16S, 276796 E, 4405894 N.

The south trailhead for the Lost Bridge Trail is at the corner of IL 29 and Main St. in Rochester.

Transportation: Amtrak trains stop in Springfield.

The Springfield bus system provides access to Rochester. Visit ride.smtd.org.

Contact: Springfield Park District, 2500 S. 11th St., Springfield; (217) 544-1751; springfieldparks.org.

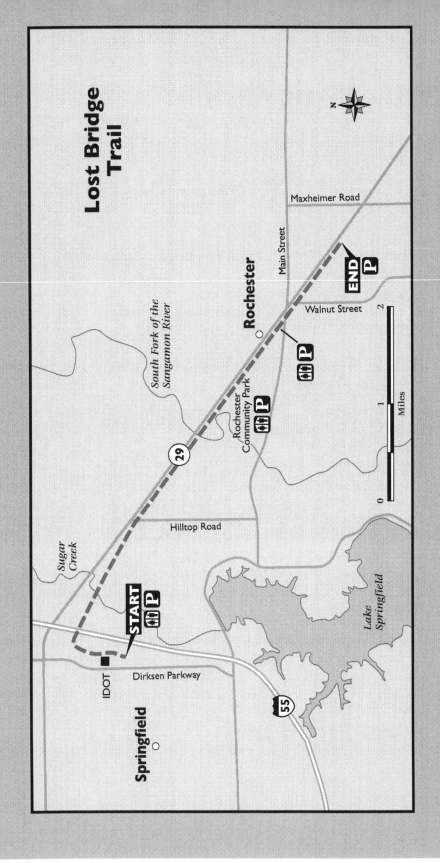

The Lost Bridge Trail runs along a railroad corridor between the east edge of Springfield and the nearby village of Rochester. The trail's name refers to an old train bridge over Sugar Creek at the beginning of the route that was sold for scrap metal by the railroad company. Fortunately one of the two old bridges that were once along this stretch of the Baltimore and Ohio Railroad remain. The remaining bridge spans the South Fork of the Sangamon River near Rochester.

Sugar Creek

The first section of the trail brushes against a reservoir that sits behind the large Illinois Department of Transportation building. While the busy interstate on the opposite shore of the little lake doesn't exactly set the stage for a peaceful environment, the grassy shore of the lake still provides a pleasant spot with an observation platform and picnic tables.

After passing the lake, a series of turns through a wooded area take you to the railroad right-of-way. You'll duck under the interstate and then cross a new wooden bridge over Sugar Creek, which carries the outflow from Lake Springfield, a large reservoir to the south.

Beyond the meanders of Sugar Creek, the surrounding landscape alternately pitches upward and drops downward. For a stretch the trail traces a raised embankment twenty-five feet above the surrounding landscape. Then the inverse occurs, and hickory-laden embankments rise about forty feet on both sides of the trail. After passing a small pond and patches of wetland, the trail shoots under a road and through a short tunnel and then makes a gradual descent toward Rochester.

Into Rochester

The minimal number of street crossings along this trail allow for a jaunt with rare interruptions. IL 29, a fairly busy road, parallels nearly the entire trail. Thankfully the road doesn't subtract much from the experience because of the heavy woods and the ravines that serve as a barrier between the trail and the highway. Before reaching Rochester, you'll cross the South Fork of the Sangamon River, and shortly after that, a spur trail veers to the right into a community park containing a duck pond, sports fields, and a concession stand.

In Rochester you'll pass a trail parking area, as well as a folksy mural on the side of a silo depicting a meeting in 1842 between former U.S. President Martin Van Buren and Abraham Lincoln, who was serving in the Illinois state legislature at the time. As the story goes, Van Buren was sidelined in Rochester while on a journey. Lincoln and his storytelling skills were called upon to entertain the former president for the evening. A friendship arose from the brief meeting, and Van Buren eventually endorsed Lincoln's presidential bid. To learn more about this historic meeting, turn left on John St. in Rochester to see a historic marker and small wayside exhibit.

Local Information

- Springfield Bicycle Club; (217)720-1568; spfldcycling.org. A local biking advocacy group.
- Visit Springfield, 109 N. Seventh Street, Springfield; (217) 789-2360; visitspringfieldillinois.com

In Rochester, a mural on the side of grain silo commemorates a local meeting between President Martin Van Buren and Abraham Lincoln.

Local Events/Attractions

- Abraham Lincoln Presidential Museum, 212 N. Sixth Street, Springfield; (217) 558-8844; presidentlincoln.illinois.gov. This museum dedicated to Illinois's most-famous figure has some high-tech attractions.
- Illinois State Museum, 502 S. Spring Street; (217) 782-7386; museum.state.il.us. Permanent and changing exhibits on the state's land, life, people, and art.

Restaurants

- Cozy Dog Drive-In, 2935 S. Sixth Street, Springfield; (217) 525-1992; cozydogdrivein.com. Credits itself with inventing the corn dog. Get ready for lots of Route 66 memorabilia.
- Public House 29, 312 Sattley Street, Rochester, (217) 576-7024; pubhouse29.com. Pub with bar food right beside the trail.
- Mockingbird Bakery, 129 S. John Street, Rochester, (217) 498-1354; mockingbirdbakery.org. One block off the trail in Rochester.

Accommodations

- Comfort Suites Near Route 66, 2620 S. Dirksen Parkway, Springfield; (217) 615-4445; bit.ly/comfort66. Located several blocks south of the trail's starting point.
- Carpenter Street Hotel, 525 N. Sixth Street, Springfield; (217) 789-9100; carpenterstreethotel.com. Affordable; located north of downtown.
- Sangchris Lake State Park, 9898 Cascade Road, Rochester; (217) 498-9208; bit.ly/sanglsp. Two large campgrounds and one small walk-in camping area.

34 RIVER TRAIL

The highlight of this route is the ascent up a high bluff heavily laden with maple and oak trees. While it may sound punishing, this 3-mile climb is well worth the effort. After passing creeks, ravines, and dense woodland on the way to the top, the final few miles of trail takes you through nearby Peoria suburbs.

Location: From the Taylor St. ball diamonds in East Peoria, the trail runs southeast to Morton.

Length: 6.6 miles one-way, with optional side trip.

Surface: Asphalt.

Wheelchair access: The trail is wheelchair accessible.

Difficulty: Medium difficulty due to the climb up the bluff.

Restrooms: There are public restrooms and water at the Taylor St. ball diamonds and Bunnell Park.

Maps: bit.ly/EPeoriaRT.

Hazards: If cycling down the bluff, keep an eye peeled for upcoming street crossings. They arrive quickly.

Access and parking: From Peoria head east on I-74. Exit at US 150/IL 116 and turn right. Just after crossing the channel, turn left onto Springfield Rd. Park in the gravel lot on the left just before the ball diamonds. From the parking area, catch the trail up on the levee; proceed to the right alongside the Farm Creek Diversion Channel. UTM coordinates: 16T, 282186 E, 4504744 N.

To park at Bunnell Park take US 150 southeast from East Peoria. Turn right onto Hawthorne Ave. and left onto Frevent Ave.

To park at the east end of the trail, take US 150 to Morton. Turn right on Bond St. and then take an immediate right on Jefferson St. Park at the picnic shelter on the right.

Transportation: The closest Amtrak stations are in Bloomington and Galesburg.

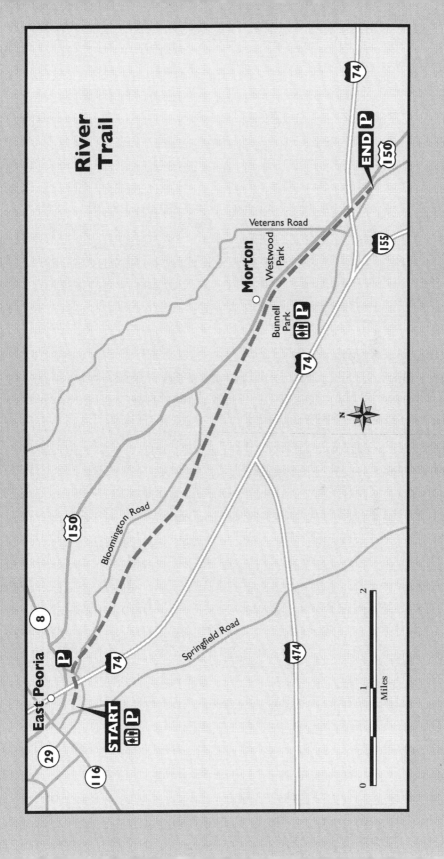

Contact: Fondulac Park District, 201 Veterans Dr., East Peoria; (309) 699-3923; fondulacpark.com.

||||||||||||||||||||||||||||||||||||||||||||||||||||||||||||||||||||||||||||||||||||||||||||

The River Trail follows a section of railroad that was once part of a 500-mile network of electric passenger trains that linked communities in central and southern Illinois. Run by the Illinois Terminal Company, these interurban trains, as they were known, followed trolley wires among cities like Champaign, Bloomington, Lincoln, Springfield, and St. Louis. Passenger service on this former railroad in East Peoria operated from 1895 until 1956, when the automobile began to take center stage. After passenger service dried up, the Illinois Terminal Company used the track to haul freight until the early 1980s.

The first 1 mile of the trail traces levees along the Farm Creek Diversion Channel and one of its small tributaries. To control the sometimes-heavy flow of water that comes down from the steep bluffs after a strong rain, these creekbeds have been widened, deepened, straightened, and lined with concrete. Often with only a trickle of water running at the bottom of the steep concrete banks, these diversion channels may look like overkill. Apparently they're not: Over the years, the dirt banks that were once built along the creek overflowed on a number of occasions and flooded downtown East Peoria.

Up the Bluff

On the way to the foot of the bluff, you'll face a few busy cross streets. Just after the diversion channel splits, a green train caboose at Veterans Rd. marks the spot where the gradual 3-mile climb to the top of the bluff begins. Since the route was graded for train travel, it's never terribly steep, but you will get a workout.

As you ascend, thick greenery on one side of the trail hides a steep ravine. The other side of the trail is open and grassy, allowing views of the nearby bluffs. One of the highlights of this trail is the bridges, some of which are thirty feet above the sandy-bottomed stream and its banks, thick with cottonwoods and sumac. Alongside the trail, little gullies—some containing trickling rivulets and others just dry rocky creekbeds—sometimes cut into the bluff. As the sides of the bluff move closer to trail, tree limbs form a thick canopy overhead.

Morton

When the landscape flattens out at the top of the bluff, you'll pass some agricultural fields and a series of grassy backyards. The trail takes a downward dip before pulling alongside US 150, which you'll accompany for the rest of the route.

The final couple miles bring you past housing subdivisions and a mobile home park and underneath I-74 before arriving at a picnic shelter nestled in the midst of a busy commercial area on the outskirts of Morton. If you're cycling back down the bluff to East Peoria, you'll find pedaling is optional for most of the way.

Back at the starting point, you can add a couple of miles to the route by heading toward the Illinois River instead of up the bluff. Be warned, though: it's an obstacle course through highly developed commercial areas requiring numerous street crossings. In future years, look for several miles of trails added to the East Peoria riverfront.

Local Information

- Peoria Area Convention & Visitors Bureau, 456 Fulton Street, Suite 300, Peoria; (800) 747-0302; peoria.org.

Local Events/Attractions

- Carl Spindler Marina, 3701 N. Main Street (Access Rd. 7), East Peoria; (309) 699-3549. Catch a 1-mile-long river trail, or rent a canoe or kayak to paddle the Illinois River.
- Peoria Riverfront, 200 Northeast Water Street, Peoria; (309) 689-3019. Enjoy parks, a marina, restaurants, a couple of museums, and a 2-mile long trail.
- Pleasant Hill Antique Mall, 315 S. Pleasant Hill Road, East Peoria; (309) 694-4040. Housed in a large former school gymnasium, located a few hundred feet from the trail.

Restaurants

- Emerald Tea Room, 132 McKinley Street, East Peoria; (309) 694-1972. Great salads; well worth a visit. Within walking distance of the trailhead.

- East Peoria Levee District, 400 W. Washington Street, East Peoria; (309) 999-1700. Plenty of chain restaurant options in this shopping area located near the trailhead.

Accommodations

- Holiday Inn & Suites East Peoria, 101 Holiday Street, East Peoria; (309) 698-3333; bit.ly/holiday-innses. Located blocks from the trail and near many restaurants.
- Jubilee College State Park, 13015 W. Fussner Road, Brimfield; (309) 446-3758; bit.ly/jubileecsp. Lots of campsites; located twenty minutes north of Peoria.

35 ROCK ISLAND STATE TRAIL

"Oh the Rock Island Line is a mighty fine line/Oh the Rock Island Line is the road to ride." This sage advice offered by Johnny Cash and countless other musicians has granted the train line celebrity status. As you explore this piece of an American icon, you'll enjoy the wooded ravines, the pastoral scenery, the many bridges over winding prairie creeks, and the quiet little towns along the way.

Location: From Glen Oak Park at Abington St. and NE Perry Ave. in Peoria, the trail runs north to Toulon.

Length: 34.1 miles one-way.

Surface: Asphalt on the southern 9 miles or so; well-compacted crushed gravel on the remaining 25 miles except for the on-street sections.

Wheelchair access: The trail is wheelchair accessible, but use caution for the on-street sections. Particularly on the south section, the trail crosses numerous busy streets.

Difficulty: Because of its length, this trail has a medium-to-hard level of difficulty.

Restrooms: There are public restrooms and water at Glen Oak Park, the Rock Island Trail parking area (just north of Alta), Kickapoo Creek State Recreation Area, in the small park on First St. in Dunlap (portable toilet), at Cutters Grove Park in Princeton, and next to the old depot on Williams St. in Wyoming, and the parking area at the north end of the trail.

Maps: bit.ly/rockislandtrl; bit.ly/rockislandtrail.

Hazards: The long tunnel under IL 6 is narrow and dark as night. If you're riding a bike, dismount. Watch for traffic as the trail crosses busy streets, particularly on the south section of the trail. Traffic is very mild on all on-street sections in the small towns of Dunlap, Princeville, and Wyoming.

Access and parking: From I-74 in Peoria, take exit 90 east on N. Gale Ave. Turn left on W. McClure Ave. and then turn right on N. Prospect Rd. Turn left on E. Frye Ave. The trail begins at the entrance to Glen Oak Park at the

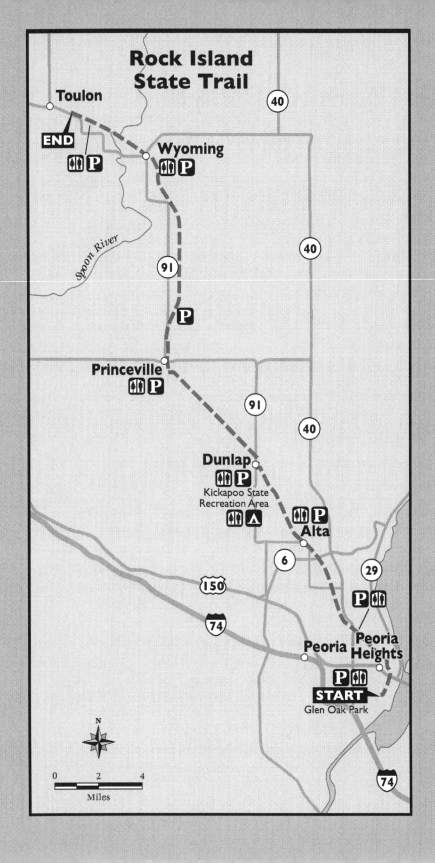

corner of Abington St. NE Perry Ave. Park inside the park on the park road. UTM coordinates: 16T, 0282782 E, 4509731 N.

To park at the Alta Rd. trailhead, take IL 6 north from Peoria to Allen Rd. Head north on Allen Rd. and bear left on W. Alta Rd. The Rock Island Trail parking area is on the right.

To reach at the parking area on Parks School Rd. north of Dunlap, take IL 6 to IL 40. Follow IL 40 north to Parks School Rd. and turn left. The parking area is on the right.

To park at the County Line Rd. parking area north of Princeville, take IL 40 north to County Line Rd. (CR 350 N.) and turn left. Parking is on the right.

To park in Wyoming at the Rock Island Depot Museum, follow IL 40 north to CR 950 N. and turn left. This road immediately becomes CR 600 N. The parking area is on the left.

To park at the north trailhead outside Toulon, follow I-74 west of Peoria. Head north on IL 78/US 150. Stay north on IL 78 as US 150 turns left. Turn right onto IL 17. The parking area is on the left after passing through Toulon.

Transportation: The closest Amtrak stations are in Bloomington and Galesburg.

Contact: Peoria Park District; 2218 N. Prospect Ave., Peoria; (309) 682-1200; peoriaparks.org.

Rock Island State Trail, 311 E. Williams St., Wyoming; (309) 695-2228; bit.ly/RISTrail. The trail office is in an old train depot alongside the trail.

IIIIIIIIIIIIIIIIIIIIIIIIIIIIIIIIIIIIIIIIIIIIIIIIIIIIIIIIIIIIIIIIIIIIIIIIIIIIIIIIIIIIIIIIIIIIIII

I nitially running from Chicago to the Quad Cities, the Rock Island Railroad Line was the first railroad to cross the Mississippi River. Eventually it branched out to fourteen states and played an important role in the settlement of the West. The railroad acquired nearly mythical status by way of a folk song first recorded in a Southern prison in the 1930s and later recorded by diverse artists as Lead Belly, Johnny Cash, Pete Seeger, and Little Richard.

This section of the railroad, a spur off the main Rock Island Line, was used for transporting grain from the Midwestern breadbasket to the distilleries of Peoria from 1871 to 1965. In the late nineteenth century the line helped establish Peoria's status as the whiskey capital of the world. (The city boasted twenty-four breweries and seventy-three distilleries between 1837 and 1919.)

Much to See in Peoria

Either at the beginning or end of your journey, consider taking a tour of Glen Oak Park, where this route starts. It's a large rambling park with wooded ravines, a music amphitheater, a lagoon, a children's museum, and the city zoo. (Another nearby spot you should visit is the Peoria Riverfront, located blocks from the trailhead and containing a host of attractions.)

After starting out from the southern tip of the Glen Oak Park, watch for the turnoff at Park Ave., where you'll cross NE Perry Ave. The trail resumes less than one block ahead on the left and soon skirts the edge of Springdale Cemetery before sending you over War Memorial Dr. on a newly refurbished bridge. Pass the offices of the Peoria Journal Star on the right, followed by the western edge of Grandview Park, another historic Peoria Park.

Just before crossing Prospect Rd., the trail passes Trefzger's Bakery, which claims to be oldest bakery in Central Illinois. The bakery, established in 1861, only recently set up shop in this historic building. In 1890s, when the Peoria area was a hub for bicycle production, this building housed a bicycle manufacturer.

At the bridge over Knoxville Ave. is a shopping mall on the right and on the left is Donavan Park, which contains a restaurant and an astronomical observatory. You'll see plenty of suburban backyards before encountering another shopping mall, which the trail loops around to avoid crossing the busy Pioneer Parkway without a traffic signal.

Heading out of Peoria

North of Pioneer Parkway, the trail passes an airstrip and accompanies sections of a meandering stream before entering a long, narrow tunnel under IL 6. Before and after the tunnel, thick woodland borders the trail.

North of the hamlet of Alta, the steady march of new housing subdivisions and accompanying roads are replacing farmland on both sides of the trail. Watch for an observation deck on the right side of the trail that overlooks a small ravine containing a winding, sandy-bottomed tributary to Kickapoo Creek.

Not far ahead is the access to the Kickapoo State Recreation Area, containing what is likely to be the best dedicated rail trail camping area in the Midwest. The park's campground is specifically for Rock Island Trail users, as well as people who are willing to hike 0.6 mile from the nearest parking lot. The park hosts several miles of trails that tour wooded areas, a restored prairie, and a stream.

Continuing ahead beautiful scenery continues to unfold. A big ravine opens up on the side of the trail, and soon a forty-foot-high bridge over Kickapoo Creek offers a bird's-eye view of the creek's pleasant, wooded banks.

Dunlap and Princeville

In Dunlap you'll encounter the first of the trail's three on-street sections. Bike route signs make each turn crystal clear (turns also are outlined below). Between Dunlap and Princeville, cyclists, walkers, and runners start to thin out. High banks on the side of the trail come and go. When the banks drop down, they reveal the dusty silos and red wooden barns scattered over the lightly rolling agricultural landscape. Entering Princeville, a nifty mural promoting the trail graces a small building containing restrooms.

As the trail parallels Santa Fe Ave. north of Princeville, you'll pass through a thick tunnel of maple trees before crossing North Creek. Farther north of Princeville, a trailside prairie restoration project may catch your eye: It's chock-full of the prairie grasses and flowers once so common throughout Illinois. A few more miles bring you to several pleasant creeks, both intermittent and year-round. Some wind along wooded banks; others wiggle through small grassy ravines.

Wyoming and the Spoon River

The next section of trail presents an opportunity to work on cadence, stride, stroke, or whatever else you do when the route is uneventful and the scenery on the dull side. A thin strip of trees—in this case, oak and hickory—line the trail for a number of miles through this section, preventing views beyond the edges of the trail. On the way into Wyoming, it becomes an exciting moment when the veil slips away: The trail rises a bit, and the trees open up, offering long views of the surrounding pastoral landscape.

In Wyoming you'll pass the old train depot containing the trail headquarters and a small museum focusing on the former railroad. After Wyoming the woodland grows thicker. Wetlands decorate one side of the trail; the Spoon River appears on the other at the bottom of a forty-foot-deep ravine. After a 0.25-mile-long alliance between trail and the river, the Spoon takes a sharp turn and passes under the trail as you mount a spectacular old train bridge. Benches on this long, steel-truss bridge suspended fifty feet above the river allow you to sit and enjoy the sights and sounds. From the bridge look to the Spoon's northeast bank for a tiny creek that flows down into the river.

The trails end nearly 3 miles ahead in Toulon, but the northernmost trail parking area is about 2 miles ahead, just outside the town of Toulon.

Resistance and Controversy

As one of the first Illinois rail trails south of the Chicago region, the Rock Island Trail encountered more than its share of controversy and resistance. Plenty of people were against the trail's development, and they butted heads regularly with the trail's dedicated group of supporters and volunteers. Those in opposition carried out many political maneuvers to prevent the trail's development. There was vandalism of the trail, too, including a fire meant to destroy to the trail's main attraction: the bridge over the Spoon River. Perseverance and good sense eventually prevailed, and the trail was christened in 1989.

The bridge over the Spoon River soars over a bend in the waterway.

Major Milepoints

8.0   If cycling, walk your bike while passing through the tunnel under IL 6. It's long, dark, and narrow.

12.9 On-street section: In Dunlap turn right onto First St.

13.0 Turn left onto Ash St.

13.1 Turn right onto Third St.

13.4 Turn right onto Hickory St. and then quickly left onto Second St.

19.2 On-street section: Turn right onto Walnut Rd.

19.9 Turn right onto North St. and then make a quick left onto N. Town Ave.

20.0 Turn left onto N. Town St.

20.6 Turn left to regain the trail.

31.8 On-street section: Turn left onto Williams St.

32.0 Turn right onto Seventh St.

32.1 Turn left onto Thomas St.

32.2 Turn right onto Sixth St. Pass a couple of houses and resume the trail on the left.

Local Information

- Peoria Area Convention & Visitors Bureau, 456 Fulton Street, Suite 300, Peoria; (800) 747-0302; peoria.org.
- Bike Peoria; bikepeoria.org. Advocates for better biking and trails around Peoria.

Local Events/Attractions

- Peoria Riverfront, 200 Northeast Water Street, Peoria; (309) 689-3019. Less than 1 mile southeast of the trailhead, the 2-mile long riverfront trail takes you past parks, a marina, restaurants, and a couple of museums:, including the Peoria Riverfront Museum which focuses on art, science, history, and technology.
- Rock Island Depot Museum, 311 E. Williams Street, Wyoming; (309) 695-2228. Memorabilia from the Chicago, Burlington, and Quincy Line that operated on this trail.
- Trefzger's Bakery, 4416 N. Prospect Road, Peoria Heights; (309) 685-9221; trefzgersbakery.com. Central Illinois's oldest bakery is located right alongside the trail.

Restaurants

- Ellen's Diner, 127 E. Main Street, Princeville; (309) 385-1700. Typical diner fare located close to the route.
- Junction City Shopping Center, 5901 N. Prospect Road, Peoria; (309) 689-0808; newjunctioncity.com. The trail runs next to this shopping mall, which offers nearly a dozen restaurant options.

Accommodations

- Four Points by Sheraton Peoria, 500 Hamilton Boulevard, Peoria; (309) 306-3424; bit.ly/fppeoria; located very close to Peoria Riverfront and many dining options.
- Kickapoo State Recreation Area, 311 E. Williams Street, Wyoming; (309) 695-2228. The very quiet campground is accessible via the Rock Island Trail and by hiking in 0.6 mile from the overnight parking lot on Fox Road; pit toilets, fire pads, picnic tables, a picnic shelter, and water.

36 SANGAMON VALLEY TRAIL

The highlights of the Sangamon Valley Trail, without a doubt, are the captivating views from soaring bridges over two small creeks and the mighty Sangamon River. In addition to these soaring bridges that take you through the treetops, there are three parks along this trail that you can explore.

Location: From Centennial Park on the western edge of Springfield, the trail runs north to Irwin Bridge Rd.

Length: 11.5 miles one-way.

Surface: Asphalt.

Wheelchair access: The trail is wheelchair accessible with few road crossings.

Difficulty: Easy.

Restrooms: In Centennial Park parking area at the south trailhead and at Stuart Park.

Maps: bit.ly/spdtrails, bit.ly/svtrail.

Hazards: None.

Access and parking: From I-72, take exit 91 and then head north on Wabash Ave. Several hundred feet ahead, turn left on Bunker Hill Rd. The trail parking area is less than 1 mile ahead on the right just after the main entrance for Centennial Park. UTM coordinates: 16S, 0263474 E, 4404379 N.

To park at Stuart Park: If heading south on I-55 into Springfield, take exit 105 and turn right on S. Sherman Blvd. Continue ahead for 10 miles as it turns into N. Peoria Rd. and then Veterans Pkwy. (IL 4). At W. Jefferson St., turn right and then take an immediate right on Winch Ln. Stuart Park is just ahead on the left.

To park at the trail's north parking area: From I-55, take exit 105 and turn right on S. Sherman Blvd. Less than 1 mile ahead, turn right on E. Andrew Rd. and continue ahead for 5.6 miles. The Cantrall Creek Rd. trail parking area is on the left.

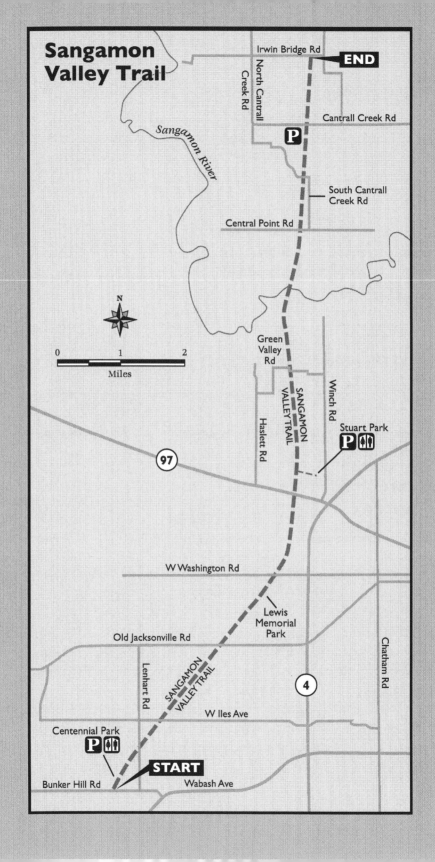

Transportation: The Sangamon Mass Transit District's #16 bus will get you very close to the south trailhead and the #4 bus will get you very close to Stuart Park; all the buses have bike racks; smtd.org.

Amtrak trains serve Springfield.

Rentals: No nearby bike rentals available, but keep watch for a bikesharing program that is to launch.

Contact: Springfield Park District, 2500 S. 11th St., Springfield; (217) 544-1751; springfieldparks.org. Plans are afoot to extend the north end of this trail several miles into Athens.

As one of the newer rail trails in the state, the Sangamon Valley Trail offers loads of charm. The charm is most evident as you pass over a series of dramatic bridges straddling a couple of creeks and one big river—all located on the northern two-thirds of the route. And if you're someone who appreciates uninterrupted trails, lengthy stretches of this trail allow you to go on autopilot without worrying about dicey road crossings.

Another attraction on this trail are three pleasant parks along the way. The first and largest of these parks, Centennial Park, provides a perfect starting point. There are picnicking spots, ponds, hiking trails, a bike repair station, and even plaques honoring two local advocates who helped get this trail and other trails in Springfield off the ground—Lynn Miller and Bill Donels.

Spring Creek and Two Parks

During the first few miles on the trail, the buffer of trees on either side of you comes and goes as the surrounding environment alternates between a newer suburban neighborhood and planted rows of soybean. Plenty of access points connect the trail to local residential streets, and at about 4 miles in, you'll see a connection to Lewis Park (the access trail is unmarked, but it appears shortly after passing the electrical switching station on the right).

After passing a towering grain elevator that once served the train cars running on this railroad, the trail mounts the first of a trio of dramatic bridges. This one, originally constructed in 1913, soars about sixty feet above Spring Creek. Part of the supporting structure of this bridge came from a bridge built over the Fox River in Geneva, Illinois, in 1883.

Coming down from the bridge, maple and sycamore hang overhead as the trail runs through a trench built to keep the path of the railroad gently graded. Along this stretch you may notice informal foot trails—complete with short bridges and benches—built on the embankment to the right. Just ahead, a short spur trail offers a connection to Stuart Park, which has a popular dog run. North of Stuart Park, a bovine audience might be in attendance as you travel through a swath of wide open agricultural land and cow pasture.

Sangamon River and Cantrall Creek

Now for the showstopper of this trail—a spectacular bridge over the big Sangamon River. The bridge, about 100 yards long, feels like a long, narrow treehouse as it sends you through the upper reaches of the wooded floodplain. Take a break and enjoy the view and the peaceful atmosphere high above one of the main rivers of central Illinois. You may notice how the river appears rather shallow—the main reason it never became the trade route through central Illinois that early settlers had hoped.

The good views continue for the next quarter mile as the trail follows the top of an embankment that sits above the surrounding landscape. When leaves have fallen, you'll get the full view of a wooded ridge to the left and agricultural fields and marshland about eighty feet below on the right.

Two miles ahead, you'll enter a stretch of trail resembling a big tunnel—earthen embankments on the sides of the trail and mature poplar, hickory, and sycamore offering a protective canopy overhead. Then comes the final bridge and another chance to soak up rural ambiance from the treetops. This high, dramatic trail bridge seems out of tune with the oddly tiny Cantrall Creek down below. As is the case with the other bridges on the trail, you can peek over the side to see the original metal and concrete railroad bridge infrastructure.

From the bridge, it's just 0.5 mile to the trail's northernmost parking area on Cantrall Creek Rd. and 1.5 miles to the north end of the trail at Irwin Bridge Rd. The Cantrall Creek Rd. parking area is a good place to start

A Railroad Built to Transport Coal

Like nearly every other railroad at the time, the rail line that now hosts the Sangamon Valley Trail was built for the sole purpose of transporting raw materials. In this case it was moving coal from mines just to the south in Macoupin County to fuel the steam engines operating on the Chicago and Northwestern Railroad. The six coal mines served by the railroad were also owned by the railroad, providing an in-house pipeline for powering the locomotives. Since this railroad wasn't built for passengers, it avoided population centers like downtown Springfield. Once diesel-powered locomotives began taking over in earnest in the 1950s, the railroad's need for coal began to decline and the need for this rail line soon disappeared.

if you're interested in a shorter trip and just seeing the great bridges of this trail.

Local Information

- Springfield Convention and Visitors Bureau, 109 N. Seventh Street, Springfield; (217) 789-2360; visitspringfieldillinois.com.
- Springfield Bicycle Club; (217)720-1568; spfldcycling.org. A local biking advocacy group.

Local Events/Attractions

- Abraham Lincoln Presidential Museum, 212 N. Sixth Street, Springfield; (800) 610-2094; alplm. org. This museum dedicated to Illinois's most famous figure has some high-tech attractions.

Restaurants

- Roots Latin Grill, 4127 Wabash Avenue, Springfield; (217) 679-7357; rootslatingrill.com. Inventive Latin food close to the south trailhead.
- Bella Milano, 4525 Wabash Avenue, Springfield; (217) 547-0011; bellamilanos.com/springfield. Italian fare close to south trailhead.

You may encounter curious onlookers in the cow pasture that sits right alongside the Sangamon Valley Trail.

Accommodations

- Courtyard by Marriott Springfield, 3462 Freedom Drive, Springfield; (217) 793-5300; marriott. com. One of a handful of chain hotels located close to south trailhead.
- Lincoln's New Salem State Historic Site, 15588 History Lane, Petersburg; (217) 632-4000; lincolnsnewsalem.com. Campground located next to a village recreated from Lincoln's youth.

37 STEVENS CREEK/ROCK SPRINGS TRAILS

If you crave riverside trails, this is one of the best in the state. As you follow Stevens Creek along the western edge of Decatur, the trail winds and wriggles about as much as the creek itself. And the lovely vistas just keep coming as you make your way to Rock Springs Conservation Area, the largest park in the county.

Location: From Greendell Park on the northwest side of Decatur, the trail meanders south alongside Stevens Creek to the Rock Springs Conservation Area.

Length: 6.5 miles with a couple of options for side trips that would add a few more miles.

Surface: Asphalt.

Wheelchair access: This route is wheelchair accessible.

Difficulty: Easy.

Restrooms: Restrooms and water are available near the trail in Fairview Park and at the Rock Creek Conservation Area.

Maps: bit.ly/decaturtrls; bit.ly/decaturbikemap.

Hazards: Flooding occurs on this route. Be sure to call ahead (217) 421-7493 for current trail conditions.

Access and parking: To reach the trailhead at Greendell Park from the north or the west, exit I-72 at IL 121 and head south. Two miles ahead, turn left on N. University Ave. and then turn left one block ahead on Green Oak Dr. The trail parking area is less than 1 mile ahead on the left. UTM coordinates: 16S, 0330799 E, 4416322 N.

To park on W. Center St. (roughly the halfway point in this route), head west on US 36 from I-72. At N. Sunnyside Rd., turn left. Where the road ends 1 mile ahead, turn right on W. Center St. The trail parking area is less than 1 mile ahead on the right.

To park at the Rock Springs Conservation Area, head east on US 36 from I-72. Turn right on N. Wyckles Rd., and then turn left on W. Rock

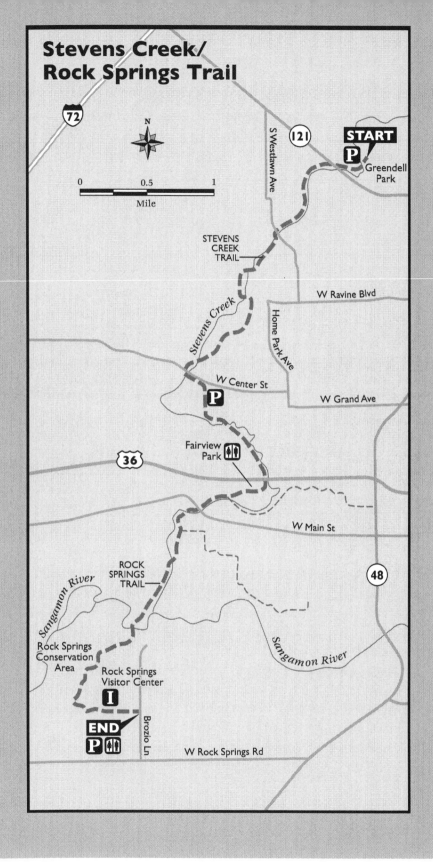

Springs Rd. Turn left on Brozio Ln. and follow signs to the visitor center, where the bike trail begins.

Contact: Decatur Park District, 620 E. Riverside Ave., Decatur; (217) 422-5911; decatur-parks.org. Plans are underway to extend this trail north 1.5 miles to Cresthaven Park.

The Trail

About 80 percent of this route follows Stevens Creek as it runs under heavy tree cover, through expansive bottomland woods, and past occasional bluffs. For a trail that runs through a fairly urban area, there's no shortage of natural beauty on the way south to Rock Springs Conservation Area.

Scenic Views along Stevens Creek

Only a mile or two into the trail you'll likely lose count of all the trail bridges you've crossed over Stevens Creek. Was that seven or eight bridges? Who knows? One thing for sure is that at each bridge you'll enjoy views up and down the riffley creek, and, as an added element, some of the bridges have mowed areas nearby that invite you to linger.

Among the many enjoyable features of this route are the wooded bluffs, mostly small, sometimes a little larger. As the trail mounts the bluffs, you're granted wider views of the creek and the surrounding bottomland. It's another way this trail gives you a feeling of constantly shifting scenery.

After crossing W. Center St. and another bridge over the creek, you'll see a historic marker kitty-corner to the trail parking area at the corner of Center and W. Hunt Streets. The plaque commemorates the namesake of Stevens Creek, Leonard Stevens, the first permanent white settler in the area who, in 1822, built a cabin on Stevens Creek. According to the sign, Stevens's forebears continued to hold much of the land in the immediate area.

If you're looking for a nice place to take a break, the bench at the Center St. trail parking area offers an ideal spot to take in the woodland, mostly poplars and pine. And you're likely to exchange friendly greetings with the occasional dog walker funneling onto the trail from the nearby suburban residential neighborhood.

Fairview Park and Its Spur Trails

Just after the trail ducks under a couple of large bridges—first a train bridge with monolithic concrete pillars and then under US 36—you'll enter Fairview Park, containing a popular dog run and plenty of spots to take a rest. If you're interested in exploring the rest of Fairview Park and want to add a couple miles to your trip, take the spur tail to the left. At the very least, pay a visit to the spur trail's nearby footbridge that soars high over Stevens Creek. And after the footbridge, you'll trace the top of a seventy-foot-high bluff towering above Stevens Creek.

Back on the main route, after crossing Stevens Creek again, there's another 1.5-mile spur trail heading left that will take you through a lovely restored prairie, a park, and on to the Sangamon River.

Explore Rock Springs

This trail just keeps getting better as you get closer to Rock Springs Conservation Area, the largest park in the county. As the maple-tree-laden bottomland woods escort you to the crossing of the Sangamon River, bluffs rise up on the sides of the trail. Soon, you'll pass through pristine prairie and start seeing offshoot foot trails that are part of the conservation area.

The trail climbs out of the floodplain through stands of oak and hickory before reaching the top of the bluff. You'll cut through a tallgrass prairie and then, just before reaching the Rock Springs parking area and nature center, you'll pass through a five-acre pine forest containing a fragrant mix of red and white pine. The conservation center has plenty of good picnicking spots, in addition to a visitor center and a historic farmstead exhibit.

Local Information

- Central Illinois Tourism Development Office, 700 E. Adams Street, Springfield; (217) 525-7980; visitcentralillinois.com.
- Decatur Area Convention and Visitors Bureau, 202 E. North Street, Decatur; (217) 423-7000; decaturcvb.com.

The lush greenery alongside Stevens Creek is a draw for local walkers.

- Decatur Bicycle Club, decaturbicycleclub.org. A local bicycling club that hosts rides and other social activities.

Local Events/Attractions

- Macon County Museum Complex, 5580 N. Fork Road, Decatur; (217) 422-4919; decaturcvb.com. Includes a log courthouse where Lincoln tried cases, a one-room schoolhouse, and several other historic buildings.
- Rock Springs Conservation Area, 3939 Nearing Lane, Decatur; (217) 423-7708; maconcounty-conservation.org. Contains ponds, hiking trails, and a homestead prairie farm exhibit; nature center has exhibits, live animal displays, and an art gallery.
- Scovill Park, 71 S. Country Club Road, Decatur; (217) 422-5911; decatur-parks.org. Has a zoo, a sculpture park, gardens, a children's museum; located on the south shore of Lake Decatur.

Restaurants

- Taproot, 170 N. Merchant Street, Decatur; (217) 330-6365; taprootdecatur.com. American fare; one of the better eateries in downtown Decatur.
- Gin Mill, 124 E. Prairie Street, Decatur; (217) 330-8073. Steak and seafood; outdoor seating in downtown Decatur.

Accommodations

- Friends Creek Regional Park, 13734 Friends Creek Park Road, Cisco; (217) 423-7708; macon-countyconservation.org. A county-owned park with a pleasant campground, hiking trails, and a historic schoolhouse.
- Holiday Inn & Suites, 5150 N. Wingate Drive, Decatur; (217) 542-5400; ihg.com/holidayinn. One of several chain hotels on the northern edge of Decatur.

Southern Illinois

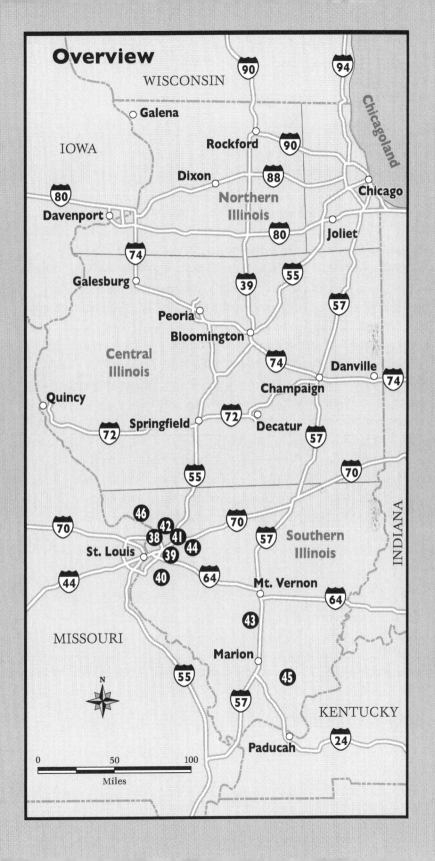

The Metro East region, located across the Mississippi River from St. Louis, claims the largest concentration of Illinois rail trails outside of Chicago. This extensive collection of trails offers many miles of uninterrupted running, walking, and cycling. You can explore Horseshoe Lake before heading up the bluffs to take a tour of communities such as Glen Carbon, Marysville, Edwardsville, and Leclaire. If you're looking for a peaceful escape, trails like the Quercus Grove, Nickel Plate, Ronald J. Foster, and Goshen Trails give you many miles of quiet rural ambiance peppered with attractive parks and pleasant small towns.

In northern Madison County, the historic river town of Alton serves as a jumping-off point for a couple of great trails that trace the shore of the Mississippi River. Heading downstream from Alton on the Confluence Trail takes you on top of a series of river levees and past a couple of museums. You'll see wetlands and a channel that was dug for river barge traffic. Heading upstream from Alton, the Vadalabene Great River Road Trail runs past miles of wooded and rocky bluffs on the shore of the Mississippi River, ending at the incomparable Pere Marquette State Park.

If Illinois had a rail trails hall of fame, the Tunnel Hill Trail would be one of the first inductees. Running nearly 50 miles from Eldorado south to the Cache River Wetlands, the trail gives visitors a taste of the breathtaking beauty within the 270,000-acre Shawnee National Forest. Ravines, rocky streams, and wooded bluffs figure prominently on the northern half of the trail. The southern half features bottomland woods, ponds, streams, and marshes within the internationally recognized Cache River Wetlands.

38 CONFLUENCE TRAIL

As you trace Mississippi River levees from Alton south to Granite City, you'll travel alongside the river and one of its channels, as well as adjoining ponds and wetlands. Be sure to give yourself time to explore a couple of museums right alongside the trail, one focusing on the Mississippi River and the other highlighting the explorations of Lewis and Clark.

Location: From Russell Commons Park in Alton, the trail follows the Mississippi River south to Granite City.

Length: 16.6 miles one-way.

Surface: Mostly asphalt; several miles of crushed gravel surface along the Chain of Rocks Canal.

Wheelchair access: The crushed gravel trail surface along the Chain of Rocks Canal can be rough in places.

Difficulty: The trail has a medium level of difficulty.

Restrooms: There are public restrooms and water at the trailhead, the Great River Museum, and the Lewis and Clark State Historic Site.

Maps: mcttrails.org; arcg.is/0TWv0D.

Hazards: While following the top of the levee, the trail regularly drops down steeply at the road crossings. Be careful navigating the gates on either side of the road crossings. Long stretches of this trail are wide open, offering no shelter from wind and sun.

Access and parking: From the St. Louis area take US 67 north across the Mississippi River. Getting off the bridge, continue left on US 67. Immediately turn left onto Ridge St. and follow it as it curves left. The park is on the left after you pass under the bridge.

From I-55 head west on IL 140. Stay on IL 140 through Alton until you reach Broadway St. Turn right on Broadway and then turn left on IL 143 and then right on Discovery Parkway. Russell Commons Park is on the right. Pick up the trail across Discovery Parkway from Russell Commons Park. UTM coordinates: 15S, 745303 E, 4307691 N.

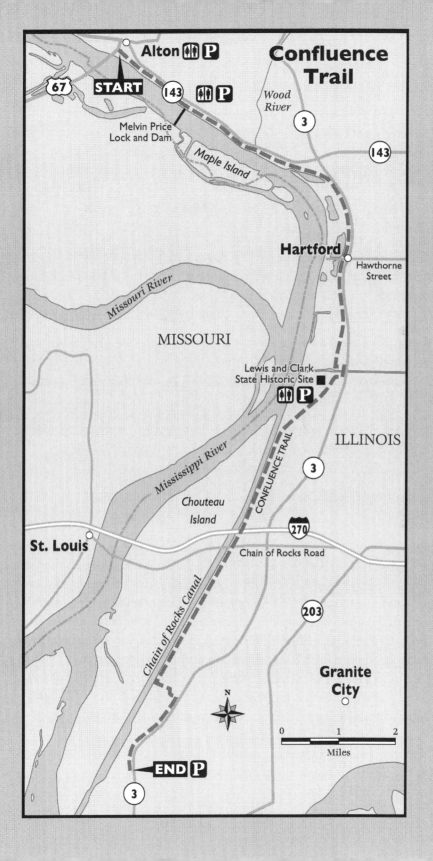

To park at the Melvin Price Locks and Dam, head southeast of Alton on IL 143. The entrance is on the right.

To park at Lewis and Clark State Historic Site, head southeast of Alton on IL 143. Turn right onto IL 3. Cross the Cahokia Diversion Channel; the entrance is on the right.

To park at the south end of the trail, head north on IL 3 from I-55 in East St. Louis. Turn left on W. 20th St. and the parking area is immediately on the left.

Transportation: Madison County's #1, #1X, #, #9, and #24X buses connects with the Confluence Trail. The bus route map at mct.org shows local bus routes and the county trails.

Amtrak stations are in Alton, St. Louis, and Carlinville.

Rentals: The Bike Factory, 616 Franklin Ave., Edwardsville; (618) 659-8706; thebikefactory.com.

Covered Bridge Bike Rental, 195 S. Main St., Glen Carbon; (618) 205-3132; coveredbridgebikerental.com.

Contact: Madison County Trails, One Transit Way, Granite City; (618) 874-7433; www.mcttrails.org.

Alton is an old river town built on the side of a bluff above the Mississippi. Its streets are lined with historic storefronts containing antiques shops, restaurants, and bars. Among Alton's famous residents are Robert Wadlow—the ten-foot-tall man who's honored with a life-sized statue near the Alton history museum and Elijah Lovejoy, an abolitionist newspaper publisher who was killed by a proslavery mob in 1837. A monument to Lovejoy is located in a cemetery several blocks from the trailhead of the Confluence Trail. The trail starts underneath the town's most striking landmark, a nearly 1-mile-long bridge over the Mississippi River built in 1994. As soon as the trail takes you up on the levee from Russell Commons Park, you'll see the bridge's dramatic design featuring a series of cables fanning out from two main high supports that look a bit like a ship's masts and riggings waiting for the sails to be hoisted.

Melvin Price Lock and Dam

As you follow this trail along the system of Metro East levees—sometimes close to the river and other times further away—the good views abound. But keep in mind you'll be going through some urban industrial areas and the trail runs alongside highways for much of the way.

This initial joyous stretch of trail runs some forty to fifty feet above the river's shoreline, where you'll see occasional herons wading in shallow water. At about the same time the Clark Bridge was built, the massive Melvin Price Lock and Dam opened just south of Alton. Of the twenty-five locks and dams on Upper Mississippi, this one is unusual because it has its own museum. The Great Rivers Museum, situated alongside the trail, allows visitors to tour the 0.3-mile-long lock and peruse an engaging collection of exhibits on the human and natural history associated with the river.

Continuing south from the lock, the trail crosses the Wood River and passes a sprawling oil refinery operation and the tiny industrial town of Hartford. From the raised levee, glimpses through the trees come and go of the river and the barges moored near the shore. When the trail moves inland away from the river, wetlands and reservoirs multiply. In a handful of spots, the trail takes a quick dip down to cross a road and then quickly rises back up on the levee.

Honoring Lewis and Clark

South of Hartford, the slender 150-foot structure on the left that looks like a guard tower at a futuristic prison is actually a monument dedicated to the Lewis and Clark Expedition. By taking an elevator or stairs to the top of this silvery tower, visitors can see the confluence of the Mississippi and Missouri Rivers.

After the wood-and-steel bridge over the Cahokia Diversion Channel, you'll arrive at the Lewis and Clark State Historic Site. The museum is located on the spot where the expedition set up camp and spent the winter of 1803–1804 before heading westward on the Missouri River. The most impressive exhibit in the museum is the full-size replica of the expedition's fifty-five-foot boat that was dragged, paddled, and sailed on the Missouri River. One side of the boat is cut away to show the boat's interior and all the carefully packed items. The grassy backyard of the museum contains a replica of the log fort built by the expedition.

Chain of Rocks Canal and Bridge

From the museum the trail runs through a swath of grassland before meeting up with the Chain of Rocks Canal, an 8.4-mile-long waterway that allows river traffic to bypass a series of treacherous rock ledges in the river's main channel. Just before pulling alongside the canal, look to the right for a view of the full Mississippi River. (The confluence with the Missouri River is 1 mile upstream and out of view.) The straight-as-an-arrow canal is treeless and edged by piles of riprap. Look for waterbirds hanging out in the many wetland areas along the trail.

Along this stretch there's an excellent side trip for cyclists that will take you across the Mississippi on a spectacular foot bridge to the 11-mile-long Riverfront Trail in Missouri (see Major Milepoints for directions). The side trip takes you on a 3-mile-long trip on the quiet Chain of Rocks Rd. to Chouteau Island. On the island, you can cross the Mississippi River on the Chain of Rocks Bridge. Once the bridge for the historic Route 66 but now only open to people on foot and on bikes, this nearly 1-mile-long bridge is one of the unsung treasures of the region. The views, seventy feet or so above the river, are breathtaking. The Missouri side of the bridge connects to the north end of the Riverfront Trail, which leads all the way to downtown St. Louis. For people with energy to burn, the 5.7-mile-long Eagle Points Trail on Chouteau Island could be another side trip. It runs south

The Levees of Metro East

The Confluence Trail follows a system of levees along the Mississippi River built and maintained by the Army Corps of Engineers. This 75-mile-long flood control system offers flood protection for nearly 300,000 people who live on the Illinois side of the river. The Army Corps levees are just some of the levees in the area. Many other local levees protect patches of farmland or small segments of a community.

from Chain of Rocks Rd. along the west shoreline of the Chain of Rocks Canal to where it meets up with the Mississippi River.

Major Milepoints

11.6   Side trip to Chain of Rocks Bridge: After passing under I-270, take the connector trail left and then turn right on S. Slough Rd.

11.9   Turn left on W. Chain of Rocks Rd.

12.2   Turn right on W. Chain of Rocks Rd. and cross the Chain of Rocks Canal.

12.9   Levee Rd. on the left will take you to the Eagle Points Trail.

14.1   Arrive at the Chain of Rocks Bridge parking area.

Local Information

- Great Rivers and Routes of Southwestern Illinois, 200 Piasa Street, Alton; (618) 465-6676; riversandroutes.com
- Illinois South Tourism, 4387 N. Illinois Street, Suite 200, Swansea; (618) 257-1488; illinoisouth.org

Local Events/Attractions

- Elijah P. Lovejoy Monument, 1299 E. 5th Street, Alton; (800) 258-6645; bit.ly/elmonument; a ninety-foot pillar topped with a bronze statue of victory honoring this hero of the Illinois abolitionists movement; at the Alton City Cemetery; open dawn to dusk.
- Lewis and Clark State Historic Site, 1 Lewis and Clark Trail, Hartford; (618) 251-5811; campdubois.com. Free museum (with a giftshop) offers a thorough introduction to the famous expedition at the site where they spent the winter.
- National Great Rivers Museum, at the Melvin Price Locks and Dam 26; IL 143 in East Alton; (618) 462-6979; mtrf.org. Delves into many aspects of Mississippi River culture. Video exhibits, a gift shop, and a model of a historic riverboat.

Restaurants

- State Street Market, 208 State Street, Alton; (618) 462-8800; statestreetmarketofalton.com; a local favorite featuring soups and sandwiches for lunch and more upscale dinner options; on the river.
- Tony's, 312 Piasa Street, Alton; (618) 462-8384; tonysrestaurant.com. Known for steaks and Italian food.

Accommodations

- The Beall Mansion, 407 E. 12th Street, Alton; (866) 843-2325; beallmansion.com. This 1903 mansion contains a museum; on the National Register of Historic Places.

- Pere Marquette Lodge and Conference Center, 13653 Lodge Boulevard, Grafton; (618) 786-2331; pmlodge.net. Rooms, cabins, campground, and a restaurant at one of the most scenic state parks in Illinois.

39 GOSHEN TRAIL

As you follow the Goshen Trail through a string of suburban Metro East communities, you'll encounter long, pleasant stretches of trail uninterrupted by roads, typically with mature trees towering overhead. Along the way, you'll also be treated with dramatic bridges, a bustling shopping area (with trailside eating options), and a nature preserve worth a visit.

Location: From the northern edge of O'Fallon in Metro East, the trail guides you north to Roxana.

Length: 19.5 miles.

Surface: Asphalt.

Wheelchair access: The trail is wheelchair accessible.

Difficulty: Moderately difficult if you're going the full distance.

Restrooms: Public restrooms are available at the south trailhead, at the Watershed Nature Center, and at the northern trailhead.

Maps: mcttrails.org.

Hazards: There are no hazards on the route.

Access and parking: From I-64, head north on N. Illinois St. (IL 159) at exit 12. Nearly 1 mile ahead turn right on Milburn School Rd. About 3 miles ahead, go north Simmons Rd. at the roundabout and then several blocks ahead, turn right on Kyle Rd. The trailhead is less than 0.5 mile ahead on the left. UTM coordinates: 16S, 0245642 E, 4278446 N.

To park at the trail parking area on Old Troy Rd.: From I-55, take exit 18 and follow Edwardsville Rd. (IL 162) west for 1 mile. Turn right on Old Troy Rd., and the parking area is immediately on the right.

To park at the north end of the trail at the Watershed Trail Parking Area, take exit 5 from IL 255 and head east on Madison Ave. Immediately turn left on Wanda Rd. and then immediately turn right on Russell Dr. The parking area is on the right.

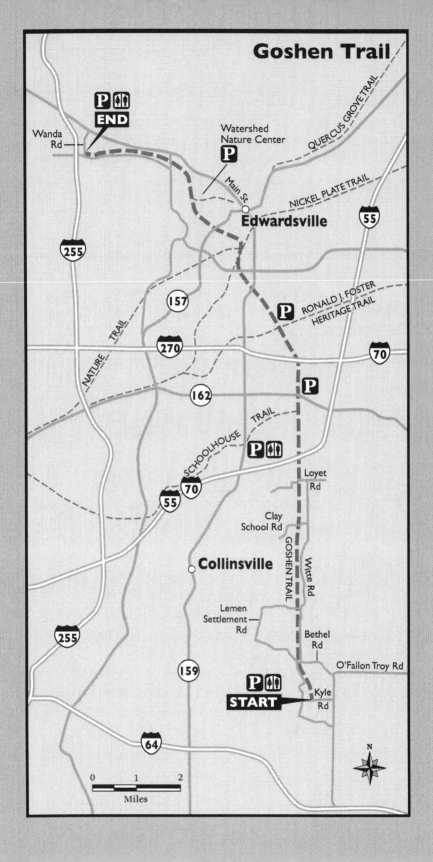

Transportation: Seven different Madison County bus lines—#7, #13X, #14X, #16, #16X, #19, #22—connect with the northern half of the Goshen Trail. The bus route map at mct.org shows the bus routes and the trails.

The closest Amtrak stations are in St. Louis, Carlinville, and Alton.

Rentals: The Bike Factory, 616 Franklin Ave., Edwardsville, IL; thebikefactory.com.

Covered Bridge Bike Rental, 195 S. Main St., Glen Carbon, IL; (618) 205-3132; coveredbridgebikerental.com

Contact: Madison County Transit Trails, 1 Transit Way, Pontoon Beach, IL; (618) 797-4600; mcttrails.org. The website offers suggestions for combining this trail with others to form a loop.

While the Goshen Trail is never busy, it's a well-used trail, for sure—particularly when compared to the more rural Madison County trails like the Nickel Plate and Quercus Grove Trails. One reason for the Goshen Trail's popularity might be related to how it connects to a number of other major trails in Madison County's famous collection of rail trails. Another draw is the 7-mile extension that was added on the south end of the trail in 2019, connecting Collinsville Township and O'Fallon with the existing trail in Edwardsville, Glen Carbon, and Troy.

Creeks, Ravines, and a Big Green Tunnel

After starting at the south end of the trail, rolling terrain dominates and big trailside ravines open on the sides of the trail. Amid the topsy-turvy landscape, the trail, of course, remains flat—a reminder of the extent that railroads went to and the brute force employed to keep the train tracks on level ground. When ravines appear on this trail, you may notice that a creek is never far away. In this case, the ravines at the trail's onset escort you to a seventy-foot-high bridge with spellbinding views above Ogles Creek.

As you leave the creek and ravines behind, mature specimens of cottonwood and oak will capture your attention as they rise to great heights from the sides of the trail. Plenty of smaller trees like sassafras and dogwood also attract your attention. Occasionally, the veil of trees falls away, revealing big expanses of farmland, sometimes coming right to the edge of the trail.

About 4 miles into the trail, you'll find loads of scenery to soak in as you mount a 200-foot-long bridge, over-active train tracks, a small creek, and Lockman Rd. Continuing on, there are more ravines and more small creeks, and plenty of mature trees that make the trail feel like a big green tunnel.

Trail Connections and a Shopping District

Trail builders were likely gritting their teeth when they constructed the awkward C-shaped route the Goshen Trail takes around I-55/I-70, which involves a block-long on-street section and two street crossings. Leaving the expressway behind, you'll soon reach another trail bridge with commanding views—this one over Canteen Creek.

As you come across a series of trail junctions that connect you with more than 100 miles of Madison County Trails, you'll notice that trail signs are unfortunately absent; instead, look to the nearby map board. First is the Schoolhouse Trail, followed by the Ronald J. Foster Heritage Trail, and the Nickel Plate Trail.

Between those last two trail junctions, the trail cuts through the suburban shopping areas of Glen Carbon and Edwardsville. While the strip malls, big box stores, a cinema multiplex, and even a golf driving range all provide an interesting distraction, the trail feels removed from the surrounding hustle and bustle as it tunnels under the traffic-laden streets, allowing you to continue on your merry way.

After passing under Governors Parkway and before meeting up with the Nickel Plate Trail, an enormous rusting water tank, a remnant of steam engines that plied the former railroad, appears on the side of the trail. You'll cross a couple of small creeks and encounter a final dose of rolling terrain as the trail curves to the east.

Watershed Nature Center

The next trail junction is with the Watershed Trail, which leads you to Watershed Nature Center, just a quarter mile off the Goshen Trail, to the right. The nature center offers a pleasant spot for respite—complete with benches to enjoy great views of a sprawling marsh active with birds. There's a 1-mile-long hiking loop around a couple of small lakes that takes you through woodland, prairie, and marshland (bikes are not allowed on the hiking trails).

Just after the Nature Trail junction, you'll enjoy more stellar views from the tree tops on a soaring bridge over Cahokia Creek. The terrain flattens for the final few miles of the trail as it runs alongside several different roads—some busy, others less so. The trail comes to an end shortly after crossing Indian Creek.

Local Information

- Illinois South Tourism, 4387 N. Illinois Street, Suite 200, Swansea; (618) 257-1488; illinoisouth.org.

Local Events/Attractions

- Bella Vista Winery, 6633 E. Main Street, Maryville, (618) 365-6280; bellavistail.com. Sandwiches, pizza, and a variety of wines; located close to the trail.
- Watershed Nature Center, 1591 Tower Avenue, Edwardsville; (618) 692-7578; watershednaturecenter.org. One-mile loop walk runs through a variety of environments; connected to Goshen trail with short spur trail.

Several bridges on the Goshen Trail take you into the treetops for commanding views of the surrounding terrain.

Restaurants

- Global Brew Tap House, 2329 Plum Street, Edwardsville; (618) 307-5858; edwardsville.global-brew.com. Regional chain that specializes in grilled cheese sandwiches; extensive beer selection; located on the trail.
- Gulf Shores Restaurant and Grill, 215 Harvard Drive, Edwardsville; (618) 650-9109; gulfshores-restaurantandgrill.com. Seafood, gumbo, sandwiches, and more; located a half mile off the trail.

Accommodations

- Holiday Inn Express Troy, 2011 Formosa Road, Troy; (618) 667-2301; bit.ly/hixtroy. Located less than 1 mile from the trail; indoor pool.
- Horseshoe Lake State Park, 3321 IL 111, Granite City; (618) 931-0270; bit.ly/hlstatepark. Forty-eight campsites located on an island; convenient location.

40 METROBIKELINK TRAIL

No question that the MetroBikeLink Trail is one of the best new multi-use trails in the state. Why? Mostly it's because the scenery is persistently interesting, toggling between town and country as you follow the route of the MetroLink commuter train through Metro East.

Location: From the Fairview Heights MetroLink Station in Metro East, the trail runs alongside the commuter train line southeast to the Scott Airforce Base.

Length: 14 miles with several options to take side trips totaling another 7 miles.

Surface: Asphalt.

Wheelchair access: Yes, the trail is wheelchair accessible as is the MetroLink commuter train.

Difficulty: Easy.

Restrooms: Restrooms available at the Pump Station parking area (the second turnoff on the right south of Swansea Station); restrooms also available at the MetroLink Belleville Station.

Maps: bit.ly/metrobikelink; scctd.org/metrobikelink.

Hazards: When passing the train stations on this trail, watch for people walking to the stations and sometimes waiting for trains on the trail. As you would in any urban setting, keep watch of what's happening around you. Every mile or two, emergency call stations are available along the trail.

Access and parking: Ample parking is available at all six of the MetroLink stations along the trail.

To park at Fairview Heights MetroLink Station: From I-64 take exit 9 south on IL 157. Less than 1 mile ahead, turn left on St. Clair Ave. The Fairview Heights MetroLink Station is just ahead on the left. UTM coordinates: 15S, 0757192 E, 4275950 N.

To park at the Belleville MetroLink Station: From I-64 take exit 12 to IL 159 south. Proceed 4 miles and turn left on N. Douglas Ave. Turn left again

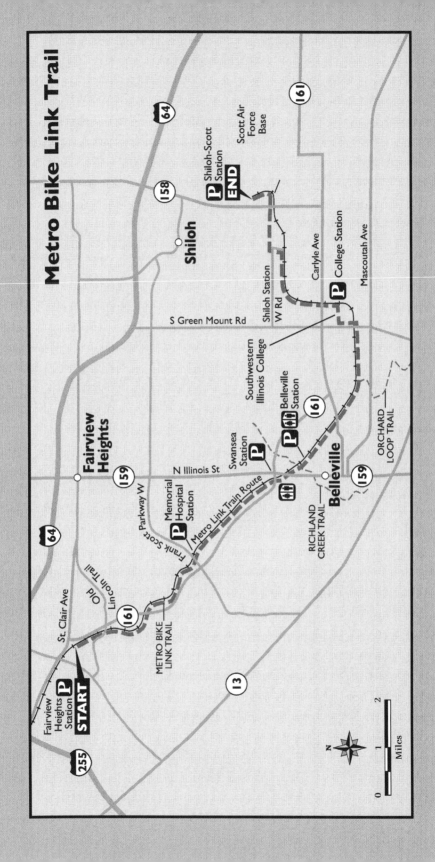

onto Scheel St. MetroLink parking is a block and a half ahead, at the end of the street.

To park at Shiloh-Scott Metrolink Station: From I-64 take exit 19B south on IL 158. Proceed for 2.3 miles to the entrance to the Metrolink station on the left.

Transportation: The MetroLink commuter train makes it very easy to reach the trail from St. Louis. Also, there are multiple Metro bus routes that serve the trail: #1, #12, #14, #15, #16, #17, #17X, #20X, #21, #21X. You can bring your bike aboard MetroLink trains and MetroBuses.

Amtrak trains serve St. Louis.

Rentals: The Bike Factory, 616 Franklin Ave., Edwardsville; thebikefactory. com.

Covered Bridge Bike Rental, 195 S. Main St., Glen Carbon; (618) 205-3132; coveredbridgebikerental.com.

Contact: St. Clair County Transit District, 27 N. Illinois St., Belleville; (618) 628-8090; scctd.org/metrobikelink.

While using the Metrolink Bike Trail, every ten minutes or so you'll hear the oddly soothing sound of metal-sliding-on-metal as the MetroLink Red Line train careens by on the nearby tracks—and if you're lucky, one of the conductors will give you a beep as they pass. The Red MetroLink Line is the older and longer of the two St. Louis regional commuter train routes, running 38 miles between Lambert Airport in Missouri and Scott Air Force Base in Illinois. The bike trail shadows just a small section of the train's route through the Metro East towns of Fairview Heights, Belleville, and Swansea. Newer trains and tracks means the trains are church-mouse quiet.

Some of the best miles of this trail are the first four or five as you snake your way underneath wooded bluffs, duck under overpasses, cross wooden bridges, mount small hills, drop back down, and follow the path of Schoenberger Creek as it wiggles its way through the bottom of a ravine.

A Coal Train

The MetroLink train and its accompanying trail use the route of a railroad built in the late 1800s to transport coal from local mines. This railroad helped trigger a coal mining boom in the area, spurring dozens of coal mines to open in Belleville and the surrounding communities. Much of the entire county, in fact, sits on top of former underground coal mines.

After the lively first section along Shoenberger Creek, the trail weaves through a mature forest, offering a pleasant leafy canopy overhead, just before reaching the Memorial Hospital MetroLink Station. After the hospital station, the trail gets squeezed in between the tracks on one side and metal fencing on the other.

Trail Connections

After ducking under one highway (IL 161) and then shooting over another (IL 159), you'll encounter turnoffs going north and south for the Richland Creek path. The first option takes you north on a winding scenic path alongside Richland Creek to Centennial Park. The next turnoff takes you south, also following the creek through a handful of smaller parks featuring some trailside sculpture and a number of street crossings. If you have time, these are both worthwhile diversions totaling about 3 miles.

As you get closer to Southwestern Illinois College, the landscape becomes a little more rural, a little less urban. Also on this section of the trail, you'll see the turnoff for the 4-mile-long Orchard Loop Trail, which takes a circuitous route south by a local school, through apple orchards, and by a local attraction called Eckert's Country Store & Farms.

College Campus and an Air Force Base

When you reach the campus of Southwestern Illinois College, stay to the right, passing the athletic buildings and sports fields. This campus—built in the early 1970s—is the largest of college's three campuses that host a total of about 10,000 students.

With the college campus behind you and the final 3 miles of the trail ahead of you, you'll pass through a suburban shopping area, and then, suddenly, agricultural land sprawls in every direction and a peaceful atmosphere reigns.

You'll encounter the end of the line—for the train and for the trail—at Scott Air Force Base. The base, which employs some 13,000 people and has more than 2,500 residents, was established in 1917 after the United States entered World War I. Over the years, it served as the main location for developing Army air balloons and dirigibles, and during World War II, was the main training center for military airplane radio operators.

At the Shiloh-Scott MetroLink Station, you'll have the option to conveniently hop on the train to head back to the starting point.

Local Information

- City of Belleville, 101 S. Illinois Street, Belleville; (618) 233-6810; bit.ly/bvtourism.

Local Events/Attractions

- Eckert's Country Store & Farms, 951 S. Greenmount Road, Belleville; (618) 233-0513; eckerts. com. Various family-oriented activities; several dining options; accessible from the Orchard Loop Trail.
- Victorian Home Museum, 701 E. Washington Street, Belleville; (618) 234-0600; bit.ly/bvi-chouse. A fine 1866 home with period decor, located blocks from the trail.

The entire MetroBikeLink Trail follows a segment of the route of the Red MetroLink commuter train that runs between St. Louis and Metro East in Illinois.

Restaurants

- 1428 Tap Haus, 1428 N. Illinois Street, Swansea; (618) 416-5512; 1428taphausbeer.com. Good selection of local beers and bar food; beer garden; located very close to the trail.
- Hofbräuhaus St. Louis-Belleville, 123 St. Eugene Drive, Belleville; (618) 800-2337; hbbelleville.com. Traditional Bavarian music, cuisine, and beer provided in large beer hall atmosphere located across the street from one of the largest Catholic shrines in the nation.

Accommodations

- Holiday Inn St. Louis-Fairview Heights, 313 Salem Place, Fairview Heights; (618) 212-1300; ihg.com. On-site bar/restaurant and indoor pool; located close to the trail.
- Horseshoe Lake State Park, 3321 IL 111, Granite City; (618) 931-0270; bit.ly/hlstatepark. Forty-eight campsites located on an island.

41 NICKEL PLATE TRAIL

There's loads to take in while on the longest trail in Metro East: lush woodland alongside Judy's Branch Creek, an assortment of trailside parks, the sprawling rural landscape, and the unusual historic community of Leclaire.

Location: From the Glen Carbon Park & Ride Lot near the intersection of IL 157 and IL 162 in Metro East, the trail heads northeast to the small town of New Douglas.

Length: 25.4 miles.

Surface: Asphalt on the western one-third of the trail and crushed gravel on the remainder.

Wheelchair access: The crushed gravel on the trail surface is hard packed and in good condition for wheelchair use.

Difficulty: Moderate to difficult because of the length.

Restrooms: Public restrooms and water at Miners Park; Edwardsville Township Park; Alhambra County Park, and restrooms are available at the Rec Plex in New Douglas (just north of the trailhead).

Maps: mcttrails.org.

Hazards: Watch for traffic at the street crossings. Long stretches of the trail offer little protection from wind and sun. Once you're out in the countryside, trailside amenities are scarce.

Access and parking: Park at the Glen Carbon Park and Ride. From I-270, take exit 9 and head south on N. Bluff Rd. (IL 157). The trail parking area is one 1 ahead on the right. (Note: The south end trail is a couple miles to the south, but this is southernmost parking area.) UTM coordinates: 15S, 0760482 E, 4292389 N.

To access the Nickel Plate Trail at Edwardsville Township Park, head north from I-270 at exit 12 on Troy Rd. (IL 159). Stay on IL 159 for 1.8 miles until turning left on Center Grove Rd. The entrance to the park is on the left.

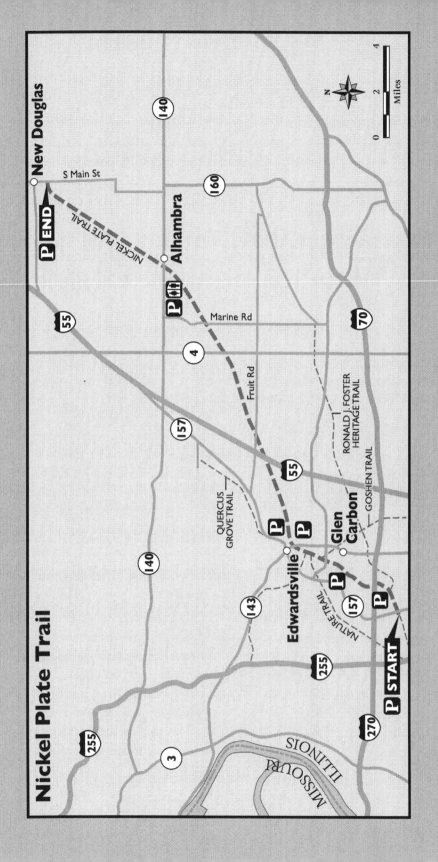

To access the Nickel Plate Trail from the Schwarz Rd. parking area, exit west on Marine Rd. (IL 143) from I-55. The trailhead parking area is at the corner of Marine and Schwarz Roads, about 2.5 miles ahead.

To park in the Alhambra, take exit 30 from I-55 and head west. Follow State St. (IL 140) for 5.2 miles to Alhambra County Park (Landolt Dr.) on the right. Access the trail in the far southeastern corner of the park.

To park at the north end of the trail in New Douglas, take exit 37 from I-55 and head east. Follow New Douglas Rd. for 6.4 miles to New Douglas. Turn right on S. Main St., and the trailhead parking is 0.5 mile ahead on the left.

Transportation: Madison County's #22 bus connects with the south end of the Nickel Plate Trail. The bus route map at mct.org shows local bus routes and the county trails.

The closest Amtrak stations are in St. Louis, Carlinville, and Alton.

Rentals: The Bike Factory, 616 Franklin Ave., Edwardsville; thebikefactory. com

Covered Bridge Bike Rental, 195 S. Main St., Glen Carbon; (618) 205-3132; coveredbridgebikerental.com. This rental service is located steps from the trail.

Contact: Madison County Trails, One Transit Way, Granite City; (618) 874-7433; mcttrails.org. The website offers suggestions for combining this trail with others to form a loop.

Within Metro East's astounding 220 miles of multi-use trails, the Nickel Plate Trail stands out as the longest and perhaps the most varied. Throughout its length, you'll experience a full range of environments within the region. The western, more urban part of the trail runs through the towns of Glen Carbon and Edwardsville while the eastern portion exposes you to the wide open farmland of rural Madison County.

Glen Carbon and Edwardsville

The first several miles of this trail bring you by a few pleasant urban parks in Glen Carbon and Edwardsville. First, though, you'll pass by a small covered bridge spanning Judy's Branch Creek on S. Main St. in Glen Carbon. Originally built in 1934, the covered bridge has been rebuilt twice over the years, most recently in 2008. For the next couple of miles after passing the access trails for Miner Park, you'll catch occasional glimpses of Judy's Branch Creek through the woodland. Just beyond where the trail passes under I-270, a spur trail on the right leads up a steep bluff to a collection of pleasant biking and hiking trails at Greenspace North Conservation Area. Not far ahead, the trail grazes another park, Edwardsville Township Park, which contains a display of a naval fighter plane.

As several trails come together, keep an eye on your route to ensure you stay on the Nickel Plate Trail. Continuing ahead, the trail runs by a satellite campus of Lewis and Clark Community College, where you'll encounter a handful of historic manufacturing buildings that were the centerpiece of Leclaire, a factory town founded in 1890 by an enlightened industrialist named N. O. Nelson.

Into the Countryside

Leaving Edwardsville, the industrial legacy of the area is again on display as you pass a brick manufacturer in operation since 1880. Brick making and coal mining both claim a long history in Edwardsville. Just after the brickyard, the trail mounts a seventy-five-foot-high earthen embankment, towering over a deep, wooded ravine containing Mooney Creek.

The landscape flattens as agricultural fields take over. After passing the Oak Brook Golf Club on the right, the trail dips down toward a swathe of wetlands and woods before crossing Silver Creek and one of its tributaries. You'll be tempted to take a photo or two at a nonprofit rescue organization for wild horses and burros called the Legendary Mustang Sanctuary, which has a large horse pen right alongside the trail on Klenke Rd. Beyond the Mustang Sanctuary is one of the most pleasing sections on the northern half of the trail: Mature trees offer a pleasant canopy overhead, and every now and then, the railroad embankment offers expansive views of the surrounding woodland.

Alhambra

Alhambra gives you the only chance on the northern 20 miles of the trail to hit a restaurant or a convenience store. You'll also find a municipal park with a small lake that offers a relaxing spot to take a break. Alhambra was reportedly named after Washington Irving's book, *Tales of the Alhambra*, about a Moorish castle in Spain. Since Alhambra means "red castle" in Arabic, it's entertaining to know that next to Alhambra in Illinois was a town that locals decided to name Green Castle. As the story goes, the two towns were engaged in a rivalry, but eventually reconciled and combined in 1884 under the name Alhambra.

The final 5 miles feature big views of the surrounding landscape interrupted occasionally by small pockets of trees. The only company you're likely to have on this peaceful stretch of trail are the songbirds flitting among the trailside prairie plants and the occasional tractor in the field. The trail ends with little fanfare in New Douglas, another tiny agricultural town with its roots in coal mining.

No Ordinary Factory Town

Called one of the nation's first examples of profit sharing and one of the most successful attempts at cooperative living, the town of Leclaire was founded in 1890 by plumbing supply manufacturer N. O. Nelson. Nelson was far out of step with the captains of industry of his time: He sought to create a company where workers were treated in an exemplary fashion, with excellent working conditions. The company offered employees affordable homes, easy access to parks and recreation, and free education. Now part of Edwardsville, more than 400 homes and a collection of manufacturing buildings (located right alongside the Nickel Plate Trail) comprise the 200-acre Leclaire Historic District.

Local Information

- Illinois South Tourism, 4387 N. Illinois Street, Suite 200, Swansea; (618) 257-1488; illinoisouth.org.

Alongside the Nickel Plate Trail is a nonprofit dedicated to rescuing horses and burros.

Local Events/Attractions

- Colonel Benjamin Stephenson House, 409 S. Buchanan Street, Edwardsville; (618) 692-1818; stephensonhouse.org. A restored home, now a museum, built in 1820 by a local politician; located one block from the trail.

- Friends of Leclaire, (618) 656-1294; historic-leclaire.org. Learn about the history of this unusual factory town and its annual festival; a video about the history of Leclaire is dated, but worth a look; bit.ly/leclairevid.
- Glen Carbon Heritage Museum, 124 School Street, Glen Carbon; (618) 288-7271; bit.ly/glenc-museum. Museum is housed in an old schoolhouse and around the corner at 148 Main Street is a display of an 1850s cabin; limited hours; easily accessible from the trail through Miners Park.
- Legendary Mustang Sanctuary, 10107 Klenke Road, Alhambra; (618) 616-8875; legendarymus-tangsanctuary.org. The nonprofit hosts events and programs.

Restaurants

- Peel Wood Fired Pizza, 921 S. Arbor Vitae, Edwardsville; (618) 659-8561; peelpizza.com. Located steps from the trail near the Leclaire Historic District; brew their own beer.
- Maedge's Restaurant & Convenience Store, 709 E. Main Street, Alhambra, (618) 488-6400; bit.ly/maedges. Basic diner combined with a convenience store; located one-third of a mile off the trail.
- Mr. Currys India Restaurant, 7403 Marine Road (IL 143), Edwardsville; (618) 692-3892; mrcur-rys.com. Affordable lunch buffet; plenty of vegetarian options; homemade sauce for sale.

Accommodations

- Holiday Inn Express & Suites Edwardsville, 1000 Plummer Drive, Edwardsville; (618) 692-7255; bit.ly/edholidayinn. Located close to Southern Illinois University Edwardsville and right alongside Madison County's Nature Trail.
- Shale Lake Cabins and Cottages, 1499 Washington Avenue, Williamson; (618) 637-2470; shalewine.com. Pleasant location close to New Douglas at the Shale Lake Winery.
- Horseshoe Lake State Park, 3321 IL 111, Granite City; (618) 931-0270; bit.ly/hlstatepark. Forty-eight campsites located on an island.

42 QUERCUS GROVE TRAIL

The Quercus Grove Trail shadows long stretches of the historic Route 66, taking you to three small towns and giving you options for seeing Route 66–related attractions along the way. Like its sister the Nickel Plate Trail, the Quercus Grove Trail takes you to the furthest reaches of the Metro East region where farms and open views prevail.

Location: Starting north of Edwardsville in Metro East, the trail runs northeast to Staunton.

Length: 15.9 miles one way.

Surface: Asphalt with a short section of crushed gravel on the north end of the trail.

Wheelchair access: Three brief on-road sections are not wheelchair friendly. The rest of the trail is wheelchair accessible.

Difficulty: Moderate because of the length.

Restrooms: Restrooms are available in Hamel Community Park, located a few blocks off the trail; Worden Community Park; and the small park at the north end of the trail in Staunton.

Maps: mcttrails.org.

Hazards: Long stretches of the trail offer little protection from wind and sun; watch for poison ivy on the sides of the trail in the more rural areas.

Access and parking: To park on Old Carpenter Rd.: If coming from I-270, head north on IL 157 at exit 9. Follow IL 157 for about 7 miles, passing through Edwardsville, to Old Carpenter Rd., where you'll turn left. The parking area is on the left. If coming from I-55 from the north, take exit 30 to Hamel and head east on E. State St. Turn left on IL 157 and follow it for 6 miles to Old Carpenter Rd., where you'll turn right. The parking area is on the left. (Note: The trail actually starts 1.5 miles south of this parking area in downtown Edwardsville, but there is no designated parking area close the south trailhead. The parking area on Old Carpenter Rd. is the

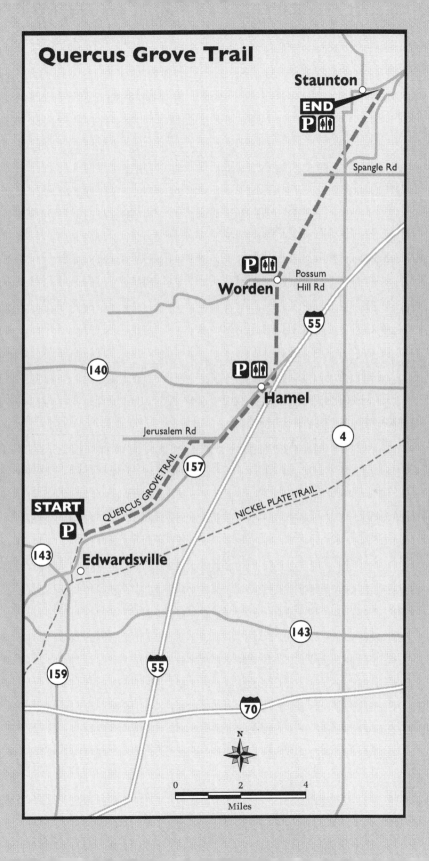

southernmost parking spot on the trail.) UTM coordinates: 16S, 0245284 E, 4302048 N.

To park in Worden, take I-55 to exit 33. Go north on IL 4, and then turn left on Possum Hill Rd. and follow it for nearly 2 miles to the entrance to Worden Community Park on the right.

To park in Staunton at the north trailhead, take I-55 to exit 41. Head west on Staunton Rd. for 2 miles. Turn left on S. Union St.; park in the small park at the water tower directly ahead.

Transportation: Madison County's #22 bus connects with the south end of the Quercus Grove Trail and several other bus lines come in close proximity. The bus route map at mct.org shows the bus routes and the county trails.

The closest Amtrak stations are in St. Louis, Carlinville, and Alton.

Rentals: The Bike Factory, 616 Franklin Ave., Edwardsville; thebikefactory.com.

Covered Bridge Bike Rental, 195 S. Main St., Glen Carbon; (618) 205-3132; coveredbridgebikerental.com.

Contact: Madison County Transit Trails, 1 Transit Way, Pontoon Beach; (618) 797-4600; mcttrails.org. The website offers suggestions for combining this trail with others to form a loop.

The entire Quercus Grove Trail runs in close proximity—and sometimes even right alongside—the historic Route 66, the roadway that once connected Chicago and Los Angeles. On the trail, you'll experience the pleasures that travelers encountered on Route 66 when it was built nearly a century ago—the joy of big open spaces punctuated every so often by the charming small towns of America.

Following the Mother Road

During the first 4 miles of the trail, thick greenery on the sides of the trail opens up every now and then to reveal the agricultural land sprawling in every direction. You'll also catch glimpses of historic Route 66 (now IL 157 on this portion), usually no more than a few hundred yards to the east.

After completing the first of the trail's three on-street sections, you'll meet up with a pleasant stretch of trail that runs directly beside the former

Route 66. On this section, you'll pass by plenty of homes, enjoying their gardens and statuary as you make your way into the small town of Hamel. Just before reaching Hamel, there's a brief section when the surrounding landscape drops down around you, revealing scenic wooded ravines.

Hamel and Worden

In Hamel, the grain silos and retailers of heavy farm equipment reveal the town's bread and butter. After the trail follows another brief on-street section, you're already on your way out of town alongside Route 66, and before you know it, the soybean fields again take over the landscape.

As the trail passes through a handsome arched railroad underpass, you'll see low spots containing ponds, likely created by the need for dirt in building the railroad embankments. The ponds seem to attract local birds like killdeers, vultures, as well as American kestrels. On the way into the tiny town of Worden, look for Osage orange and walnut trees.

Worden Community Park offers a pleasant trailside spot to take a break. North of the park, you may notice the tree-covered mound on the left, which was created by waste material (typically shale) removed during coal mining. A few mines around Worden were in operation from the 1880s until the 1940s.

Staunton

The final on-street section of the trail starts in DeCamp Junction, once a small coal-mining settlement that now contains a roadhouse that got its start in 1931 on Route 66. The roadhouse, called DeCamp Station, has sports leagues that play in the back alongside the trail.

After crossing the former Route 66 (now IL 4) on the way into Staunton, you'll enjoy the fanciful decor in some peoples' backyards adjoining the trail, including a large cluster of bird houses made from dried gourds—likely home for purple martins. Similar to Worden and DeCamp Junction, coal mining had a long tradition in Staunton, starting after the civil war and continuing until World War II, and for a time, the town had the largest coal mining union in the state.

Get Your Kicks on Route 66

Introducing many to the thrill of the open road and coinciding with the ascendance of the automobile in the US, Route 66 continues to mesmerize people. Established in 1926, it ultimately stretched 2,448 miles from Chicago to Los Angeles. The route in Illinois—roughly what is now the route of I-55—used existing roads, but changed several times over the years. Plenty of Route 66 roadside attractions still exist in Illinois and there's even a bike route that traces much of the former roadway through Illinois (see Local Information).

Want to catch another local Route 66 landmark? After coming to the end of the trail in Staunton, head east a few blocks to Henry's Rabbit Ranch to see a vintage gas station, half-buried cars, and, yes, rabbits.

The arched tunnel marks a spot on the Quercus Grove Trail where two railroads crossed paths.

Major Milepoints

3.9 On-street section, 0.8 miles. At Jerusalem Rd. (very little traffic), continue 0.8 miles to the right to IL 157. Pick up the trail on the east side of IL 157, and go left.

6.3 On-street section, 0.5 miles. Cyclists confident in traffic can continue ahead on IL 157 for 0.5 miles to catch the rest of the trail. Less confident cyclists and people walking and running can take a slightly longer, but quieter route by turning left on Park Ave., passing through Hamel Community Park, and then turning right on W. State St. Then turn left on Meyer Ave., followed by a right on Schroeder Ave. to reach the next section of trail.

12.4 On-street section, 0.8 miles. At Spangle Rd. (very little traffic) head left for 0.25 miles to reach the rest of the trail.

Local Information

- Illinois Route 66 Scenic Byway, 1045 S. 5th Street, Springfield; (217) 670-1805; illinoisroute66.org
- Illinois South Tourism, 4387 N. Illinois Street, Suite 200, Swansea; (618) 257-1488; illinoisouth.org
- Ride Illinois Route 66 Trail Guide; rideillinois.org/maps/route-66-trail-guide.

Local Events/Attractions

- Henry's Rabbit Ranch, 1107 Old Route 66, Staunton, (618) 635-5655; henrysroute66.com. A recreation of vintage gas station, a collection of half-buried automobiles, plenty of Mother Road memorabilia, and an abundance of rabbits.
- Route 66 Creamery, 11 S. Old Route 66, Hamel. Ice cream shop located close to the trail in a renovated train depot.
- Shale Winery, 1499 Washington Avenue, Williamson; (618) 637-2470. Food, events, and rental cabins, located just outside of Staunton.

Restaurants

- Weezy's Route 66 Bar & Grill, 108 S. Old Route 66, Hamel; (618) 633-2228. Serving travelers since the late 1930s; dining room has a Route 66 theme.
- DeCamp Station, 8767 State Route 4, Staunton; (618) 637-2951; decampstationil.com. Friendly vibe at this bar and grill featuring its own softball diamond and volleyball courts in back.

Accommodations

- Holiday Inn Express & Suites Edwardsville, 1000 Plummer Drive, Edwardsville; (618) 692-7255; bit.ly/edholidayinn. Located close to Southern Illinois University Edwardsville and right alongside Madison County's Nature Trail (which connects to the Quercus Grove Trail).
- Shale Lake Cabins and Cottages, 1499 Washington Avenue, Williamson; (618) 637-2470; shalewine.com. Pleasant location outside of Staunton at the Shale Lake winery.

43 REND LAKE TRAIL

This trail meanders through a series of campgrounds and day-use areas on the wooded shores of Rend Lake in south central Illinois. While touring one of the top recreation spots in the state, you'll encounter a marina, a beach, an enormous dam that impounds the lake, and loads of inviting picnicking options where you can soak up expansive views of this large scenic lake.

Location: Starting on the southeast shore of Rend Lake, which is located 25 miles north of Carbondale, the trail meanders northwest near the shore of the lake.

Length: 9.8 miles one-way.

Surface: Asphalt.

Wheelchair access: The route is wheelchair accessible.

Difficulty: The trail is easy.

Restrooms: There are public restrooms and water at the South Marcum Campground, the Dam West Recreation Area, Rend Lake Visitor Center, and both the South Sandusky and North Sandusky Campgrounds.

Maps: bit.ly/rendtrail.

Hazards: No hazards.

Access and parking: Coming from the north on I-57, exit on IL 154 heading east. Turn right on IL 37. Turn right onto Petroff Rd. (Illinois St.) and right onto Mine 24 Rd. Park at the Spillway Recreation Area, on the right just before mounting the Rend Lake Dam: 16S, 328423 E, 4211645 N.

Trail users can park at multiple points along the trail between the Rend Lake Visitor Center and the North Sandusky Recreation Area. Just follow Rend City Rd. north from the visitor center to access the different campgrounds and day use areas.

Transportation: The closest Amtrak station is in DuQuoin, located about 15 miles southwest of Rend Lake.

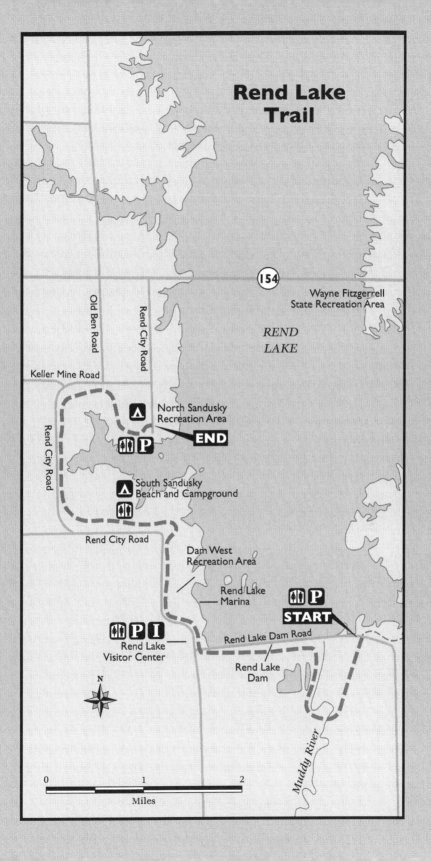

Rentals: No bike rentals in the area.

Contact: United States Army Corps of Engineers, Rend Lake Visitor Center, 11981 Rend City Rd., Benton; (618) 724-2493; rendlake.com.

R end Lake is a relatively new addition to the landscape of southern Illinois. Built in the early 1970s by damming up the Big Muddy River and Casey Creek, state and federal agencies created the 19,000-acre reservoir as a water supply for a two-county area. The lake, shaped like a broad Y, also was built to serve as a prime recreation spot.

Anglers from southern and central Illinois come for the largemouth bass, crappie, bluegills, and channel catfish. But, as the travel brochures point out, Rend Lake is much more than an oversized fishing hole: The 13-mile-long lake draws pleasure boaters, water skiers, and beachgoers. The wooded shores lure throngs of campers, hikers, hunters, and wildlife watchers; and the Rend Lake Recreation Complex on the east side of the lake offers golf, lodging, and a shooting facility.

Starting from the southeast corner of the lake, the Big Muddy River spillway is the first sight you'll encounter south of Rend Lake Dam Rd. Continuing south, the pedestrian bridge over the Big Muddy River takes you to rich wetlands fed by the river's backwaters. While following an arm of the river, watch for legions of turtles and frogs, as well as large pike and catfish sunning themselves near the shore.

After a peaceful 1.2-mile-long ramble between the seventy-foot-high Rend Lake Dam on the right and dense stands of oak, hickory, maple, and cypress on the left, you'll once again cross the Rend Lake Dam Rd. before reaching the Rend Lake Visitor Center. At the visitor center, you can check its exhibits of live reptiles, fish, and honeybees. There's also a native plant garden and plenty of picnicking spots.

Campgrounds and Picnic Areas

The next several miles take you through wooded areas mixed in with a series of picnic areas and campgrounds along the western shore of Rend

Lake. On the right, watch for the entrance to one of the busier places on the lake, the Rend Lake Marina, featuring many dozens of slips (and boat rentals). Another mile ahead brings you to the South Sandusky Recreation Area, which hosts the only sandy beach on the lake.

As you weave through the South Sandusky and the North Sandusky Campgrounds, enjoying the rolling terrain blanketed with cypress and silver maples trees, you'll have opportunities to explore the lake's wooded coves by taking several detours on the quiet campground roads. Between the two camping areas, the trail crosses Sandusky Creek and travels alongside Rend City Rd. The trail ends near the North Sandusky Day Use Area.

Local Information

- Illinois South Tourism, 4387 N. Illinois Street, Suite 200, Swansea; (618) 257-1488; illinoisouth. org
- Rend Lake Area Tourism Council, (618) 435-4000; rendlake.com.

Local Events/Attractions

- Franklin County Historic Jail Museum, 209 W. Main Street, Benton; (618) 435-5777; historicjail. com. Local history museum housed in a former jail, just south of Rend Lake.
- Pheasant Hollow Winery, 14931 IL-37, Whittington; (618) 629-2302; pheasanthollowwines. com. Dining, live music and entertainment, and of course, local wine.

Visit Wayne Fitzgerrell State Recreation Area

If you're on a bike, you can explore more of Rend Lake with a 3.5-mile side trip to Wayne Fitzgerrell State Recreation Area from the north end of this trail. The 4-mile-long crushed-gravel trail in the state park runs to Rend Lake College. To reach the state park from the North Sandusky Recreation Area, go north on N. Rend City Rd. and then right onto IL 154 (no trail on this fairly busy stretch of road, but an ample-size shoulder keeps you away from traffic). After entering the park on the left, take the third street on the left. Stay right at the next junction. The crushed-gravel bike trail starts from the parking area on the left.

- Wayne Fitzgerrell State Recreation Area, 11094 Ranger Road, Whittington; (618) 629-2320; bit. ly/wfitzsra. The park, located on the east side of Rend Lake, contains a 4-mile bike trail.

Restaurants

- Bagels & Brews, 102 N. Park Street, Sesser; bagelsbrews.coffee; Coffee and sandwiches a few miles from the trail.
- Jack Russell Fish Company, 106 E. Main Street, Benton; (618) 439-3474; jackrussellfishcompany. com. Offers fish and seafood.

Accommodations

- Rend Lake Cabins in the Woods, 1 Rend Lake Cabin Drive, Benton; (618) 927-0371; rendlakecab-ins.com. Good selection of cabins very close to the trail.
- Wayne Fitzgerrell State Park, 11094 Ranger Road, Whittington; (618) 629-2320; bit.ly/wfitzsra. One of many camping options at Rend Lake. Huge RV camping area; tent camping sites in the park's north section.

44 RONALD J. FOSTER HERITAGE TRAIL

Like the other rail trails in Madison County, the Ronald J. Foster Heritage Trail takes you through a variety of interesting environments. At the beginning, near the village of Glen Carbon, the trail shadows the wooded banks of Judy's Branch Creek, and continuing east you'll encounter ravines, restored prairie, dense woodland, and a trestle bridge over Silver Creek. After Silver Creek, wide-open farmland prevails all the way to the trail's terminus in the town of Marine.

Location: From the Metro East town of Glen Carbon, the trail heads east to Marine.

Length: 12.2 miles one-way.

Surface: Asphalt on the west section of the trail; rougher chip-and-tar surface on much of the eastern section.

Wheelchair access: The trail is wheelchair accessible.

Difficulty: The trail is mostly easy; the eastern end offers little protection from sun and wind.

Restrooms: There are public restrooms at the trailhead in Citizens Park, Goshen Trail intersection (water only), and at the east end of the trail in Marine Village Park.

Maps: mcttrails.org.

Hazards: Watch for traffic while crossing a few busy streets.

Access and parking: Park at Citizens Park on Main St. in Glen Carbon. From I-270, head south on IL 157. Turn left onto Main St. and use the trailhead parking area on the right. Catch the trail in the southwest corner of the park. UTM coordinates: 16S, 240546 E, 4292822 N.

To reach the trailhead parking area where the Glen Carbon Trail meets the Goshen Trail, head north on IL 159 from I-270. Turn right onto Cottonwood Rd. and continue ahead as it becomes Old Troy Rd. The parking area is on the right.

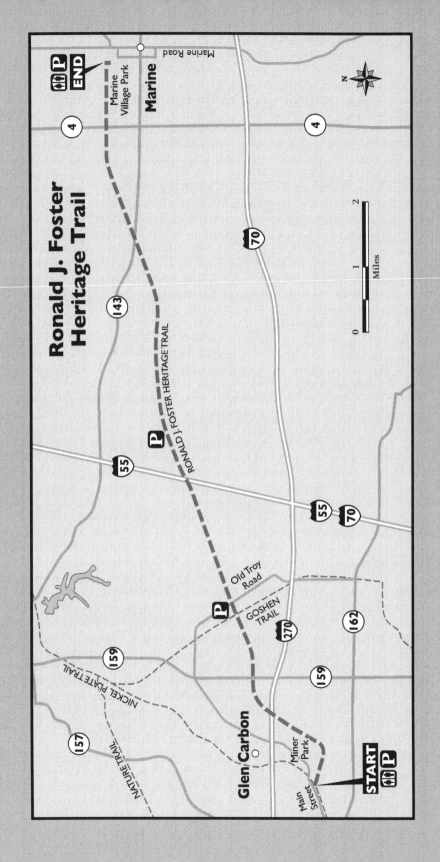

To access the trail from Kuhn Station Rd., exit west on IL 143 from I-55. Turn right onto Staunton Rd. and then left onto Goshen Rd. Turn right onto Kuhn Station Rd.

To access the east end of the trail at Marine Village Park, head north on IL 4 from I-70. At IL 143 turn right. In Marine turn left onto Verson St.

Transportation: Madison County's #13, #13X, #16, #16X, and #19 buses connects with the south end of the Ronald J. Foster Heritage Trail. The bus route map at mct.org shows local bus routes and the county trails.

The closest Amtrak stations are in St. Louis, Carlinville, and Alton.

Rentals: The Bike Factory, 616 Franklin Ave., Edwardsville; (618) 659-8706; thebikefactory.com.

Covered Bridge Bike Rental, 195 S. Main St., Glen Carbon; (618) 205-3132; coveredbridgebikerental.com. This rental service is located steps from the trail.

Contact: Madison County Trails, One Transit Way, Granite City; (618) 874-7433; mcttrails.org.

IIIIIIIIIIIIIIIIIIIIIIIIIIIIIIIIIIIIIIIIIIIIIIIIIIIIIIIIIIIIIIIIIIIIIIIIIIIIIIIIIIIIIIIIII

As the name suggests, the village of Glen Carbon owes its existence to local coal mines. The village, located on Mississippi River Bluffs, lies on top of seven veins of bituminous coal. Since the Glen Carbon mines were located along Judy's Branch Creek, it's no coincidence that the railroad followed the route of the creek as well. Now users of the Ronald J. Foster Heritage Trail can follow the same route.

The trail, which is named after a long-time mayor of Glen Carbon, starts with a pleasantly wooded character, broken up occasionally with sections of restored tallgrass prairie laden with compass plants, milkweed, black-eyed Susans, and thistles. Watch for Judy's Branch Creek as it winds through the ravines that border the trail. The interpretive signs along the way share details about the coal mines that operated near the former railroad. After I-270, the woodland grows more dense and trees hang overhead. Embankments rise up intermittently on the sides of the trail. After ducking under IL 159, there's access on the left to hiking trails and picnicking spots at Greenspace East Park (walk your bike; no riding allowed). Near the junction with the Goshen Trail (at 3.2 miles), check out the grain elevator, built in 1913 for loading grain on railcars.

From Town to Country

Soon the atmosphere becomes remote. Agricultural land dominates. Now and then ravines and woodland are peppered among the rows of crops. Beyond the trailhead parking lot on Kuhn Station Rd., the trail begins to make a long, gradual descent toward Silver Creek. The Silver Creek trestle bridge rises some fifty feet above the creek and runs for more than a hundred yards through treetops of maple and elm. Just after the bridge you'll encounter the creek again as it curves beside the trail.

After Silver Creek, cross-streets rarely interrupt the final 4 miles of trail that unwind in front of you. A slight embankment puts you about ten feet above the surrounding cornfields, offering views of farms and wooded patches in the distance. The trail ends at the edge of a quiet pond

Patches of restored prairie decorate the sides of the Ronald J. Foster Heritage Trail.

in Marine Heritage Park. Curiously, this Illinois prairie town was named "Marine" because its early settlers were sailors.

Local Information

- Illinois South Tourism, 4387 N. Illinois St., Suite 200, Swansea; (618) 257-1488; illinoisouth.org.

Local Events/Attractions

- Liberty Apple Orchard, 8308 Kuhn Station Road, Edwardsville; (618) 659-9217; libertyappleorchard.com. U-pick options; small store in an old schoolhouse with cider, treats, and snack; located just off the trail.
- Glen Carbon Heritage Museum, 124 School Street, Glen Carbon; (618) 288-7271; bit.ly/glencmuseum. Museum is housed in old schoolhouse and around the corner at 148 Main Street is a display of an 1850s cabin; limited hours; located blocks from the trail.

Restaurants

- Weeping Willow Tea Room; 123 Glen Crossing Road, Glen Carbon; (618) 205-8557; weepingwillowtearoom.com. Sandwiches, salads, soup; located blocks from the trail.

Accommodations

- Holiday Inn Express & Suites Edwardsville, 1000 Plummer Drive, Edwardsville; (618) 692-7255; bit.ly/edholidayinn. Located close to Southern Illinois University Edwardsville and right alongside Madison County's Nature Trail.
- Horseshoe Lake State Park, 3321 IL 111, Granite City; (618) 931-0270; bit.ly/hlstatepark. Forty-eight campsites located on an island.

45 TUNNEL HILL STATE TRAIL

Get ready for one of the most captivating trails in Illinois. You'll see ravines, rocky streams, sprawling wetlands, and wooded bluffs. In between the seven towns, as well as several ghost towns that disappeared after the trains stopped running, you'll cross twenty-three trestle bridges, some of which are astounding spans of metal latticework reaching out over deep ravines.

Location: From Eldorado, which is located about 40 miles east of Carbondale, the trail runs southwest nearly to the Ohio River.

Length: 53.6 miles one-way.

Surface: Crushed gravel.

Wheelchair access: While the trail is wheelchair accessible, use caution at some street crossings in Harrisburg and others like IL 146 in Vienna. The tunnel is the highest point on the path, with gradual inclines and declines on each side.

Difficulty: Due to the length, the extended inclines, and a long, extremely dark tunnel, this trail is rated as difficult.

Restrooms: There are toilets and water at the trail parking areas in Harrisburg, Carrier Mills, Stonefort, New Burnside, Tunnel Hill, Vienna, Karnak, and at the Cache River State Natural Area Visitor Center.

Maps: bit.ly/tunnelhst.

Hazards: If cycling, consider walking your bike through the long tunnel—it's extremely dark. And you may want to bring a light. Amenities are spaced out widely on the trail; prepare accordingly. Use caution as the trail crosses a few busy roads along the way, particularly at the dicey intersection with Poplar St. in Harrisburg.

Access and parking: From I-57 to the north, head east on I-64 to exit 89. Turn right on Brehm Ln. and then turn left on IL 142. In Eldorado, turn right on Eldorado Rd. and then left on Russell Rd. At Carter St., turn right. The

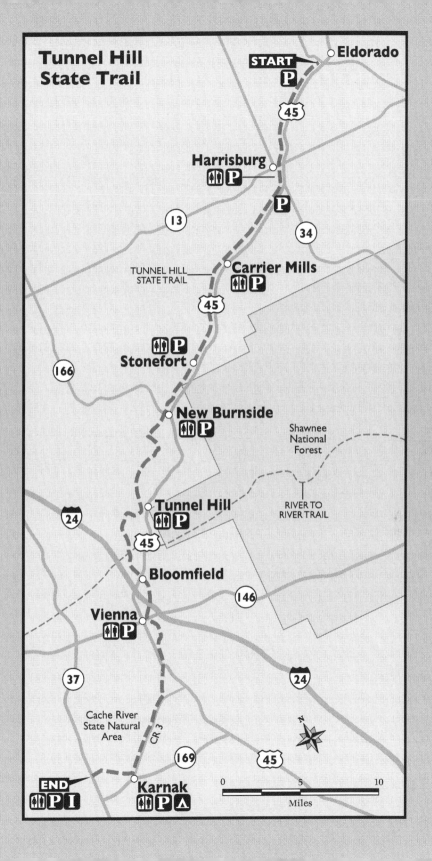

trailhead is on the right just before reaching US 45, but you'll park in the lot left that sits between US 45 and Kennedy St.

From I-57 in Marion, head east on IL 13 to Harrisburg. Turn right onto US 45 (Commercial St.) and right a couple blocks ahead onto Walnut St. The trailhead parking area is on the right at Front St. Turn right on Veterans Dr. and the trail parking is on the right.

To reach the Carrier Mills parking area from Harrisburg, head south on US 45. In Carrier Mills turn right onto Main St. and then left onto Railroad St.

To reach the Stonefort parking area from Harrisburg, take US 45 to Cedar St. in Stonefort. Turn right Cedar St. at the old train depot and then right on Roosevelt St.

To reach the New Burnside parking area, turn right onto IL 166 as you're heading south on US 45. Turn left onto Second St. The parking area is at the corner of Second and Main Streets.

To get to the Tunnel Hill parking area from I-24, head east at exit 7 on Tunnel Hill Rd. (CR 12). The parking area is on the left between Main and Colfax Streets.

To reach the trail parking area in Vienna from I-24, take exit 16 west on IL 146 (Vine St.) into Vienna. Park in the community park on the right.

To reach the parking area in Karnak from I-57, take exit 18 east on Shawnee College Rd. (CR 7). Turn left onto IL 37 and right onto IL 169. In Karnak turn left onto First St.

To reach the south terminus of the trail at the Cache River State Natural Area Visitor Center, exit I-57 heading east at Cypress Rd. (exit 24). At IL 37 turn right. The visitor center is on the left.

Transportation: The closest Amtrak station is in Carbondale.

Rentals: Sandburn Junction Greenhouse and Nursery, 490 Sandburn Ln., Vienna; (618) 771-2825; sandburnjunction.com. Located very close to the trail; primitive camping available as well.

Contact: Shawnee National Forest, Hidden Springs Ranger Station, 602 N. First St., Vienna; (618) 658-2111; fs.usda.gov/Shawnee.

Tunnel Hill State Trail, 400 E. Vine Street, Vienna; (618) 658-2168; bit.ly/tunnelhillst; trail headquarters located at the trailhead in Vienna.

Before becoming the Tunnel Hill Trail, this was a railroad that carried passengers, as well as coal, salt, wood, and food items such as peaches and apples between Vincennes, Indiana, and Cairo, Illinois. Fun fact: the railroad was developed in part by Ambrose Burnside, a Union Civil War general and US Senator most remembered for his distinctive style of facial hair. (Reportedly, Burnside's friends transposed the syllables in his name to come up with "sideburns.") His legacy lives on in a town named in his honor you'll encounter at roughly the halfway point.

Harrisburg and the Pioneer Village

The first 20 miles of the trail—from Eldorado through Harrisburg, Carrier Mills, and Stonefort —runs alongside US 45 rather closely for most of the way. While US 45 isn't unbearably busy, it does possess a steady stream of

The trail bridge soars over Little Cache Creek, which is located a couple miles south of the tunnel.

traffic. And the initial several miles of the trail through farmland to Harrisburg provides very little buffer between the trail and the highway.

While passing an array of restaurants and stores in Harrisburg, keep in mind that amenities dwindle fast once you're out of town. Vienna, nearly 35 miles south of Harrisburg, offers the next best collection of restaurants, stores, and lodging options.

As the trail curves right on the outskirts of Harrisburg, look for the sign pointing to the Saline County Pioneer Village and Museum. The museum, located just a couple of blocks north of the trail on Feazel St., is housed in a stately brick building that once served as the county poorhouse. Also on the grounds is a cabin built by French settlers, a small fort, a Quaker church, a school, an old jail cell, and a cabin that reportedly belonged to river pirates along the Ohio River.

Carrier Mills, Stonefort, and New Burnside

At one time, this railroad carted away vast amounts of coal that was scraped from the surface of this landscape. Even though the forest and human efforts have mitigated some of the profound effects of strip mining, you'll often see small, unusually shaped ponds in the area, which indicate where mining was carried out. Between Carrier Mills and Stonefort, some of these telltale ponds appear alongside the trail. One mile south of Carrier Mills, free African Americans founded the settlement of Lakeview, first named Pond Settlement, between 1818 and 1820. Lakeview is the oldest African American settlement in Illinois and the founding families hold an annual reunion.

South of Stonefort, just as the trail permanently splits from US 45, the rugged terrain of the Shawnee Hills arrives front and center. Hills rise up around you, and the trail starts snaking through little ravines.

After passing through the tiny town of New Burnside, signs along the trail will point out the former location of Parker City, one of a handful of ghost towns along the trail. Thanks to its location at the junction of two railroads, Parker City contained hotels, stores, forty houses, and was home to more than 200 residents. After both railroads were abandoned, the town soon dried up and disappeared, and all that's left now is the railroad depot's foundation.

Over the next several miles the trail threads its way through a scenic ravine carved out by Sugar Creek. Steep wooded bluffs decorated with occasional sandstone outcroppings swell up on each side of the trail. Continuing through the ravine, the trail gradually rises all the way to the trail's namesake feature, Tunnel Hill. During much of this very gradual climb, the trail sits fifty feet or more above the densely wooded—sometimes swampy—bottomland.

Ravines, Bluffs, and a Long Tunnel

The trail burrows into the hillside just south of the hamlet of Tunnel Hill. At one time this dark and damp tunnel extended farther: In 1929 about 300 feet of the tunnel collapsed; now it's 543 feet long—with no lights. If you're on a bike, pay heed to the signs recommending that you dismount. Pedaling through total the darkness within a tunnel is disorienting— vaguely dreamlike—and slightly dangerous. After emerging from the tunnel, you'll start a gradual descent from the highest point on the trail.

About 2.5 miles after the tunnel, the trail crosses a 450-foot-long trestle bridge that towers ninety feet above a deep, dramatic ravine. The bridge guides you through upper reaches of tulip, fir, oak, and maple trees. A glance down from the side of the bridge reveals a trickling tributary to Little Cache Creek.

Little Cache Creek and its tributaries continue to define the landscape for the next several miles. Through the trees on the right, the creek widens as a result of damming. Another trestle bridge overlooks the solid sandstone creekbed that once hosted the creek—before a dam corked its flow. Just before the bridge, you'll encounter the junction with the River to River Trail, a hiking and equestrian trail that runs across southern Illinois, from the Ohio River on the east to the Mississippi River on the west. Continuing ahead, 100-foot bluffs shoot upward. Keep an eye on the creek as it wriggles from one side of the trail to the other, sometimes disappearing for short stretches.

Vienna and the Cache River Wetlands

Getting closer to the Vienna, the landscape starts to level off as agriculture fields replace the ravines and bluffs. Wetlands come and go; barns are visible in the distance. In Vienna the trail passes through a pleasant community park that contains the Foreman Depot Museum, a restored train depot from the early 1900s featuring exhibits about local railroad history.

South of Vienna, the last of the hills give way to bottomland, swampland, and a scattering of ponds. The trail runs beside CR 3 for 5 miles as you pass through the villages of Belknap and Karnak. Fortunately CR 3 contains little traffic, and there is typically a leafy buffer between the trail and the road. South of Belknap, look for the signs directing you across CR 3 to a small viewing spot, where you may see egrets, herons, and other wetland-loving creatures. Because of the rich biological variety, these wetlands and others around the Cache River have been designated as one of only fifteen worldwide Wetlands of International Importance by the United Nations Education, Scientific, and Cultural Organization (UNESCO).

After crossing the Cache River you'll arrive in Karnak, where there's a long-abandoned, vine-covered wooden train depot next to the trail.

The tunnel was carved through a hill of sandstone and shale.

‡IIIIIIIIIIIIIIIIIIIIIIIIIIIIIIIIIIIIIIIIIIIIIIIIIIIIIIIIIIIIIIIIIIIIIIIIIIIIIIIIIIIIIIE

Shorter Trips to Consider

Some of the best natural scenery along the trail can be found on the 16-mile (one-way) trip between Vienna and New Burnside. Within that stretch of trail, shorter trips can be enjoyed between Tunnel Hill and Vienna (9.6 miles, one-way), Tunnel Hill and New Burnside (6.4 miles, one-way), and from Tunnel Hill south to the longest bridge on the trail spanning Little Cache Creek (2.7 miles, one-way). If you like wetlands, the trip between Karnak and the Barkhausen-Cache River Wetlands Center can't be missed (2.8 miles, one-way).

ΠIIIIIIIIIIIIIIIIIIIIIIIIIIIIIIIIIIIIIIIIIIIIIIIIIIIIIIIIIIIIIIIIIIIIIIIIIIIIIIIIIIIIIΠ

As the trail turns west in Karnak, stands of elm and maple rise along the trail, and wetlands flood the low spots. Cross the Cache River once more before reaching the end of the trail at the Barkhausen-Cache River Wetlands Center.

Local Information

- Illinois South Tourism, 4387 N. Illinois Street, Suite 200, Swansea; (618) 257-1488; illinoisouth. org.
- Saline County Tourism Board; 1600 S. Feazel Street, Harrisburg; (618) 253-8910; visitsaline-county.com.

Local Events/Attractions

- Barkhausen-Cache River Wetlands Center, 8885 IL 37 South, Cypress; (618) 657-2064; bit.ly/cachewetlands. Located at the south end of the trail; plenty of exhibits about local flora and fauna, as well as viewing platforms and short hiking trails.
- Saline Creek Pioneer Village and Museum, 1600 S. Feazel Street, Harrisburg; (618) 253-7342. Displays local artifacts; the grounds contain a collection of historic buildings; close to the trail.
- Foreman Depot Museum; 298. E. Vine Street, Vienna; (618) 658-8547. Contains photographs and artifacts of early Johnson County railroads. The trail passes the museum in Vienna City Park.
- Stonefort Depot Museum, 28-36 Chestnut Street, Stonefort; (618) 252-5112; heritech.com/stonefort_depot. Small museum alongside the trail focusing on railroad and local history; limited hours.

Restaurants

- The Bar BQ Barn, 632 N. Main Street, Harrisburg; (618) 252-6190. Local favorite specializing in barbecue sandwiches.
- Ned's Shed, 101 N. First Street, Vienna; (618) 658-9507. A longtime fixture in Vienna; known for its burgers. Located 0.5 mile west of the trail on IL 146.

Accommodations

- Ferne Clyffe State Park, P.O Box 10, 90 Office Drive, Goreville; (618) 995-2411; bit.ly/fernecsp. One of many great camping options in the area; other options are the Saline County State Fish and Wildlife Area close to the north half of the trail and Jackson Falls, Bell Smith Springs, Dixon Springs State Park, and Lake Glendale Recreation Area close to the south half. There's also no-frills camping directly alongside the trail in Karnak.
- Perkins House Inn, 504 W. Vine Street, Vienna; (618) 528-9776; perkinshouseinn.com. Historic hotel located blocks from the trail.

46 VADALABENE GREAT RIVER ROAD TRAIL

The drama and beauty of this route are mesmerizing. Sometimes it's difficult to keep your eyes on the trail as you wend your way between the Mississippi River on one side and the soaring bluffs on the other. After passing through the river town of Grafton, the trail ends at one of the most impressive state parks in Illinois.

Location: From Piasa Park, located just north of Alton on IL 100, the trail runs northwest alongside the Mississippi River to Pere Marquette State Park at the confluence of the Illinois and Mississippi Rivers.

Length: 20.5 miles one-way.

Surface: Asphalt (some areas in rough condition).

Wheelchair access: The trail is wheelchair accessible, but much of the central portion is simply the extra-wide shoulder of IL 100. Fast-moving traffic runs fairly close.

Difficulty: This trail has a medium level of difficulty since most of it is exposed to the elements. Also, much of it runs close to traffic on IL 100.

Restrooms: There are public restrooms and water at the trailhead, the gas station at Piasa Creek, the visitor center east of Grafton, and the visitor center and lodge at Pere Marquette.

Maps: mcttrails.org.

Hazards: The central portion of this route follows the extra wide shoulder of IL 100 and isn't suitable for young kids. Use caution on this section: IL 100 is a busy road, particularly on summer weekends. The two ends of the route offer several miles of paved trail that is separate from the roadway and is more family friendly.

Access and parking: From the St. Louis, Missouri, area, take US 67 north across the Mississippi River. Turn left onto IL 100 in Alton. The parking area is on the right at the foot of the bluff decorated with the large painting of the Piasa Bird. UTM coordinates: 15S, 742986 E, 4308901 N.

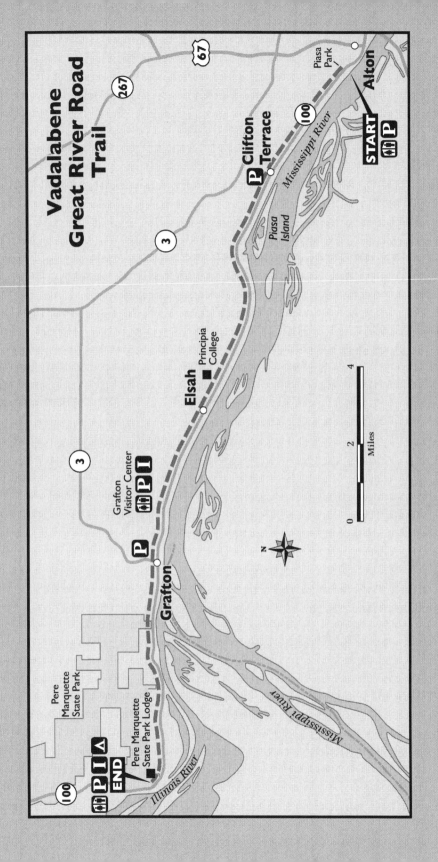

From I-55 head west on IL 140. Stay on IL 140 through Alton until you reach Broadway St. Continue ahead on Broadway Street, which eventually turns into IL 100. The parking area is on the right.

All alternative parking spots are easily accessible from IL 100. A small park in Clifton Terrace offers parking. You also can park at the visitor center alongside the trail outside Grafton and at Pere Marquette State Park.

Transportation: Madison County's #1, #8, #9, #10, #11 and #24X buses connect with Alton. The bus route map at mct.org shows local bus routes and the county trails.

Amtrak stations are in Alton, St. Louis, and Carlinville.

Rentals: The Bike Factory, 616 Franklin Ave., Edwardsville; (618) 659-8706; thebikefactory.com.

Covered Bridge Bike Rental, 195 S. Main Street, Glen Carbon; (618) 205-3132; coveredbridgebikerental.com. Contact: Illinois Department of Transportation, 2300 S. Dirksen Parkway, Springfield; (618) 346-3100; dot. state.il.us.

The rocky bluffs and wide river make this one of the most scenic multiuse trails in the state. The trail's only notable drawback is its close proximity to IL 100, which tends to be especially busy with traffic on summer weekends (to avoid some traffic, consider a midweek trip or go early in the day on a weekend). Within the first few miles you'll see the first of a series of roadside parks. When the trail occasionally wanders slightly up the bluff, you'll get some relief from being elbow to elbow with traffic.

Heading Upriver

On the opposite shore of the Mississippi River in the small town of Portage des Sioux, Missouri, look for a twenty-five-foot fiberglass sculpture of a human figure dedicated to Our Lady of the Rivers. The sculpture, which sits on twenty-foot pedestal, was erected after the town was spared from a major flood in 1951. Now the monument is the site of an annual blessing of the boats.

In the river you're likely to see barges passing among a handful of islands. You'll see signs for Principia College, a Christian Science school founded up on the bluffs in 1897. At the turnoff for the college, consider a quick visit to the tiny village of Elsah, which looks as though it hasn't changed for a hundred years. A few klicks ahead brings you to a water park where kids can hop on a slide that goes down the bluff into a pool.

The village of Grafton is lined with shops, bars, and eateries, many catering to the tourist set. In Grafton the trail drops down by the river and runs behind the main business strip through an open and grassy flood-plain sprinkled with a few houses. To check out the many businesses along IL 100, you may want to simply walk (or walk your bike) along the sidewalk instead of using the path by the river. Leaving Grafton, the trail passes the old stone building that houses the Illinois Youth Center and then runs underneath a stone cross that marks the point where Jacques Marquette became the first European to enter what is now Illinois.

Pere Marquette State Park

The final part of this route will dazzle you. This is where the trail winds along the side of the river bluff, and zigzags through rugged terrain, dense with stands of maple and sassafras trees. As the trail crosses a bridge about a hundred feet up on the bluff, you can see the Illinois River, the nearby wetlands, and the Grafton car ferry below. As you come down off the bluff, the Pere Marquette riding stables signal your entrance into one of the best state parks in Illinois.

At Pere Marquette State Park, be sure to drop in at the Great Lodge, which contains a magnificent open room built with stone and logs. From the lodge, cyclists with a thirst for punishment may want to take what is likely the steepest climb in the entire state. The initial mile of this road climbs about 350 feet. As a reward at the top, you're granted stunning views of the Illinois River and its backwaters. On a clear day, the Gateway Arch is visible in downtown St. Louis. At the visitor center near the lodge, you can also pick up a map showing the park's excellent collection of hiking trails that lead to dramatic overlooks up the bluff.

The Vadalabene Great River Road Trail traces the route of IL 100 between the Mississippi River and its wooded river bluffs.

On the return trip to Alton, you'll be using the wide shoulder on the opposite side of the road for much of the route. This is closer to the river and puts you farther away from the bluffs, allowing better views of the high bluffs and the craggy cliffs.

The Piasa Bird

This route starts at the foot of the bluff adorned with the painting of a Piasa Bird—a dragonlike creature with antlers, wings, and a long tail. According to local lore, the Native American people who once lived in the area were plagued by this ferocious flying creature that lived in the cliffs above the river. After the bird was finally killed by archers wielding poison arrows, Native Americans painted an image of the Piasa Bird on a rock wall to commemorate the event. The current image is a reproduction of the original pictograph.

Local Information

- Great Rivers and Routes of Southwestern Illinois, 200 Piasa Street, Alton 62002; (618) 465-6676; riversandroutes.com
- Illinois South Tourism, 4387 N. Illinois Street, Suite 200, Swansea; (618) 257-1488; illinoisouth. org.

Local Events/Attractions

- Aire's Resort, 800 Timber Ridge Drive, Grafton; (618) 786-7477; aeriesview.com. Dining and lodging options, as well as a winery, a zipline tour, and a chair lift that takes you up the bluff from Grafton.
- Alton Museum of History and Art, 2809 College Avenue, Alton; (618) 462-2763; altonmuseum. com. Exhibits on Piasa Bird lore, Lincoln-Douglas debates, and Robert Wadlow, Alton's "gentle giant."
- Argosy Casino Alton, 1 Piasa Street, Alton; (618) 474-7500; argosyalton.com. Three floors of gaming with a restaurant; located on the river.
- Pere Marquette State Park, 13112 Visitor Center Lane, Grafton; (618) 786-3323; bit.ly/pmspark. One of the most scenic parks in the state; horseback riding, stellar hiking trails, and rock climbing.

Restaurants

- Grafton Winery & Brewhaus, 300 W. Main Street, Grafton; (618) 786-3001; shopgraftonwinery. com. Wines and beers produced on onsite; standard food options; large patio overlooking the river.

- Pere Marquette Lodge and Conference Center, 13653 Lodge Boulevard, Grafton; (618) 786-2331; pmlodge.net. Breakfast, lunch, and dinner served in the impressive Great Lodge.

Accommodations

- The Beall Mansion, 407 E. 12th Street, Alton; (866) 843-2325; beallmansion.com. This 1903 mansion—on the National Register of Historic Places—contains a museum.
- Pere Marquette Lodge and Conference Center. Rooms, cabins, and a campground.
- Ruebel Hotel and Saloon, 217 E. Main Street, Grafton; (618) 786-2315; ruebelhotel.com. Offers twenty-two rooms in a historic hotel above a restaurant; cottages and lodge rooms also available.

Honorable Mentions

Here are some additional multi-use trails in Illinois that deserve a visit.

BLOOMINGDALE TRAIL
Biking, inline skating, running, wheelchair accessible, walking.

Location: Between Ashland and Ridgeway Avenues on Chicago's near northwest side.

Length: 2.75 miles.

Surface: Concrete.

Contact: Chicago Park District, 541 N. Fairbanks Ave., Chicago; (312) 742-7529; the606.org.

Snapshot description: A unique and stunningly designed urban trail guides you alongside Chicago rooftops.

THE DES PLAINES RIVER TRAIL (COOK COUNTY)
Location: Between Lake Cook Rd. and North Ave. in northern Cook County.

Length: Roughly 20 miles, but with some gaps.

Surface: Dirt; crushed gravel.

Contact: Forest Preserves of Cook County, 536 N. Harlem Ave., River Forest; (800) 870-3666; fpdcc.com.

Snapshot description: Some sections are lovely while others are plagued with drainage, access, and flooding issues. The county has plans to improve the trail.

GENERAL DACY TRAIL
Location: Shelbyville in south central Illinois.

Length: 6 miles.

Surface: Crushed limestone, asphalt.

Contact: US Army Corps of Engineers, Lake Shelbyville Project Office & Visitor Center, 1989 State Highway 16, Shelbyville; (217) 774-3951; dacey-trail.org

Snapshot description: Follows the wooded shoreline of Lake Shelbyville and its dam; can be made into a loop.

KANKAKEE RIVER STATE PARK TRAIL

Location: Along the Kankakee River about 50 miles south of Chicago.

Length: 10.2 miles.

Surface: Gravel; asphalt sections.

Contact: Kankakee River State Park, 5314 IL-102, Bourbonnais; (815) 933-1383; www2.illinois.gov/dnr.

Snapshot description: Great views, lush woodlands, and a canopied trail through a state park that offers plenty to do.

METRO EAST LEVEE TRAIL

Location: Just south of East St. Louis, along the Mississippi River.

Length: 7.6 miles.

Surface: Rough gravel.

Contact: Metro East Parks and Recreation, 104 United Dr., Collinsville; (618) 346-4905; meprd.org.

Snapshot description: A mix of urban and rural areas, wetlands and crop-land, and drainage canals and ponds. Rough surface in sections.

PECATONICA PRAIRIE TRAIL

Location: Just west of Rockford, between Meridian Rd. and Farwell Bridge Rd.

Length: 29.5 miles.

Surface: Crushed limestone with some asphalt portions.

Contact: Pecatonica Prairie Trail Commission, (815) 233-1357; pecatoni-caprairietrail.com.

Snapshot description: A very quiet rural trail running through a couple of small farming towns; trail surface can be slightly rough in places.

SKOKIE VALLEY TRAIL

Location: Between Lake-Cook Rd. and Rockland Rd. in Chicago's north suburbs.

Length: 9.5 miles.

Surface: Asphalt.

Contact: Lake County Division of Transportation, 600 W. Winchester Road, Libertyville; (847) 377-7400; lakecountyil.gov

Snapshot description: Follows a powerline right-of-way through a scenic suburban environment; look for extensions to the south in future years.

INDEX

ABOUT THE AUTHOR

Through his books and speaking appearances, Ted Villaire has helped many thousands of people get outside and connect with the natural world in the Prairie State. He's author of *60 Hikes within 60 Miles: Chicago, Camping Illinois, Road Biking Illinois, Best Bike Rides Chicago,* and *Easy Hikes Close to Home: Chicago.* In addition to writing books, he's worked as a news reporter for various daily and weekly newspapers and has written for both local and national magazines. He currently serves as communications director at the Active Transportation Alliance in Chicago. Villaire attended Aquinas College in Grand Rapids, Michigan, and DePaul University in Chicago and lives on the Northwest side of Chicago. Get in touch with him and learn more about his books by visiting tedvillaire.com.